D1427374

MURRAY WALKER'S

1996 Grand Prix Year

**Photography by
LAT Photographic**

PUBLISHER
Richard Poulter

EDITOR
Simon Arron

ART EDITOR
Ryan Baptiste

PRODUCTION MANAGER
Steven Palmer

BUSINESS DEVELOPMENT MANAGER
Simon Maurice

SALES PROMOTION
Clare Kristensen

**Murray Walker's
1996 Grand Prix Year**
is published by Hazleton Publishing
3 Richmond Hill
Richmond, Surrey
TW10 6RE, England
Produced in association with **Shell**

Colour reproduction by
Masterlith Ltd, Mitcham, Surrey

Printed in England by
Ebenezer Baylis & Son Ltd, Worcester

© **Hazleton Securities Ltd 1996**
No part of this publication may be reproduced, stored in a retrieval
system or transmitted, in any form or by any means, electronic,
mechanical, photocopying, recording or otherwise, without prior
permission in writing from Hazleton Securities Ltd.

ISBN: 1-874557 179

DISTRIBUTORS

UNITED KINGDOM
Biblios Ltd
Star Road
Partridge Green
West Sussex
RH13 8LD
Tel: 01403 710971
Fax: 01403 711143

AUSTRALIA
Technical Book and
Magazine Co. Pty. Ltd,
295 Swanston Street
Melbourne VIC 3000
Tel: (03) 9663 3951
Fax: (03) 9663 2094

NEW ZEALAND
David Bateman Ltd
PO Box 100-242
North Shore Mail Centre
Auckland 1330
Tel: (9) 415 7664
Fax: (9) 415 8892

NORTH AMERICA
Motorbooks Int.
PO Box 1,
729 Prospect Avenue,
Osceola,
Wisconsin 54020, USA
Tel: (1) 715 294 3345
Fax: (1) 715 294 4448

SOUTH AFRICA
Motorbooks
341 Jan Smuts Avenue
Craighill Park
Johannesburg
Tel: (011) 325 4458/60
Fax: (011) 325 4146

CONTENTS

We Race

**Where cars are a passion,
the oil is Shell.**

You Win

DURING 1996...

- After 11 years of outstanding success in Adelaide, the Australian GP moved to Melbourne where it was equally impressive.
- Seven of the top drivers changed teams
- 1995 Indy champion Jacques Villeneuve, son of Gilles, switched to Formula One, started his first Grand Prix from pole position and very nearly won the race. At the Nurburgring he won only his fourth GP.
- The entry list was reduced to 22 cars from 11 teams, and was further reduced during the season by the demise of the Forti team.
- Qualifying was confined to one hour-long session on Saturday , with a requirement to lap within 107 per cent of the pole position time.
- Higher cockpit sides and larger driver-openings were introduced for safety reasons; rear "winglets" were banned to reduce downforce.
- Jackie Stewart announced the 1997 debut of Stewart GP, with massive support from Ford
- New V10 engines were introduced by Ferrari, Renault, Mercedes-Benz, Mugen Honda, Peugeot, Ford and Yamaha.
- Renault announced its withdrawal from Formula One at the end of 1997, after eight years of dominant success with its innovative V10.
- Tom Walkinshaw abandoned his attempts to build Ligier into a winning team, and bought the Footwork (Arrows) team which was renamed TWR-Arrows.
- Only three drivers were still running at the end of the Monaco GP - the lowest figure ever .
- At Monaco, Olivier Panis gave Ligier its first win since 1981 (Jacques Laffite, Canada) and Mugen Honda its first ever F1 victory.
- Michael Schumacher won his first Grand Prix for Ferrari (in Spain), with a drive of overwhelming brilliance in appalling weather conditions.
- Ferrari failed to finish nine times from 10 starts at five successive races (Canada, France, Britain, Germany and Hungary).
- Williams equalled Ferrari's record by winning its eighth constructors' championship.
- Williams caused surprise and dismay by deciding not to renew Damon Hill's contract for 1997. To general amazement, Hill signed with TWR-Arrows for 1997.
  Marlboro and McLaren announced that their tremendously successful 23-year partnership would finish at the end of 1996.

CAREER PERFORMANCES: 1996 DRIVERS

Driver	Nat	Team	Starts	Wins	Poles	Fastest laps	Points
Jean Alesi	F	Benetton	118	1	1	4	189
Luca Badoer	I	Forti	34	-	-	-	-
Rubens Barrichello	BR	Jordan	64	-	1	-	46
Gerhard Berger	A	Benetton	196	9	11	19	359*
Martin Brundle	GB	Jordan	158	-	-	-	98
David Coulthard	GB	McLaren	41	1	5	4	81
Pedro Diniz	BR	Ligier	33	-	-	-	2
Giancarlo Fisichella	I	Minardi	8	-	-	-	-
Heinz-Harald Frentzen	D	Sauber	48	-	-	-	29
Mika Hakkinen	SF	McLaren	79	-	-	-	91
Johnny Herbert	GB	Sauber	96	2	-	-	67
Damon Hill	GB	Williams	67	21	20	19	326
Eddie Irvine	GB	Ferrari	48	-	-	-	28
Ukyo Katayama	J	Tyrrell	78	-	-	-	5
Pedro Lamy	P	Minardi	32	-	-	-	1
Giovanni Lavaggi	I	Minardi	7	-	-	-	-
Tarso Marques	BR	Minardi	2	-	-	-	-
Andrea Montermini	I	Forti	21	-	-	-	-
Olivier Panis	F	Ligier	49	1	-	-	38
Ricardo Rosset	BR	Footwork	16	-	-	-	-
Mika Salo	SF	Tyrrell	35	-	-	-	10
Michael Schumacher	D	Ferrari	85	22	14	25	362
Jos Verstappen	NL	Footwork	31	-	-	-	11
Jacques Villeneuve	CDN	Williams	16	4	3	6	78

*Includes 1 point from 1984 that was not valid for the Championship

1996 RACE STATISTICS

Race	Winner	Pole	Fastest lap
Australia	Damon Hill	Jacques Villeneuve	Jacques Villeneuve
Brazil	Damon Hill	Damon Hill	Damon Hill
Argentina	Damon Hill	Damon Hill	Jean Alesi
Europe	Jacques Villeneuve	Damon Hill	Damon Hill
San Marino	Damon Hill	Michael Schumacher	Damon Hill
Monaco	Olivier Panis	Michael Schumacher	Jean Alesi
Spain	Michael Schumacher	Damon Hill	Michael Schumacher
Canada	Damon Hill	Damon Hill	Jacques Villeneuve
France	Damon Hill	Michael Schumacher	Jacques Villeneuve
Britain	Jacques Villeneuve	Damon Hill	Jacques Villeneuve
Germany	Damon Hill	Damon Hill	Damon Hill
Hungary	Jacques Villeneuve	Michael Schumacher	Damon Hill
Belgium	Michael Schumacher	Jacques Villeneuve	Gerhard Berger
Italy	Michael Schumacher	Damon Hill	Michael Schumacher
Portugal	Jacques Villeneuve	Damon Hill	Jacques Villeneuve
Japan	Damon Hill	Jacques Villeneuve	Jacques Villeneuve

Bottom left. Thanks to the new high cockpit sides, it wouldn't be so easy for Jean Alesi to see who he was about to hit next.

Bottom centre. "I don't know what you're laughing about. I never spun a Tyrrell four times in seven laps." Returnee Mika Hakkinen confronts the press, including recent F1 testee Tony Dodgins (centre left).

Bottom right. Famous names: pre-season title favourite Damon Hill (in pre-season title-favourite car) acquaints himself with his new teammate, and son of another racing legend: Jacques Villeneuve, left.

When 22 cars turned up in Australia for the first race of 1996, the expectations for a great year of Grands Prix were high, and no wonder. For no less than seven of Formula One's top drivers had switched teams since the previous season. And that wasn't all.

The young Canadian sensation Jacques Villeneuve, son of the late, great Gilles, whose charismatic driving for Ferrari from 1978-1982 had made him a racing legend, had defected to Formula One after blowing everybody away in American Indycar racing. In Grand Prix terms he was an unknown quantity, but he was certainly an exciting new threat to the establishment and, in a Williams-Renault, a potential race winner.

There is nothing strange about driver moves from one team to another, but for so many of the top men to transfer at the same time was more than unusual and created intrigue. All the leading teams had a new look about them, and none more so than Ferrari. In the five years since 1990, its last good season, the great Maranello team had only won twice despite massive efforts to regain its former dominance.

New cars, new engines, different personnel at every level, different drivers. They'd tried everything but still not achieved championship form. Now though, at enormous expense, double world champion Michael Schumacher was a Ferrari driver with a new John Barnard-designed car, a new V10 to break the Maranello V12 tradition and the rapid, if comparatively inexperienced Eddie Irvine to partner him. If this didn't do the trick,

"No less than seven of Formula One's top drivers had switched teams since the previous season"

nothing would. Ferrari wasn't the only contractor whose reputation was on the line. McLaren, for so long one of the top teams, had endured two terrible seasons with no wins and only eight podium finishes. The 1995 car had been an embarrassing failure, much to the dismay and discomfort of engine partner Mercedes. When the new MP 4/11 appeared it was a revelation. As good looking as its predecessor had been ugly and mighty quick in testing. But with the race speed of Mika Hakkinen in doubt after his heavy crash in Australia, and David Coulthard new to the team, there was no guarantee that it was going to return to the top.

Continuity can be a major plus to a team where everyone knows each other, their working methods, the car and its engine. Which put Williams in a strong position. It had been with Renault since 1989, with Damon Hill since 1991 and had been testing with Villeneuve for the whole of the winter to give him experience of the team and the tracks that were new to him.

Williams was in great shape and so was Hill. Despite his 1995 mistakes, for which he had been so vilified, Damon had been the only real opposition to Schumacher. Second to his German rival in each of the previous two championships Damon meant to finish 1996 at the top. With all that he had going for him, he was the favourite to do so.

What about Benetton? With three championships in the last two seasons, including a first-ever constructors' title in 1995, the Enstone team was on top of the world. But of the 240 points the team had scored in 1994/95, a staggering 194 had been won by Schumacher. Benetton had effectively been a one-man team as Johnny Herbert had found to his cost. Now they had established stars in Gerhard Berger and Jean Alesi, but Berger had not taken at all happily to the 1995 Schumacher-orientated Benetton in winter testing. The new 196 would be a different car designed to accommodate Gerhard's needs, as well as Alesi's very different driving style, which mirrored Schumacher's. But it was by no means a foregone conclusion that the team would be as dominant as it had been with its German ace.

In 1996, after the loss of Lotus, Larrousse, Simtek and Pacific, due to their inability to raise the massive budgets that money-hungry Formula One demands, the entry list was down to 22 cars from 11 teams. Of the remaining seven constructors, two in particular, Jordan and Sauber, looked likely to threaten the top four.

Eddie Jordan had painstakingly built his Silverstone-based team since 1991 and now it had to win. In the enormously experienced, talented, and still-hungry Martin Brundle, he at least had a driver who could help them develop a car. In the young but capable Rubens Barrichello, he had someone who was also a potential winner if the conditions were right. With Gary Anderson having designed it, the new 196 would be good - but would he have overcome the 1995 car's reliability problems? And would the much-revised Peugeot V10 be good enough?

Sauber was under pressure too. No lack of driver talent with Heinz-Harald Frentzen, who could undoubtedly win races in the right car and who had two

Lofty: Benetton launched its 1996 programme in the amphitheatre at Taormina, Sicily. Would that be the highest position the B196 reached all season?

years' experience of the team partnered by Johnny Herbert. Johnny was determined not to be overshadowed by H-H at Sauber as he had been by Schumacher at Benetton. But the new Ford V10 was an unknown racing quantity and the Swiss team had yet to produce a really good car.

The rest looked as though they would be struggling to get many points. With Mika Salo now knowing all the circuits, an impressive new Yamaha V10 and a much better car, which would hearten the demoralised Ukyo Katayama, Tyrrell was looking brighter. Ligier appeared less so, despite its Mugen-Honda engine. But Arrows was expecting to fly with the

excellent Hart V8 and the spectacular Dutchman Jos Verstappen at the wheel.

For Minardi and Forti though, with their far less powerful customer' Ford ED V8 engines, the problem was going to be to qualify within the new time limit of 107 per cent of pole position.

Another innovation was that qualifying was to be during a single one-hour session on Saturday afternoon, with Friday's action confined to two setting-up periods. The cars would all be different to those of the previous year, although not dramatically so.

There were bigger driver-openings to reduce the likelihood of

Ferrari unveiled the new F310 from beneath a glorified dog blanket. Not a wholly inappropriate choice, as it would turn out.

"History shows that whenever the governing body tries to reduce performance by legislation, the engineers find ways to thwart it"

head injuries and no rear winglets in order to reduce downforce and thereby slow the cars. At least that was the intention, but history shows that whenever the governing body tries to reduce performance by legislation, the engineers find ways to thwart it. The three-litre cars of 1995, for instance, had been little slower than their 3.5-litre 1994 predecessors; sometimes, indeed, they were faster.

Like the last GP of 1995 the first of 1996 was to be Down Under - but not in Adelaide. After 11 wonderful years the Australian race moved to Melbourne, where the historic Albert Park circuit had been completely rebuilt as part of a superb new sports complex. No one had any doubt that the venue would be ideal, with potentially the largest and most enthusiastic crowd of the year, but it was going to feel very strange to start the season there.

Be that as it may, there were plenty of intriguing conundrums to be answered.

Let battle commence. . .

Far left. Eddie Jordan: Optimistic after landing the generous backing of B&H.

Middle left. Ukyo Katayama: things couldn't get worse than they had been last season. Well, not until the first race, anyway.

Left. Johnny Herbert tells his new colleagues at Sauber what life had been like at Benetton...

**Main pic:
Odd couples.
Villeneuve out-
qualified Hill,
and leads; Irvine
outqualified
Schumacher,
and stays ahead
- briefly. The
Ulsterman
would finish
third, behind the
Williams twins,
after the world
champion
dropped out.**

**"D'you always
drive that fast?"
The victorious
Hill consoles his
new team-mate;
Villeneuve had
almost equalled
Giancarlo
Baghetti's
unique feat of
winning his first-
ever World
Championship
Grand Prix.**

**Martin Brundle
contemplates
which way up
the world is
really supposed
to be, in the
wake of his
unconventional
start to the
season.**

For 11 years the high point of the Grand Prix season had been the last event of the year in Adelaide. Everyone loved this superb street circuit, with its friendly atmosphere, immaculate organisation, great restaurants, wines and people. It was the ideal place to finish a tiring and stressful year and nobody wanted it to lose the Australian Grand Prix.

But now it had. Just four months after the end of the 1995 season we were back in Australia for the first event of 1996 -in Melbourne, a very different city. Amongst the virtues of Adelaide had been its intimacy and compactness. Melbourne, the self-styled sporting capital of Australia, was three times the size. What was it going to belike? Would the rebuilt Albert Park circuit, scene of previous non-championship Australian Grands Prix (Stirling Moss won there in 1956), be up to the job? Would Australia have lost its appeal without the magic of Adelaide?

Certainly not. Melbourne would be a sensational success. A marvellous city, a magnificent circuit, the same friendly and laid-back efficiency. Even the weather was brilliant. Australia 1996 was as good as ever.

Melbourne wasn't the only thing that was new. There were new cars to comply with revised safety regulations, second-generation three-litre engines and major driver changes. No less than seven top drivers had switched teams and there was a new wild card in the pack - Jacques Villeneuve. How was the young Canadian prodigy, son of the great Gilles, and the man who had dominated America's Indycar scene in 1995, going to adapt to Formula One with Williams?

He had been brilliant in winter testing but racing is something else, pointed out the cynics who remembered Michael Andretti's 1993 failure with McLaren. Jacques' Formula One debut was to surpass many greats of the past. Better than Senna. Better than Prost. Better even than Fangio. At Melbourne he instantaneously became a global star, and a potential 1996 world champion.

The first Grand Prix of the year is always

AUSTRALIA

a bit of a mystery. Some of the teams have done a lot of testing. Some very little. New car, driver and team combinations have yet to settle down.

Nowhere have all the teams tested together. So anticipation was high as the cars, headed by Ferrari's new boy, double world champion Michael Schumacher, raced out of Albert Park's magnificent garage complex on to the lakeside circuit for the familiarisation session on Thursday. Driver reactions? "It's a fun track," said Damon Hill. "Fast, and reminiscent of Montreal," said Olivier Panis. "Flows well and enjoyable to drive," said Martin Brundle. Jacques Villeneuve thought it was fun too - and well he might. In his first competitive Formula One appearance he was fastest of all, a full second quicker than Damon Hill.

To say that the Grand Prix scene was electrified would be a masterpiece of understatement.

Times would count for the grid, with no one more than 107 per cent away from the pole position time being allowed to start. Hill had been fastest in Friday's two free

sessions and the astounding Villeneuve had again been quickest on Saturday morning. So clearly the Williams-Renault was the class of the field. At the end of qualifying the buzz was electric. Jacques Villeneuve was in pole position for his first Grand Prix! It was only the third time in the history of Formula One that a debutant would be starting from pole (Mario Andretti, Watkins Glen 1968 and Carlos Reutemann, Buenos Aires 1972 were the previous cases).

Sensational. With Hill second, only 0.1s adrift, Ferrari newcomer Irvine third, brilliantly out-qualifying Schumacher, a happily recovered Mika Hakkinen fifth and Benetton's Jean Alesi sixth there was a new and exciting look at the front of the Melbourne grid.

Then came the horror..

Villeneuve's first Grand Prix start was immaculate but Hill's wasn't. Damon was out-dragged by both Irvine and

Schumacher before all hell broke loose at Turn Three. As Martin Brundle arrived at some 180 mph from a frustrated 19th on the grid, he hit Coulthard's McLaren, flew through the air over Johnny Herbert's Sauber, barrel-rolled over the gravel trap and slammed into the unyielding concrete wall. It seemed inconceivable that he was unhurt but, amazingly, he clambered from his totally destroyed Jordan and ran back to the pits for medical clearance to restart. It was an incredible demonstration of courage, determination and fitness. Villeneuve made another perfect start and this time Damon go it right as he slotted into second place ahead of Irvine, Schumacher, Alesi and Hakkinen. All through the winter Schumacher had been saying that the new Ferrari F310 with its V10 engine was insufficiently tested and developed to guarantee reliability. But we remembered how, in 1989, Nigel Mansell had won his first race for Ferrari in identi-

Jean Alesi practises refusing to listen to a lecture from Flavio Briatore; Briatore practises refusing to acknowledge the French-Sicilian's response.

"It was only the third time in the history of Formula One that a debutant would be starting from pole"

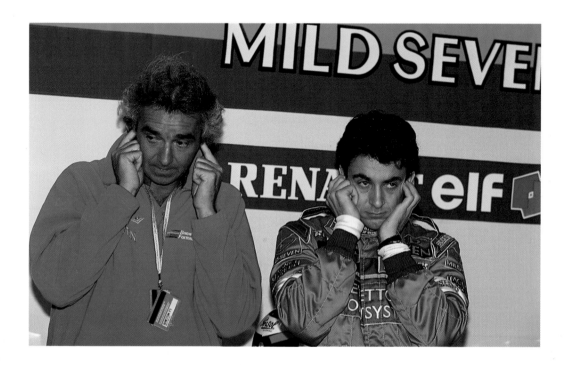

cal circumstances. And now Schumacher was right with the two Williams as they pulled away from the rest.

Had Ferrari been sandbagging? Perhaps, because Irvine was fourth and staying ahead of Alesi, Hakkinen, Barrichello and a slow-starting Gerhard Berger.

Melbourne couldn't have hoped for more. Villeneuve at the front with Hill and Schumacher right behind, constantly challenging. There are places to pass at Albert Park but no one did. It was that close. Irvine dropped back and Alesi caught the Ferrari as Hakkinen, Barrichello, Berger and the excellent Mika Salo formed a high-speed, sixth-to-ninth, nose-to-tail traffic jam. Then, at Turn Three on the 11th of 58 laps, Alesi impetuously tried the impossible - to dive inside Irvine's Ferrari. If Jean thought he could intimidate Eddie he had made his first mistake of the day. His second was when he was in the wrong place

as Irvine claimed the corner. Out went the Benetton with a shredded sidepod.

Something had to happen to break up the leading trio, and Schumacher was the first of the leaders to come in, on lap 19 (12.9s). In third, out fourth behind Irvine. Eddie was next on lap 21. In third, out seventh. But, still as one, Villeneuve and Hill raced on, and on, and on. On lap 27 Villeneuve set the fastest lap of the race (1m 33.421s, 126.960 mph), but Hill was right behind him. Not until lap 29 did Jacques come in to make it plain that both he and Hill were on a one-stop strategy, whereas the Ferraris would be stopping twice.

So, Schumacher's battle with the Williams drivers hadn't been as impressive as it had looked, as he had been running a much lighter fuel load. When Villeneuve stopped and Hill took the lead, Jacques was over 40s ahead of Schumacher. No contest there, but Damon's stop would be

The class of '96 surrounds world champion Schumacher (centre front), the only man whose reported annual salary made Alan Shearer sound inexpensive.

Back in the country where he had almost lost his life only a few months earlier, Mika Hakkinen proved that his latent natural speed was still intact.

crucial. Villeneuve's had taken 17.6s and Hill's, on lap 31, took 18.5. As Damon shot out of the pit lane Villeneuve, on hotter tyres, was right behind him and in Turn Four he scrambled back into the lead. Terrific!

Behind the Williams duo Schumacher slowly entered the pits for an unscheduled stop. Brake trouble. Off came the Ferrari nosecone to get at the master cylinder, but although Michael rejoined he went off at Turn Three before driving in to retire. His prophesy had come true.

Damon was really pressuring Villeneuve. There was nothing in it between them, but as Jacques completed lap 34 he slid sideways on to the grass coming out of Turn One and very nearly lost the Williams. As Hill drew level in a situation ominously reminiscent of his move on Schumacher at Adelaide in 1994, Jacques gathered it all up and Damon sensibly backed off. Better to stay second than take them both out. Irvine was third, Berger had climbed to fourth thanks to some excellent Benetton

pit work, Hakkinen was fifth, and Salo and Frentzen were fighting for the last point. But all eyes were on Jacques and Damon.

Everyone could see, from the haze of smoke at the back of his car, that Villeneuve was losing oil - and lots of it. It was equally plain that the shining white of Hill's car was changing to a slimy brown. But Jacques stayed ahead, getting closer and closer to becoming only the second driver in the history of Formula One to win his first World Championship Grand Prix (Giancarlo Baghetti was the first, taking his only GP win on his debut for Ferrari at Reims in 1961).

Jock Clear, Villeneuve's race engineer was screaming into the radio for Jacques to slow down to save his engine and a maximum 16 points for Williams in the constructors' champi-

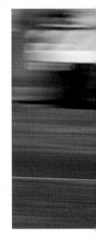

onship. As the red light on his dashboard came on and the team gave him a pit board advising him to slow down, the young Canadian moved over and Hill sailed past. It was all over.

So Damon won his 14th Grand Prix to equal the record of his double world champion father Graham. Both Hill and Villeneuve richly deserved to win. It was a day which showed that the others had got a lot to do before the two South American races.

The over-150,000 crowd went home with a comforting glow. They had seen a great race on a great circuit which had more than justified the contentious move to Melbourne. But most of all they had seen a truly great drive by a new young star who could well become one of the best of all time.

"Most of all they had seen a truly great drive by a new young star who could well become one of the best of all time"

Below: In his first race for Benetton since 1986, Gerhard Berger picked up a fistful of points.

Volunteers conduct aero-dynamic experiments on the FIA's behalf, to see if it is possible to generate closer racing.

FERRARI

Debut race for Michael Schumacher in all-new John Barnard-designed F310 with first Ferrari V10 engine, supported by Eddie Irvine. But car late and reliability suspect after very little testing. Irvine excites establishment by qualifying third ahead of Schumacher (Michael in spare car after rear wing problem, but still only third time in 70 GPs that he had been outqualified by a team-mate). Both Schumacher and Irvine out-drag Hill at start before race stopped when Brundle crashes. After passing Irvine to third, lap two, following second start, two-stop Schumacher (in lighter car) impressively races with one-stop Villeneuve and Hill until lap 19 tyre/fuel stop. Increasingly distant Irvine battles for fourth with Alesi. Schumacher regains third from Irvine, lap 20, but then drops back with loss of brake fluid. Into pits, lap 31, for long, 63.2s, stop during which nose cone removed for attention to master cylinder. Rejoins, now ninth, but goes off at Turn Three and limps back to pit to retire. Irvine and Alesi collide, lap 10, during over-ambitious passing attempt by Jean. Eddie continues unharmed to finish excellent third, with fourth fastest lap, 14.5s behind stricken Villeneuve, in first race for Ferrari. Team not unhappy in view of lack of testing and optimistic for future after further development.

BENETTON-RENAULT

A disheartening start to the season. For first race with Benetton Jean Alesi and Gerhard Berger qualify only sixth and seventh after myriad problems. Alesi blows engine on Saturday and Berger goes into wall, necessitating switch to spare. Jean then hits crewman Michael Jakeman during warm-up practice stop, fortunately without serious injury. Alesi passes Hakkinen to fifth, lap one, and charges to close on Irvine. Catches Eddie and collides with Ferrari during typically "hit or bust" passing move, lap 10. Retires as a result. Berger third fastest in warm-up but down to ninth after bad start and is stuck behind Hakkinen, Barrichello and Frentzen. Passes H-H and battles with Hakkinen/Barrichello but does not progress until benefiting from usual slick Benetton team work at first stop, lap 24. Up to fourth, lap 32, following Schumacher retirement. Retains place after second stop, lap 41, and finishes there.

WILLIAMS-RENAULT

Perfect result and a new star is born. Jacques Villeneuve electrifies Grand Prix scene following enormously impressive times in pre-race testing by taking pole position for first GP; Damon Hill second, only 0.14s slower. Villeneuve makes perfect start and leads away prior to race being stopped after Brundle's lap one crash. A second faultless start sees Villeneuve lead Hill into Turn One. Jacques and Damon then race together, a second or less apart, until lap 29 when JV pits. Hill in from lead two laps later. Exits pit lane just ahead of Jacques who, on hotter tyres, forcefully scrambles past back into lead at Turn Four. Hill pressures Villeneuve non-stop. Jacques slides off, lap 32, but Damon obliged to back off to avoid hitting team-mate. Villeneuve's engine now losing oil and dousing Hill behind. Team instructs him to slow down to save engine and Damon takes lead, lap 54, prior to winning second successive Australian GP and equalling his father Graham's 14 GP wins. Villeneuve sets fastest lap. Maximum points for Williams-Renault in constructors' championship and a stunning debut for Villeneuve.

McLAREN-MERCEDES

New car and engine but depressing result. Happily-recovered (from 1995 Adelaide crash) Mika Hakkinen fifth on grid but 1.7s off pace. Even worse in Sunday warm-up when 2.5s off Hill's time. One-stop Mika races strongly to finish fifth in fine comeback, albeit nearly lapped by Hill. Coulthard has nightmare McLaren debut. Starts 13th after handling problems. Heavily involved in lap one, turn three, melee which causes Brundle's crash and has to restart from pits in spare car set up for Hakkinen. Progresses to 12th, but throttle jams, lap 25, forcing retirement. On this showing new car no better than last year's failure.

LIGIER-MUGEN

Much improved Mugen V10 but much reduced sponsorship - and signs of a developing split between technical director Tom Walkinshaw and powerful Gallic elements anxious to return team to all-French format. Olivier Panis starts 11th. Ex-Forti teamster Pedro Diniz 20th and last. Panis starts well first time but passed by Verstappen at second departure. Races well to finish lapped seventh after two stops. Diniz rammed by Brundle after second start but plugs on to finish 10th, two laps down.

JORDAN-PEUGEOT

Delighted team joins big league after announcing massive sponsorship deal with Benson and Hedges which leads to new all-gold livery. Barrichello eighth on grid after being fifth on Friday, but Martin Brundle only 19th after engine and traction problems. Martin then has gigantic 180 mph lap one crash at Turn Three after hitting Herbert's Sauber and Coulthard's McLaren. Almost unbelievably emerges unharmed from shattered car and calmly runs back to pits to get medical clearance for restart. Takes second start from pit lane in spare car but hits early-braker Pedro Diniz at Turn Three and retires. "A weekend from hell!" says Martin. Barrichello races up to sixth with Hakkinen and Berger. Down to seventh after lap 25 stop before retiring, lap 30, with failed engine.

SAUBER-FORD

Johnny Herbert joins Heinz-Harald Frentzen to race new car with Ford V10 which fails to impress. Heinz-Harald starts ninth two seconds off pace. Herbert 14th in unbalanced car. Neither happy. Frentzen stops on parade lap (electrics) but is able to take second start in unbalanced spare. Does his best and finishes eighth, one lap down and two seconds off pace. Herbert's car damaged in first-start crash and unable to take second start as Frentzen takes spare. A weekend to forget.

ARROWS-HART

New car, new drivers and even better Hart V8 (although still without air valves). Dutchman Jos Verstappen a sensational fourth fastest in Thursday familiarisation runs, seventh fastest on Saturday morning and qualifies 12th. Up to 10th behind Frentzen and Salo, lap 10, prior to early stop, lap 13. Then, sadly and most unusually, engine fails, lap 16. Brazilian newcomer Ricardo Rosset qualifies 18th for first GP. Spins, lap five, trying to pass Pedro Lamy but is happy to finish 10th, two laps down.

TYRRELL-YAMAHA

Unlike most of the teams Tyrrell leave Melbourne happy. New 024 with very impressive new Yamaha V10 is vast improvement on 1995 car and Mika Salo qualifies 10th despite having to use spare after rear suspension problem with race car. Ukyo Katayama has cockpit-fit, gearbox and engine problems which limit pre-race laps before qualifying 15th. Both drivers stall engines due to clutch problem at first start so are lucky that race is stopped. Team tells Salo to drive conservatively in view of anticipated attrition and Mika finishes sixth, one lap down. Still-uncomfortable Katayama unable to drive flat out and has to slow with overheating engine. Lapped three times but finishes 11th.

MINARDI-FORD

A tough time for enthusiastic Italian team with little-changed version of 1995 car and "customer" Ford ED V8 engine. Rentadriver Taki Inoue fails to come up with money and is thankfully replaced by impressive 1995 Italian Formula Three champion Giancarlo Fisichella who qualifies 16th, a place ahead of team mate Pedro Lamy. Both drivers overcome by clutch problems in race. Lamy has to switch to spare when race car clutch fails on grid. Hit by Rosset after second start. Stops three times for safety belts to be tightened before retiring for safety reasons. Fisichella starts well but retires from 13th, lap 33, when clutch fails.

FORTI-FORD

With a little-updated version of the totally inadequate 1995 car the Forti team, now without Pedro Diniz's substantial financial backing, does not stand a chance. Ex-1995 Minardi teamster Luca Badoer does no laps in Thursday familiarisation sessions and Andrea Montermini car catches fire in garage on Friday. Neither manages to lap within 107 per cent of pole time, so neither qualifies. New car not expected until race four at the Nurburgring...in late April.

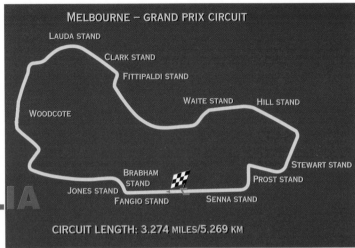

FORMULA 1 WORLD CHAMPIONSHIP

RACE 1

AUSTRALIA

10 March 1996

MELBOURNE – GRAND PRIX CIRCUIT

LAUDA STAND
CLARK STAND
FITTIPALDI STAND
WAITE STAND
HILL STAND
WOODCOTE
STEWART STAND
BRABHAM STAND
PROST STAND
JONES STAND
FANGIO STAND
SENNA STAND

CIRCUIT LENGTH: 3.274 MILES/5.269 KM

STARTING GRID

VILLENEUVE 1m 32.371s	**HILL** 1m 32.509s
IRVINE 1m 32.889s	**SCHUMACHER** 1m 33.125s
HAKKINEN 1m 34.054s	**ALESI** 1m 34.257s
BERGER 1m 34.344s	**BARRICHELLO** 1m 34.474s
FRENTZEN 1m 34.494s	**SALO** 1m 34.832s
PANIS 1m 35.330s	**VERSTAPPEN** 1m 35.338s
COULTHARD 1m 35.351s	**HERBERT** 1m35.453s
KATAYAMA 1m 35.715s	**FISICHELLA** 1m 35.898s
LAMY 1m 36.109s	**ROSSET** 1m 36.198s
BRUNDLE 1m 36.286s	**DINIZ** 1m 36.298s

Did not qualify

BADOER (Forti FG01B) 1M 39.202s	**MONTERMINI** (Forti FG01B) 1M 42.087S

RACE CLASSIFICATION

Pos	Driver	Nat	Car	Laps	Time
1	Damon Hill	GB	Williams FW18-Renault V10	58	1h 32m 50.491s
2	Jacques Villeneuve	CDN	Williams FW18-Renault V10	58	+38.020s
3	Eddie Irvine	GB	Ferrari F310-Ferrari V10	58	+1m 02.571s
4	Gerhard Berger	A	Benetton B196-Renault V10	58	+1m 17.037s
5	Mika Hakkinen	SF	Mclaren MP4/11-Mercedes V10	58	+1m 35.071s
6	Mika Salo	SF	Tyrrell 024-Yamaha V10		+1 lap
7	Olivier Panis	F	Ligier JS43-Mugen Honda V10		+1 lap
8	Heinz-Harald Frentzen	D	Sauber C15-Ford V10		+1 lap
9	Ricardo Rosset	BR	Footwork FA17-Hart V8		+2 laps
10	Pedro Diniz	BR	Ligier JS43-Mugen Honda V10		+2 laps
11	Ukyo Katayama	J	Tyrrell 024-Yamaha V10		+3 laps

Retirements	Nat	Car	Lap	Reason
Pedro Lamy	P	Minardi M195B-Ford V8	42	Broken exhaust
Michael Schumacher	D	Ferrari F310-Ferrari V10	32	Brakes
Giancarlo Fisichella	I	Minardi M195B-Ford V8	32	Clutch
Rubens Barrichello	BR	Jordan 196-Peugeot V10	29	Engine
David Coulthard	GB	McLaren MP4/11-Mercedes V10	24	Jammed throttle
Jos Verstappen	NL	Footwork FA17-Hart V8	15	Engine
Jean Alesi	F	Benetton B196-Renault V10	9	Accident
Martin Brundle	GB	Jordan 196-Peugeot V10	1	Spin
DNS Johnny Herbert	GB	Sauber C15-Ford V10		First start accident

FASTEST LAP Jacques Villeneuve 1m 33.421s lap 27 (126.960mph)

DRIVERS' CHAMPIONSHIP

Damon Hill	10
Jacques Villeneuve	6
Eddie Irvine	4
Gerhard Berger	3
Mika Hakkinen	2
Mika Salo	1

CONSTRUCTORS' CUP

Williams-Renault	16
Ferrari	4
Benetton-Renault	3
McLaren-Mercedes	2
Tyrrell-Yamaha	1

Results and Data © FIA 1996

Hill demon-
strates just
how like a wet
Tuesday in
Morecambe
Sao Paulo can
sometimes be.

Sao Paulo didn't seem quite so bad this year. Maybe it was down to familiarity, but the foul, omni-present smog seemed a bit thinner, the smoke-belching trucks slightly less noxious, the bumper-to-bumper traffic less aggressive and the general frenzy of life a whisker calmer.

None of these impressions were realistic, of course. The degrading favelas, where people live in indescribable conditions without power, water and sanitation, were still there and the dreary River Tiete still foamed with chemical pollution. Sao Paulo is most definitely not Formula One's favourite place, but it again hosted an excellent Grand Prix. Mostly because of Interlagos.

The superb 2.7-mile track tests both car and driver with its two 180mph straights, its

ROUND 2

BRAZIL

occasion that stirs the senses.

For years, Brazil has traditionally been the first race of the season but this time it followed Australia where Williams had been the class of the field. With only a three-week gap and the need to fly the cars from Melbourne to their European bases, rebuild them and then get them to Brazil there had been no real time to continue the much-needed development of the Ferraris, McLarens, Benettons and Jordans which had failed to challenge the Williams-Renaults, but everyone had done their best.

Was it going to be good enough? In a word, no.

Ferrari, despite all its money, top technicians, the world's best driver and a bold new car, was in trouble. The new titanium transverse gearbox had been cracking in Melbourne and had to be replaced with the 1995 'box and diffusor. The result was twitchy handling, which Eddie Irvine demonstrated by going off heavily on his very first lap of practice. Schumacher lost time with a water leak on Saturday morning and also crashed during the race warm-up.

Both Benetton drivers went off on Saturday morning and the new McLaren-Mercedes MP4/11, on which so many hopes rested, was not to the liking of either Mika Hakkinen or David Coulthard. The new Ford V10 engine at Sauber hadn't enough grunt, and Ligier was in disarray after Tom Walkinshaw had announced his imminent departure with his personnel and sponsorship funds. The Scot was in the process of purchasing the financially beleaguered Arrows team to further his Formula One ambitions. However, the hero of Brazil, Rubens Barrichello, and the doughty Martin Brundle were both delighted with their Jordans, despite running with reduced revs from their Peugeot V10s in the interests of reliability.

To no one's surprise it was Damon Hill

varied corners and its gradients. In the past it has also tested them most unwelcomely with its appallingly bumpy surface but this year it had just been resurfaced for the better. No longer were the drivers' feet being bounced off the pedals and their shins smashed against the bulkheads.

Throw in searing heat and tens of thousands of wildly enthusiastic, chanting, horn-blowing Paulistas and you've got an

Below. A
Torrentmeister
Alesi harasses
Villeneuve.
Taking part in
only the second
wet race of his
career, the
Canadian would
get to find out
about the low
friction surface
properties of
Brazilian gravel.

who set the pace in qualifying. In Melbourne his astounding new team-mate Jacques Villeneuve had been fastest, but in Sao Paulo the young Canadian was disadvantaged in that his rivals knew the circuit. Hill, with three races at Interlagos behind him, was untouchable. His 12th career pole position was nearly a second faster than anyone else. Villeneuve was third after methodically working away at learning the track.

But Brazil didn't give a hoot about that, "Rubinho" was second on the grid! Rubens Barrichello, calm and confident, and fired up by the support of his countrymen, had gone faster than everyone except Hill. He felt that his second place was even better than his 1994 pole position in Belgium. "I was lucky to be on the track at the right moment there, but here I was fighting with the big boys!"

With the Ferraris of Schumacher and Irvine fourth and 10th, the Benettons of Alesi and Berger fifth and eighth, Brundle's Jordan sixth, the McLarens of Hakkinen and Coulthard seventh and 14th it looked as though Brazil would be a Williams benefit.

It was, but not in the way that people expected. The rain saw to that.

After two days of perfect sunshine and idyllic conditions for the warm-up, the heavens opened 40 minutes before the race was due to start. When it rains at Sao Paulo, it deluges. In next to no time the track was awash in parts, with the pit lane like a river. Out came the wet-weather tyres but, as the rain died down and the skies began to clear, would the race be started? It took a brave decision but yes, it would.

At one o'clock sharp the red lights went out and the 22 cars (the Fortis had qualified within the 107 per cent time limit) surged away with giant roosters of water pluming up from their rear wheels. Lucky Damon. He was in front with a clear track, and he made the most of it.

"The conditions were pretty risky early on, but I was eager to get a gap between myself and whoever was behind me." That he did, and on lap three he led by nearly 10s - from Villeneuve. With a superb start the young Canadian star had got past Barrichello, as had Jean Alesi, and as Hill remorselessly pulled away a battle royal developed for third place, a second and a half behind Villeneuve. Alesi led it with Barrichello right behind him, Schumacher fifth, looking for a way past the Jordan, and Brundle and Frentzen fighting for sixth. It was a terrific spectacle.

After 17 of the 71 laps Frentzen, who was enhancing his considerable reputation even

Left: Coulthard
seeks arboreal
shelter after life
as a McLaren
driver failed to
get any easier.

Right:
Schumacher
scored his first
points for
Ferrari, albeit
a lap adrift of
his erstwhile
arch-rival.

"Lucky
Damon.
He was
in front
with
a clear
track,
and he
made
the
most
of it...
on lap
three he
led by
nearly
10s"

"Paulistas voted with their feet by leaving the circuit in their thousands after the retirement of Barrichello"

more in the underpowered Sauber, got past Schumacher's Ferrari. A new experience for Michael, although he took the place back on the next lap as, ahead of him, Alesi and Barrichello fought equally hard for third. Time after time Rubens would try to scrabble past the Benetton; and time after time he was rebuffed, as Alesi managed to keep Villeneuve in his sights. Then, on lap 27, Jacques lost it. It was only the second time in his entire career that he had raced in the wet. He had been coping magnificently with the conditions, but as Alesi made another bid for second the back of the Williams stepped out and Villeneuve was gone. Six points lost, but nothing to be ashamed of.

On lap 22 Coulthard had been the first of the top men to change to slicks as track conditions improved. Although he managed another eight laps, he paid the penalty for switching too soon by spinning out. After watching the Scot, most of the others decided to stay on rain tyres and go for a two-stop strategy. Schumacher came in on lap 24, Frentzen on lap 26, Hakkinen and Brundle on lap 30 and Barrichello on lap 34. But Hill and Alesi stayed out and they made the right decision.

On lap 40, with a dry line now most of the way round the circuit, Damon made his sole stop to take on slicks. On lap 42 Alesi

Irvine's Ferrari career started with a bang of one sort, and continued with a bang of another. On his first lap out on Friday...

did the same and then the others had to come in to change from their overheating wets to dry-weather Goodyears. With the right rubber and a stop less, Hill and Alesi were literally home and dry. No one could touch them now. They just had to keep going.

By lap 45, Berger had long since retired in a Benetton which had never performed and the gallant Frentzen had lost fifth when his engine failed; he had been 10s ahead of Schumacher at the time, too. So, with 26 laps to go Hill was nearly 25s ahead of Alesi. Schumacher lay an amazing 72s behind the Williams, and Barrichello was swarming all over the Ferrari's gearbox. Hakkinen was a lapped fifth, with Mika Salo's Tyrrell right behind him. Everyone was on their last set of tyres. It was now a run to the finish.

Hill and Alesi were uncatchable, and Jean was making no real impression on the leader as Damon watched the gap and responded when he needed to.

The battle between Schumacher and Barrichello for third place raced on unabated though until, on lap 60, Rubens made another lunge to get past the Ferrari. Not only did he fail but he spun out as, later, did his team-mate Brundle. On lap 62, Hill had the enormous satisfaction of lapping Schumacher; three laps later, he completed his day by setting the fastest lap. It was all over bar the shouting, and there was precious little of that as the depressed Paulistas voted with their feet by leaving the circuit in their thousands after the retirement of Barrichello.

Hill had driven superbly to win his 15th GP, having lapped everyone except Jean Alesi. Now he led the championship by a 14 points after only two races. Too early even to be thinking about being number one in 1997, but very comforting nevertheless. Only Jean Alesi could feel anything like as happy. Ferrari had failed Schumacher. Benetton had failed Berger. Ford had failed Frentzen and Johnny Herbert.

Hakkinen may have finished fourth, but he had been lapped. Coulthard had never been at ease in his McLaren. Barrichello

Above. Carrying the hopes of Brazil on his shoulders, native Paulista Barrichello qualified on the front row, but failed to finish. Germany's stock of F1 drivers follows.

and Brundle had blown Jordan's chances. Two of the others could be mighty pleased with themselves though. Mika Salo finished an excellent fifth for Tyrrell and Dutchman Jos Verstappen had raced in seventh for 12 laps until the Hart engine in his underfunded Arrows had, most unusually, let go.

After the race ex-McLaren driver and Eurosport TV commentator John Watson told me he had jokingly suggested to FIA President Max Mosley that all circuits should be required to have a sprinkler system to wet the track randomly during every Grand Prix. "Wet/dry races are always the most exciting," said John; he wasn't wrong. Brazil 1996 had gripped everyone from start to finish. Now there was only a week to the next South American race, won in 1995 by Damon Hill...

Left. "It'd be good for my begonias if it was like this at home." Peter Sauber contemplates the meteorological advantages of Brazil over Switzerland.

25

FERRARI

Team fits 1995 gearbox and diffusor to new 310 after problems with transverse titanium box at Melbourne. Both drivers unhappy with rear end stability and twitchy handling. Irvine crashes heavily on Friday and, unable to use spare car, loses whole day. Schumacher also loses time on Saturday morning when water leak necessitates engine change. Michael then goes off in race car during Sunday warm-up and breaks rear suspension. Schumacher/Irvine start fourth/10th, with Michael 1.36s off Hill's pole time. As a result of the pre-race storm, team opts for high-downforce set-up which penalises performance as track dries. Schumacher passed by Alesi at start and battles for third with Jean and Barrichello for 16 laps until caught and passed by Heinz-Harald Frentzen on lap 17 - a new experience for Michael. Regains fifth before first of two stops, lap 24. Rejoins 12th and up to fourth at second stop for slick tyres, lap 40. Passes fired-up Barrichello to third when Rubens pits, lap 44, but is lapped by both Hill and Alesi before finishing third. Irvine ships water on formation lap and drops to 13th. Up to fifth prior to originally intended sole stop, lap 35, but has to come in again for slicks, lap 43. Finishes lapped seventh. "Now we have a lot of work to do as we must improve in many areas," says Schumacher. Where had we heard that before?

BENETTON-RENAULT

Good weekend for Alesi. Awful for Berger. Jean fastest on Friday with Gerhard second but both go off on Saturday morning, losing valuable set-up time. Berger further affected by lack of top speed due to reduced air-box pressure caused by his height. Result is fifth (Alesi) and eighth on the grid. Jean drives excellent race. Up to third, lap one, and stays ahead of Barrichello and Schumacher in fierce 23-lap battle. To second after Villeneuve goes off, lap 27, and stays there with correct one-stop strategy to finish second, 18s down, as only driver unlapped by Hill. Berger slides down field as loses hydraulic pressure before retiring, lap 27. Reigning champion Benetton 17 points behind Williams in constructors' contest after two races.

WILLIAMS-RENAULT

The class of the field again. Hill takes 12th career pole position nearly a second faster than anyone else and dominates race. Leads almost every lap with perfect-strategy, one fuel/tyre stop. Laps everyone except Alesi. Sets fastest lap (1m 21.547s, 118.645mph) and wins 15th GP by 18s to increase championship lead to 14 points. Despite going off in qualifying, Villeneuve starts very impressive third for first race at Interlagos. In only second wet race in whole career, passes Barrichello to take second, lap one, and stays there, some 15s behind Hill, ahead of Alesi/Barrichello/Schumacher battle. Succumbs to non-stop pressure from Jean, lap 27, by sliding off track and out of race. Williams now 17 points clear of Benetton in constructors' championship.

McLAREN-MERCEDES

Another grimly uncompetitive race for the new MP4/11. "There's no real reason why we should go any better here than in Australia," says David Coulthard, who proves to be right. Using new tyres both Coulthard and Hakkinen faster than Hill on Friday, but Mika disappointed seventh on grid, 1.5s off Hill, and very unhappy Coulthard 14th, unable to balance car. Following major set-up changes Hakkinen improves to excellent third in warm-up, Coulthard has more trouble. Stops twice with failed pneumatic pressure and has to have engine changed before race. Cautious Mika down 10 places in wet on first lap but, now delighted with handling, advances to fourth by first stop, lap 30. In again, lap 43, for slicks and, with wrong strategy, finishes seventh. Coulthard shoots up five places to ninth on first lap. Slides off and down to 14th, lap 20. Rejoins and on drying track makes early stop for slicks, lap 22, but disadvantaged when rain returns. Spins out of race, lap 30.

LIGIER-MUGEN

Major drama for team when Tom Walkinshaw, fed up with inability to run it as he wishes, buys ailing Arrows organisation and announces progressive withdrawal of TWR people and sponsorship monies from Ligier. Panis excellent sixth fastest on Friday but spins in qualifying due to seized shock-absorber; starts 15th. Drives strong two-stop race in well-handling car, finishing lapped sixth to score team's first 1996 point despite throttle sticking for last 20 laps. Pedro Diniz qualifies 18th at home track but relegated to 22nd and last on grid after breaking several rules during qualifying. Then drives praiseworthy race, showing much-improved form, to finish eighth, two laps down.

JORDAN-PEUGEOT

So near and yet so far. Now well-funded team announces appointment of the excellent Gianni Morbidelli as test driver. Barrichello and Brundle both superb in qualifying with Rubens starting inspired second on grid for home GP, just a few hundred metres from his family home. Martin sixth even though penalised by faulty gearchange. To underline vastly improved Jordan-Peugeot performance, Brundle sets fastest time in warm-up with Rubens fourth. Barrichello passed by Villeneuve and Alesi on lap one but then has terrific battle with Jean, closely followed by Schumacher and Frentzen. To third after Villeneuve slides off and then to second past Alesi until first stop, lap 34. In for slicks, lap 43, and passed by Schumacher. Harries Michael for third but spins out, lap 60. Brundle, unhappy with handling in wet, spins down to 11th, lap 16. Stops twice (rain tyres lap 30, slicks lap 44 when fifth). Down to ninth after stalling in pits before also spinning out, from seventh, lap 64. Very promising for team but no points again.

SAUBER-FORD

Cosworth raises rev limit for Ford V10 but both Frentzen and Herbert still very frustrated by lack of driveability and power from new engine. H-H starts ninth despite losing set-up time with engine problem on Friday; Herbert 12th. Neither finishes. Benefiting from wet conditions which reduce performance gap, Frentzen drives magnificently to close with fifth-running Schumacher's Ferrari and then pass it on lap 17. Schumacher regains place but Frentzen back to fifth when Michael pits, lap 24. H-H then drops to eighth following lap 26 stop. Climbs back to fifth - 10s ahead of Schumacher - but has to retire, lap 36, when engine pneumatic-valve system fails. Even worse for Herbert who has engine problem on grid and has to start from pit lane in spare car. Climbs to 15th but then retires with engine problem, lap 29. Both drivers very disheartened.

ARROWS-HART

Financially beleaguered team's future brightens when Tom Walkinshaw announces departure from Ligier and takeover of Arrows. Very impressive Jos Verstappen, eighth fastest on Friday and in warm-up, qualifies 13th after being delayed in traffic. Brilliantly up to sixth on lap three in waterlogged conditions. Passed by Frentzen and Brundle but retakes Martin and runs seventh until retiring, lap 19, with engine problem. A great effort. Newcomer Ricardo Rosset starts 17th on his home track. Climbs to 14th before having colossal 150mph slide into wall on lap 11. Undoubtedly saved by new safety rules when front wheel comes back and hits new higher-cockpit side.

TYRRELL-YAMAHA

Another encouraging race. Both Mika Salo and Ukyo Katayama practice starts in testing following poor getaways in Australia Salo qualifies 11th with Katayama 16th after leaving his main effort too late. A very good race for Salo, who is deliberately cautious in opening wet laps. Climbs through field to third on lap 35 following a terrific scrap with compatriot Hakkinen. Down to seventh after lap 43 stop for slicks but finishes lapped fifth, in points for fourth successive race. With misted-up open visor Katayama hit in eye by stone at start and then spun by Lamy on lap two. Races hard at rear of field but loses lap by entering pits for slicks when Salo already there. Finishes ninth, two laps down.

MINARDI-FORD

Giancarlo Fisichella replaced by 20-year-old Brazilian, ex-Formula 3000 hotshoe Tarso Marques for the two South American races. Marques does very well to qualify 19th for first F1 race, marginally downgraded to 21st for missing the "stop-for-weighing" red light on Saturday afternoon. He would have had to start last if Pedro Diniz hadn't transgressed even more. Tarso decelerates after start to avoid confrontation ahead, spins out and stalls. End of race. Lamy makes astonishing progress to 11th on first lap but spins down to 20th in unsuccessfully trying to dodge Katayama. Soldiers on at rear of field and finishes 10th, three laps down.

FORTI-FORD

In an atmosphere of concern about whether the Brazilian team can continue much longer in its uncompetitive state, ex-Ferrari and Ligier team manager Cesare Fiorio joins to do the same job for Forti. Luca Badoer and Andrea Montermini qualify 21st and 22nd, both over five seconds off the pace but within the 107 per cent time limit, for their first race of 1996. Upgraded to 19th and 20th on the grid by the demotion of Marques and Diniz. Montermini, with estimated settings for the wet, spins three times before retiring from last place on lap 27. Luca Badoer continues at back to give team its first finish of year - 11th, four laps down.

FIA FORMULA 1 WORLD CHAMPIONSHIP

RACE 2

BRAZIL

31 March 1996

AUTODROMO JOSE CARLOS PACE, INTERLAGOS, SÃO PAULO

SUBIDA DO LAGO

CURVA DO SOL

DESCIDA DO SOL

BICO DE PATO

MERGULHO

PINHEIRINHO

FERRA DURA

SUBIDA DOS BOXES

CIRCUIT LENGTH:
2.687 MILES/4.325 KM

STARTING GRID

	HILL 1m 18.111s
BARRICHELLO 1m 19.092s	
	VILLENEUVE 1m 19.254s
SCHUMACHER 1m 19.474s	
	ALESI 1m 19.484s
BRUNDLE 1m 19.519s	
	HAKKINEN 1m 19.607s
BERGER 1m 19.762s	
	FRENTZEN 1m 19.799s
IRVINE 1m 19.951s	
	SALO 1m 20.000s
HERBERT 1m 20.144s	
	VERSTAPPEN 1m 20.157s
COULTHARD 1m 20.167s	
	PANIS 1m 20.426s
KATAYAMA 1m 20.427s	
	ROSSET 1m 20.440s
DINIZ 1m 20.873s	
	MARQUES 1m 21.421s
LAMY 1m 21.491s	
	BADOER 1m 23.174s
MONTERMINI 1m 23.454s	

RACE CLASSIFICATION

Pos	Driver	Nat	Car	Laps	Time
1	Damon Hill	GB	Williams FW18-Renault V10	71	1h 49m 52.976s
2	Jean Alesi	F	Benetton B196-Renault V10	71	+17.982s
3	Michael Schumacher	D	Ferrari F310-Ferrari V10		+1 lap
4	Mika Hakkinen	SF	McLaren MP4/11-Mercedes V10		+1 lap
5	Mika Salo	SF	Tyrrell 024-Yamaha V10		+1 lap
6	Olivier Panis	F	Ligier JS43-Mugen Honda V10		+1 lap
7	Eddie Irvine	GB	Ferrari F310-Ferrari V10		+1 lap
8	Pedro Diniz	BR	Ligier JS43-Mugen Honda V10		+2 laps
9	Ukyo Katayama	J	Tyrrell 024-Yamaha V10		+2 laps
10	Pedro Lamy	P	Minardi M195B-Ford V8		+3 laps
11	Luca Badoer	I	Forti FG01B-Ford V8		+3 laps
12	Martin Brundle	GB	Jordan 196-Peugeot V10		+7 laps

Retirements	Nat	Car	Lap	Reason
Rubens Barrichello	BR	Jordan 196-Peugeot V10	59	Spin
Heinz-Harald Frentzen	D	Sauber C15-Ford V10	36	Engine
David Coulthard	GB	McLaren MP4/11-Mercedes V10	29	Spin
Johnny Herbert	GB	Sauber C15-Ford V10	28	Engine
Jacques Villeneuve	CDN	Williams FW18-Renault V10	26	Spin
Gerhard Berger	A	Benetton B196-Renault V10	26	Hydraulics
Andrea Montermini	I	Forti FG01B-Ford V8	26	Spin
Ricardo Rosset	BR	Footwork FA17-Hart V8	24	Accident
Jos Verstappen	NL	Footwork FA17-Hart V8	19	Spin
Tarso Marques	BR	Minardi M195B-Ford V8	0	Accident
FASTEST LAP		Damon Hill 1m 21.547s lap 65 (118.646mph)		

DRIVERS' CHAMPIONSHIP

Damon Hill	20
Jacques Villeneuve	6
Jean Alesi	6
Mika Hakkinen	5
Eddie Irvine	4
Michael Schumacher	4
Gerhard Berger	3
Mika Salo	3
Olivier Panis	1

CONSTRUCTORS' CUP

Williams-Renault	26
Benetton-Renault	9
Ferrari	8
McLaren-Mercedes	5
Tyrrell-Yamaha	3
Ligier-Mugen Honda	1

Results and Data © FIA 1996

To Buenos Aires, Argentina. It's first thing on Monday morning after the Brazilian GP, and no one is unhappy to be leaving the high-rise frenzy, grimness and pollution of Sao Paulo.

For adjoining countries there's a wealth of difference between Brazil and Argentina. Portuguese is the language in Brazil; it's Spanish in Argentina. In Sao Paulo, there's an uneasy atmosphere; it is calmer and altogether nicer in Buenos Aires, which is European in feeling, with a mix of truly impressive traditional public buildings and modern architecture. And the restaurants are unsurpassed. They don't so much give you a steak as the whole animal!

If only the Oscar A Galvez Autodromo on the outskirts of the city was as good as the circuit at Interlagos, then the Argentine experience would be truly sublime. But, sadly, it isn't. The Almirante Brown Park in which it is situated is pleasant enough but the configuration of the flat, Scalextric-like track, with a welter of second- and third-gear corners, makes it mostly 'point and squirt'. Yes, there is a reasonably long straight with a 160 mph bend, but it was marred by two colossal bumps where the cars actually took off. They were so severe that Johnny Herbert's fire extinguisher activated itself in his Sauber's cockpit. Some cars' chassis were even delaminating.

What's more, the whole track needed resurfacing - especially the bit where some lunatic, aggrieved by the results of a recent touring car race, had gouged lumps out of it with a mechanical digger!

Damon Hill had now won three Grands Prix in succession, the last of 1995 and the first two of 1996. With a 14-point lead in the championship he was on a roll in a car which was undeniably the best. There had been no time for development or testing since Brazil, only for transportation. So there was no logical reason to expect any change in the pecking order. Some people tend to be dismissive of the season-opening

Above: Hill won the race; Villeneuve was quickest off the blocks in the assembly area.

Forti takes novel steps to guarantee TV exposure: Luca Badoer escaped uninjured, though the ensuing safety car was harmful to Hill's lead.

long-haul races, and contend that the racing doesn't really start until the teams get to Europe. But the points count just the same. Hill would be in great shape if he could score another maximum.

However, he had a potential rival. At Sao Paulo Michael Schumacher had predicted, "The track at Buenos Aires will suit the Ferrari much better than Interlagos. We can't cope with the bumps which are everywhere here, but they're not so bad at BA and we'll be able to set the car up stiffer."

Despite the kidney-pounders on the back

straight, he was right.

On a track where it is as difficult to pass as at Monaco and Hungary, Michael went for it and produced one of the most exciting spectacles we'd seen for a long time. Fighting the nervous F310 every inch of the way, and looking like flying off the track all the time, he was blindingly quick. Fastest on Friday morning; only a tenth off Damon in the afternoon; quickest again on Saturday morning.

So, his first pole for Ferrari? Well, no, but it was mighty close. Right until the closing

Jean Alesi asks a passer-by whether or not she knows any means of getting through the first couple of corners without hitting things.

Right: For the second time in three races, Jacques Villeneuve belied his rookie F1 status by trailing team-mate Damon Hill across the line. The French-Canadian's stock was growing...

minutes of qualifying, Schumacher's name was at the top of the monitors as Hill calmly waited in the garage. Then out rolled Damon to put in a banzai lap which was just 0.2s faster. It was Damon's 13th career pole and Michael's first front row for Ferrari. 'The Colliding Rivals' were together again; would they get round the first corner?

Jacques Villeneuve was an impressive third, despite the fact that Buenos Aires had been yet another new track to him. The Benettons of Alesi and Berger were next, with Barrichello's Jordan sixth and the underfunded Arrows of Jos Verstappen a brilliant seventh - ahead of Hakkinen, Coulthard, Irvine, Frentzen and Panis.

The Benetton mechanics worked all night on new set-ups for their drivers, and it was worth it. Alesi and Berger were first and second in Sunday's warm-up, two seconds faster than their qualifying times and a second faster than Hill's. True, track conditions were better, but there were excellent prospects for the race.

Hill got it exactly right as the lights went out, moving straight into the lead with Michael, Jean and Gerhard tucked up behind him as Villeneuve slipped to ninth after a bodged getaway. David Coulthard was one of those to profit, vaulting from ninth to fifth.

As Hill and Schumacher fought for the lead, Villeneuve was on the move. He passed Hakkinen on lap three, Verstappen on lap four, Barrichello on lap five and Coulthard on lap 12. By now, fourth-placed Berger was only 15s in front of the French-Canadian.

On lap 21 out of 72, 10s covered a calm and assured-looking Hill, Schumacher (6.5s adrift of the leader), Alesi and

Berger. Then in came Schumacher for what was to be the first of three stops. Alesi was next, followed by Hill, Berger and Villeneuve. With all now on their second set of Goodyears, there were two dramatic happenings, both involving Ligier's Pedro Diniz, which transformed the race.

As Pedro attempted to lap Badoer he clipped the sluggish Forti and, in a flash, Luca was upside down, and struggling to escape. Eventually he succeeded; as he did so out came the safety car to slow things down whilst the Forti was craned away. Damon's advantage was simultaneously worn away. Schumacher was now a car's length in arrears as the field closed up.

Meanwhile, Diniz had been in for a new nose and to refuel. As he rejoined and braked for Turn Three petrol gushed out of a jammed return valve and enveloped the engine. The whole car erupted into a gigantic high-speed fireball and it was a relief

Sauber tries a means of weight-saving: don't bother to attach the monocoque.

"There were two dramatic happenings, both involving Pedro Diniz, which transformed the race"

David Coulthard scored his best result yet for McLaren...but seventh place earned him no points. The following Barrichello got fourth.

"Alesi squandered a seemingly certain second place. Pitting for his second stop, he stalled and lost some 17s"

that Pedro, with his helmet ablaze, managed to sprint from the Ligier after it had gyrated into the gravel. The marshals did a good job and rapidly extinguished the fire as the field, with their tyres cooling, trolled around behind the official Renault Clio.

At the end of lap 32 it pulled in and the race recommenced. With 40 laps to go only five seconds covered the top 10. Now it was Damon's turn to apply the pressure. With a clear track ahead he got the hammer down and gradually eased away from the Ferrari. By lap 40 he had built a gap of five seconds - back to where he was before the safety car came out. Schumacher, now on a revised two-stop strategy, came in for what was scheduled to have been his last stop.

But he was in trouble. Shortly after the safety car withdrew, a piece of debris from a collision between the Minardi of Tarso Marques and Martin Brundle's Jordan had been flung up by Hill's Williams. "I instinctively ducked my head," said

Michael. "A few laps later I realised that something was wrong and finally the (rear) wing broke." For the second time in three races Schumacher was out. "It was a shame because the car was quite good and I am sure I would have finished on the podium."

So Alesi was now second with only three seconds covering himself, Berger and Villeneuve - for whom the safety car had been an unexpected bonus. When it came out he was 46s behind Hill; when it went the gap was 2.3!

It was at this point that Alesi squandered a seemingly certain second place. Pitting for his second stop, he stalled and lost some 17s. He dropped to eighth, with Berger up to second harried by Villeneuve. Coulthard was a more encouraging fourth, albeit with Verstappen virtually attached to his diffusor. As team-mate Schumacher cruised in to retire, Eddie Irvine was sixth.

On lap 53, with 19 to go, the race looked set. With their second stops completed,

Hill led Berger by 11s. Gerhard had the persistent and enormously impressive Villeneuve four seconds behind him and was maintaining the gap. Alesi had charged up to fourth but seemed unlikely to improve and Barrichello was a safe fifth. The battle was for sixth with 3.6s covering Coulthard, Irvine, Panis and Verstappen.

But you should never take anything for granted in Formula One. On lap 57 Berger retired with his rear suspension knackered by the back straight launch pad. Three laps later, the audacious Verstappen, apparently not realising that his Arrows team's budget

was a fraction of McLaren's, cheekily passed Coulthard and set about catching the equally well-funded Ferrari of Irvine. He not only caught it, he passed it on the last lap. To be fair to Eddie, he was stuck in sixth gear at the time - and he managed to regain the place when Jos out-braked himself. It had been a typically gutsy effort by the young Dutchman.

So Hill, who had never really looked in trouble for the whole race, made it four in a row. His third win of the year increased his championship lead to a very healthy 18 points. What we didn't know at the time though was that, with a nasty attack of the Brazilian trots, he hadn't eaten for two days and that his radio hadn't worked for the whole race.

It had been a mighty fine drive, as had those of Villeneuve, who finished second for the second time in his first three Grands Prix, and Alesi. In a magnificent recovery charge after his pit stop debacle, Jean set the fastest lap of the race and finished third, only 2.5s behind Villeneuve.

With Barrichello fourth to score Jordan's first points of the season, and Verstappen doing likewise for Arrows behind Irvine, there were five different constructors in the top six. But it had been Williams' day again - and it looked likely to remain that way for a while. There were three weeks to go before the start of the European season, however, so there was time for the rest to respond.

You take the low road... Verstappen tries the conventional approach; Irvine evaluates the frictional properties of grass.

FERRARI

Track suits highly-strung F310 better than Interlagos; Schumacher almost overcomes car deficiencies with driving brilliance. Is breathtakingly spectacular and aggressive during practice and holds pole position for much of qualifying. Finally yields as Hill goes faster, but starts on front row for first time in a Ferrari. Gets away well and retains second place, gradually dropping back until 6.5s adrift of Damon at first of three planned stops, lap 21. Rejoins fourth and back to second, 4.3s down, lap 25. Is right behind Hill when safety car pulls off, lap 32, but then falls back again. Revises strategy and comes in for second and final stop, lap 40. Slows and retires, lap 41, with rear wing damage caused by Badoer/Diniz collision debris thrown up by Hill's Williams on lap 34. "It was a shame because the car was good and I am sure I would have finished on the podium." Irvine, unable to cope with handling problems like Michael, starts 10th, 1.7s off the pace. On two-stop strategy is seventh by lap 26 and fifth by lap 47. Finishes fifth, stuck in sixth gear, after re-passing Jos Verstappen on last lap. Team due to hold much-needed development tests at Monza.

BENETTON-RENAULT

Car performance improved by revised internal air-box configuration. Alesi qualifies fourth, Berger fifth. Both drivers concerned about set-up. Mechanics work all Saturday night to effect successful changes; Alesi fastest in warm-up and Berger second. Jean and Gerhard run close third and fourth to Schumacher and retain places after first stops, laps 22 (Jean) and 24. Both move up after Schumacher retires. Alesi at second stop, lap 44, and drops to sixth, a massive 43s behind Hill. Berger, now second and going well after second stop, lap 47, has to retire, lap 56, with broken rear suspension caused by appalling back straight bumps. Alesi charges hard with series of fastest laps and finishes excellent third, 2.6s behind Villeneuve, having posted fastest lap of race (1m 29.413s, 106.556mph).

WILLIAMS-RENAULT

Another stunning race. Hill dramatically snatches pole from Schumacher in closing minutes of qualifying and then superbly dominates race, despite not having eaten for two days (Interlagos intestines). His radio is also AWOL. Leads by 10s at first stop, lap 24, and rejoins still ahead. Stays in front after safety car pulls in and extends lead over Berger to 31s at second stop, lap 51. Rejoins in lead and wins fourth successive GP (third of 1996, 16th of career, to equal Stirling Moss's record) by 12.1s. Now leads championship by commanding 18 points. Jacques Villeneuve again has to learn new circuit but qualifies excellent third, despite going off and losing set-up time on Saturday morning. Down to ninth after bad start caused by failure to release hand clutch properly. Fights back magnificently and, boosted by safety car, is only 2.3s behind leader on lap 32. Benefits from Schumacher and Berger retirements and Alesi's bodged pit stop to finish second. Williams now 29 points ahead of Benetton in constructors' championship.

McLAREN-MERCEDES

Still in the mire. With continued poor grip and balance, Hakkinen and Coulthard start despondent eighth and ninth, both some 1.5s off pole time. David storms up four places to excellent fifth on first lap. Passed by Villeneuve, lap nine, but stays in points through two stops, laps 26 and 50, until suffering embarrassment of being demoted by Verstappen, lap 60. Finishes seventh. Hakkinen retires from 11th, lap 20, with jammed throttle.

LIGIER-MUGEN HONDA

Team announces restructuring following defection of TWR personnel, notably Frank Dernie and Tony Dowe. Olivier Panis qualifies 12th in rebuilt car after off on Friday. Has bad start and drops to 15th. Is then stuck due to race-long traffic. Benefiting from retirements, finishes eighth. Pedro Diniz qualifies 18th after several offs with oversteer. In attempting to lap Badoer collides with his Forti when 14th, lap 25. In for new nose and fuel. Petrol gushes over engine through jammed return valve as soon as Diniz brakes, causing instant conflagration. Pedro very lucky to escape with minor hand burn.

JORDAN-PEUGEOT

Team uses engine-cover high wing for extra downforce. Barrichello consistently good in practice and qualifies contented sixth, a second slower than Hill. Drives strong race, taking advantage of safety car for early single stop, and gives team first 1996 points by finishing fourth. In contrast at track he does not like, Martin suffers acute oversteer and starts frustrated 15th for first race at BA. Having returned from Brazil to the UK for his father's funeral, Martin is 13th, lap 34, after lap 30 stop, when he is rear-ended by Tarso Marques and retires with no rear wing.

SAUBER-FORD

With revised set-up and new exhaust system to improve engine response, car suits Argentina better than Brazil. But drivers discouraged by comparative lack of power from new Ford-Cosworth V10. Using low downforce set-up to compensate for lack of grunt, both Frentzen and Herbert spin during qualifying. H-H starts 11th, with despondent Herbert 17th. "The car is a long way off and we don't know why." Frentzen runs 11th, at tail of five-car procession headed by one-stop Barrichello. Stops from ninth, lap 20, and rejoins 12th. Tries to pass Coulthard from seventh when safety car pulls off, lap 33, but spins out. Herbert now 10th behind Barrichello but drops back with disappearing brakes. Drives to finish and does so, lapped and ninth.

ARROWS-HART

Now a part of the very switched-on TWR organisation and with another brilliant race weekend for budding superstar Jos Verstappen, things at last looking up for Arrows (still entered as Footwork, for various complicated reasons). Despite not using uppermost 500 rpm to enhance Hart V8 reliability, Verstappen fourth fastest on Friday and Saturday mornings on a track he loves; qualifies superb seventh, just 1.27s off pace, despite only being able to do seven laps due to gearbox problem. "But for this I think I could have got fourth again." Consternation all round. Jos then drives blinder of a race. Is ninth and 4.2s behind Hill when safety car pulls off. Has second stop from fifth, lap 45, and audaciously passes Irvine's Ferrari to retake that position on last lap - only to be repassed through braking too late. Finishes sixth. Ricardo Rosset starts 20th for first race in Argentina. Pits from 18th, lap 23, but retires two laps later with broken fuel pump.

TYRRELL-YAMAHA

A bitterly disappointing weekend. Team arrives in Argentina with car it believes is really suited to its twisty circuit. Super-confident Salo happy fifth fastest on Friday, only 0.446s off Hill. Then it all falls apart. Mika goes off on fourth Saturday lap, and loses half session of setting-up time. With less grip in afternoon qualifies hugely disappointed 16th. Spins down to 19th, lap seven, and then has sticking electronic throttle. After three stops trying to effect cure is obliged to retire, lap 37. Ukyo Katayama qualifies 13th, ahead of Salo for first time in 1996. Battles past Brundle to 12th, lap 15, before taking early stop from 10th, lap 21. Retires from 13th, lap 29, when driveline fails. Nothing to show after great expectations.

MINARDI-FORD

Promising young Brazilian Tarso Marques continues with team for second South American race and, despite gearbox software problem, qualifies very impressive 14th, ahead of team-mate Pedro Lamy. Lamy has same problem but, unlike Marques, does not get new ECU and qualifies 19th. After early stop from 15th, lap 16, Marques passed by Brundle when safety car pulls off, lap 32. Rams Martin's Jordan, destroying front wing and suspension. Angrily accuses Martin of brake-testing him twice. Lamy takes sole intended stop from 12th and last-but-one, lap 39, but drive flange fails as he exits pits.

FORTI-FORD

George Ryton joins as new designer. Frank Lagorce appointed test driver as Carlo Gancia reports imminent crash-tests for eagerly awaited new car. Both Badoer and Montermini qualify within 107 per cent limit - Luca 21st and Andrea 22nd. Collision with Diniz removes Badoer from 20th, lap 25, and brings out safety car whilst overturned Forti is craned off. Montermini plugs round to finish 10th, three laps down.

AUTODROMO OSCAR ALFREDO GALVEZ, BUENOS AIRES

ASCARI
OMBÚ   ESSES
SENNA'S S
CONFITERIA CURVE
HAIRPIN
CURVE 1

CIRCUIT LENGTH:
2.646 MILES/4.259 KM

FIA FORMULA 1 WORLD CHAMPIONSHIP

3

RACE

ARGENTINA

7 April 1996

STARTING GRID

HILL 1m 30.346s	**SCHUMACHER** 1m 30.598s
VILLENEUVE 1m 30.907s	**ALESI** 1m 31.038s
BERGER 1m 31.262s	**BARRICHELLO** 1m 31.404s
VERSTAPPEN 1m 31.615s	**HAKKINEN** 1m 31.801s
COULTHARD 1m 32.001s	**IRVINE** 1m32.058s
FRENTZEN 1m 32.130s	**PANIS** 1m 32.177s
KATAYAMA 1m 32.407s	**MARQUES** 1m 32.502s
BRUNDLE 1m 32.696s	**SALO** 1m 32.903s
HERBERT 1m 33.258s	**DINIZ** 1m 33.424s
LAMY 1m 33.727s	**ROSSET** 1m 33.752s
BADOER 1m 34.830s	**MONTERMINI** 1m 35.651s

RACE CLASSIFICATION

Pos	Driver	Nat	Car	Laps	Time
1	Damon Hill	GB	Williams FW18-Renault V10	72	1h 54m 55.322s
2	Jacques Villeneuve	CDN	Williams FW18-Renault V10	72	+12.167s
3	Jean Alesi	F	Benetton B196-Renault V10	72	+14.754s
4	Rubens Barrichello	BR	Jordan 196-Peugeot V10	72	+55.131s
5	Eddie Irvine	GB	Ferrari F310-Ferrari V10	72	+1m 04.991s
6	Jos Verstappen	NL	Footwork FA17-Hart V8	72	+1m 06.913s
7	David Coulthard	GB	McLaren MP4/11-Mercedes V10	72	+1m 13.400s
8	Olivier Panis	F	Ligier JS43-Mugen Honda	72	+1m 14.295s
9	Johnny Herbert	GB	Sauber C15-Ford V10		+1 lap
10	Andrea Montermini	I	Forti FG01B-Ford V8		+3 laps

Retirements	Nat	Car	Lap	Reason
Gerhard Berger	A	Benetton B196-Renault V10	56	Suspension
Michael Schumacher	D	Ferrari F310-Ferrari V10	46	Broken rear wing
Pedro Lamy	P	Minardi M195B-Ford V8	39	CV joint
Mika Salo	SF	Tyrrell 024-Yamaha V10	36	Electronics
Martin Brundle	GB	Jordan 196-Peugeot V10	34	Accident damage
Tarso Marques	BR	Minardi M195B-Ford V8	33	Accident
Heinz-Harald Frentzen	D	Sauber C15-Ford V10	32	Spin
Pedro Diniz	BR	Ligier JS43-Mugen Honda V10	29	Fuel leak/fire
Ukyo Katayama	J	Tyrrell 024-Yamaha V10	28	Transmission
Ricardo Rosset	BR	Footwork FA17-Hart V8	24	Fuel pump
Luca Badoer	I	Forti FG01B-Ford V8	24	Accident
Mika Hakkinen	SF	McLaren MP4/11-Mercedes V10	19	Sticking throttle
FASTEST LAP		Jean Alesi 1m 29.413s lap 66 (106.556mph)		

DRIVERS' CHAMPIONSHIP

Damon Hill	30
Jacques Villeneuve	12
Jean Alesi	10
Eddie Irvine	6
Mika Hakkinen	5
Michael Schumacher	4
Gerhard Berger	3
Mika Salo	3
Rubens Barrichello	3
Olivier Panis	1
Jos Verstappen	1

CONSTRUCTORS' CUP

Williams-Renault	42
Benetton-Renault	13
Ferrari	10
McLaren-Mercedes	5
Jordan-Peugeot	3
Ligier-Mugen Honda	1
Footwork-Hart	1

Results and Data © FIA 1996

ROUND 4

EUROPE

I feel sorry for the Nurburgring. Whenever enthusiasts talk about it they qualify their remarks by *moaning* that it isn't a patch on the original 'Ring.

No, it isn't. But that's irrelevant.

The original Nurburgring, built after the first World War to relieve massive unemployment was, and still is, a stunning circuit which winds its way through the beautiful, heavily-forested, Eifel mountains and it hosted some great races. Niki Lauda's fiery crash in 1976 put a stop to Grands Prix though. It just isn't possible to apply today's safety standards to a twisty, bumpy, 14-mile lap. So a new 2.8-mile track was built alongside, money no object. First used in 1984, it seemed bland in comparison to its majestic neighbour but, as other tracks were increasingly sanitised in the laudable interests of safety, it was eventually perceived as acceptable. And, when it was re-entered on the F1 schedule in 1995, it provided one of the best races in ages.

Frankly, it was great to be back in Europe after six successive long-haul races. The teams could live comfortably out of their enormous transporters; you didn't have to sit in an aeroplane for 12 hours; and, unlike South America, the plumbing worked!

It had been three weeks since Argentina and the teams had made good use of them, testing and developing their cars for the relentless round of races which would gruellingly continue for the next 24 weeks.

All we had to worry about in Germany was

Above. "I could certainly get used to this Michael".It might have been a home win for Schumacher... if only young Jacques hadn't stolen the show

Left: A couple of interested onlookers notice the presence of Herr M Schumacher, a native of nearby Kerpen.

Right: Barrichello leading the way again for Jordan, but reported to have an eye on Indycar racing in 1997.

the weather. The previous European GP had been held in October, when conditions were absolutely foul: bitterly cold, wet, driving winds and black skies. "Bring your Damart underwear, there's a 25% chance of snow in the Eifel region in April!" they told us. But we didn't need it. For the whole four days there was glorious sunshine, blue skies and a terrific atmosphere. Could Damon Hill make it five in a row? Two teams in particular hoped to stop him: Ferrari, which had got its new gearbox, rear suspension and undertray to work since Argentina; and Benetton, which had also done a lot of rewarding work on aerodynamics and suspension. Against the dominant Williams-Renaults they seemed optimistic, but with Schumacher and Alesi - who had engaged in such a thrilling battle in 1995 - it was at least possible. As Damon himself had said, the statistical chances of his continuing to win were getting ever slimmer.

How right he was.

Up to the race itself you'd have said that nothing could stop Hill. Supremely confident and cheerful, he was fastest in every one of the practice sessions and took his third successive pole position with a daunting 0.7s advantage over team-mate Jacques Villeneuve, who had again had to learn a new circuit in the limited practice.

> ## "Once again, it looked as though the Maranello team was in danger of coming apart at the seams"

It was another dour day on home soil for Heinz-Harald Frentzen, though he chose to speak no evil.

Below. The FIA has approved a new range of flame-resistant swimsuits.

Left. Coulthard got ahead briefly on the drag to the first corner, but winner Villeneuve reasserted himself by the time they got there.

Schumacher was third, but dismayed to be 1.2s off Damon's pace. "I expected our car to be a lot closer on the smooth surface here, Luca di Montezemolo wasn't impressed either. He had made a verbal swipe at his English designer John Barnard after the South American races and, once again, it looked as though the Maranello team was in danger of coming apart at the seams.

Nor was Benetton full of the joys of spring. Alesi was fourth, Berger eighth. A major rethink about set-up elevated them to a close second (Alesi) and third to Hill in the pre-race warm-up, but they'd have to be supersonic at the start to get by the opposition.

They weren't. In fact, they were paralytic.

Both had the special handbrake they use to prevent creeping and incurring a penalty at the start lock on. Alesi slipped to 13th, Berger to 19th. Out of 20.

Nor were they alone. Hill's start was awful, and he dropped to fifth, delaying Schumacher who was passed by Barrichello, fifth on the grid, and Coulthard, who shot up to an amazing second from sixth. And the leader? Villeneuve, with an absolutely perfect getaway which saw him almost a second ahead after the first lap.

With a clear track in front of him Jacques simply raced away.

He was over seven seconds ahead of Coulthard by lap 10. Behind David's resurgent McLaren-Mercedes there was a titanic scrap for third place. Before the race Schumacher had publicly praised Hill for leading from the front in every race so far but had tartly qualified his words by adding, "his weakness is when he has to pass someone, as we have seen in the past."

Now Michael had to eat his words. On lap six Hill sailed past him, smoothly, cleanly and with positive assurance. He was now setting about Barrichello for third place. It wasn't until lap 22 that the nose-to-tail battle (with Mika Hakkinen close behind) was broken by Hill making his

Far right: Jean Alesi waited until lap two before attempting the impossible (and the impassable).

first stop, which destroyed any remaining hopes he may have had about winning. It took over 20s whilst technical boss Patrick Head examined the rear of Damon's car for suspected damage. There didn't seem to be any, so out he went, now down to 11th.

Meantime the Benetton challenge was over. An agitated Alesi had rammed Salo's Tyrrell and retired for the second time in four races as the result of a collision; Berger had been into the pits for new tyres after flat-spotting his left front during his brake problem at the start.

Then it was time for the first round of pit stops. When the top four - Villeneuve, Coulthard, Barrichello and Schumacher - had been in, Jacques was still in command. On lap 27, he had a nine- second gap to Schumacher, who had passed Coulthard and Barrichello during their pit stops. This was where Michael showed his genius.

effectively decided on lap 45. By David Coulthard.

As Schumacher emerged from the pits after his second stop, he just failed to get out in front of the McLaren and had to tuck in behind it. Whilst he ducked and dived trying to find a way past he was losing time. Before his stop he had been 0.7s behind Villeneuve. When Jacques rejoined the track after his lap 46 stop the gap was 3.5s, with 21 laps to go.

On lap 48, Villeneuve led Schumacher by 2.7s, Coulthard by 27s, Barrichello by 30s and Hakkinen by 36s (despite his penalty). Hill was sixth, and flying. He passed Hakkinen to take fifth on the next lap as Mika took a second penalty. On lap 55 the tension increased as Hill set the fastest lap of the race, closing to within 1.5s of Barrichello. The remaining laps were captivating as Villeneuve and Schumacher circulated within half a second of each other

"I hoped it would turn out like last year, but Villeneuve did not make the slightest mistake"

Michael Schumacher

Right: "Who's been sleeping in my car?" Advantage is taken of Pedro Diniz's absence.

Lap by lap he reduced the interval until, on lap 37, he was right behind the Williams. Breathtaking. But he could make no further progress as Villeneuve faultlessly stuck to his rightful racing line.

With Coulthard third, after Hakkinen had shot himself in the foot with a pit speeding penalty, Hill was in the wars again. Trying to lap Pedro Diniz's Ligier as he stormed back through the field he had the Brazilian move over on him to cause the inevitable collision. Had Schumacher been right? Whatever, Damon lost three places, leaving himself with everything to do again. He did so superbly, but the race for victory - which no longer involved him - was

as Michael sought an opportunity to repeat the astounding passing manoeuvre he had pulled on Alesi to secure victory six months earlier.

On lap 58 Hill took Barrichello for fourth, but there would be no way past his former team-mate Coulthard. "I made my car impassably wide everywhere," said the Scotsman.

Nor was there any way past for Michael Schumacher. "I hoped it would turn out like last year, but Villeneuve did not make the slightest mistake. We had an enjoyable fight and I am delighted with this result," he claimed.

Equally elated was Jacques, who won his

first Grand Prix - only his fourth F1 start - by 0.7s. It was closer than that for third, with Coulthard only 0.6s ahead of Hill, and closer yet for fourth with Barrichello literally under Damon's rear wing.

To round off a wonderful day, Martin Brundle was sixth in his Jordan-Peugeot to compensate for the thoroughly depressing start to his season. Eddie Jordan hit the nail on the head after the race, commenting: "The real winner today was the sport." Indeed so.

It was a wonderful result for Williams who, with first and fourth places, now led the constructors' championship by a massive 39 points. It was heartening for Ferrari, McLaren and Jordan, but disappointing for Benetton, who were surely thinking of putting bromide in Alesi's coffee? Above all, it was a magical race for 24-year-old Jacques Villeneuve. At Imola, one week hence, he would be racing an F1 car at a circuit he knew for the very first time. A worrying thought for Damon Hill?

Below: Poleman Hill's poor start saw him boxed in fourth place, between Barrichello and Schumacher, until the first round of stops.

FERRARI

Team reverts to 1996 gearbox, rear suspension and floor after successful testing at Mugello. Schumacher also uses special helmet to improve airflow through overhead airbox to engine. Michael second fastest to Hill on Friday and Saturday morning but, disappointed with F310's performance on smooth track, qualifies third, 1.2s off Hill's pole time. Is delayed behind poor-starting Hill and demoted to fourth by Barrichello. After fierce battle is cleanly passed by old enemy Hill, lap six, and runs fifth in nose-to-tail battle with Coulthard/Barrichello/Hill. Up to second, lap 27, 8.7s behind Villeneuve following first tyre/fuel stops. Brilliantly reduces gap to 0.6s by lap 37. Cannot pass Jacques and takes second stop, lap 44. Rejoins immediately behind Coulthard, who delays Michael enough to prevent him taking lead when Villeneuve stops, lap 46. Schumacher reduces lap 47 gap to Villeneuve from 3.5s to 0.5s by lap 52, but again cannot pass the Canadian and finishes second, 0.76s down after superb race. Eddie Irvine disappoints by qualifying seventh, two seconds off pace due to inability to set up car to his satisfaction. Clutch problem causes bad start. Down to ninth and then 11th, lap five, further delayed by electrical glitch. Hit by Panis at chicane, lap seven, and pulls in to retire.

BENETTON-RENAULT

Designer Ross Brawn expresses optimism following post-Argentina testing of new suspension parts. But disappointment when Alesi, troubled by "massive understeer", qualifies eighth with Berger eighth after inexplicable loss of engine revs. Major set-up changes on Saturday night result in Jean/Gerhard being very encouraging second and third fastest in warm-up prior to unproductive race. Both drivers have special braking system (to prevent creeping on grid) lock on at start. Alesi 13th out of 20 at end of lap one; Berger 19th. Charging Jean hits Salo's Tyrrell at start of lap two and is immediately out after second collision in four races. Black mark. Berger pits for check-up and resumes 18th. Loses further time when stalls at pit stop but just manages to avoid being lapped before finishing ninth, having set third fastest lap of race. Alesi and team incur fines totalling $22,500 for Jean crossing track and leaving circuit without seeing stewards after retiring. Not a good trip.

WILLIAMS-RENAULT

Another great race. Trouble-free Friday and Saturday yields 14th career pole position for Damon Hill with impressive Jacques Villeneuve second on grid. Damon bogs down at start as Jacques races into lead which he increases to 13s by first major tyre/fuel stops. Hill, down to fifth, charges hard and cleanly passes Schumacher's Ferrari to take fourth, lap six. Has long stop, over 20s, lap 22, whilst car checked for suspected rear-end damage. Rejoins 11th and charges again. Collides with Diniz's Ligier, lap 28, and drops three places. In superb recovery drive is back in points by lap 48. Meantime, Villeneuve retains lead despite non-stop pressure from Schumacher's Ferrari after both Jacques' stops, laps 26 and 43, and superbly wins his first Grand Prix. Hill continues to recover and records fastest lap (1m 21.363s, 125.585mph) on way to catching third-placed David Coulthard. Cannot pass the McLaren and finishes fourth. Hill's championship lead over Villeneuve down to 11 points, but Williams' constructors' lead up to commanding 39 points ahead of Ferrari.

McLAREN-MERCEDES

Team flat-out on new car to replace disappointing MP4/11, but Nurburgring sees some much-needed progress with Coulthard sixth on grid. Hakkinen has embarrassing engine failure right in front of massed Mercedes-Benz grandstand at start of qualifying and has to use spare car to start ninth. Coulthard makes sensational start, rocketing to second past Alesi, Barrichello, Schumacher and Hill. Eventually loses place to Schumacher after second stop, but manages to hold off charging Hill in great nine-lap battle to score his first McLaren podium. Hakkinen runs sixth until lap 22 and is third ahead of Coulthard, lap 31, when comes in for 10s pit speeding penalty. Has second tyre stop from fifth, lap 44, prior to another penalty stop, lap 50, again caused by entering limit area too fast. Despite losing over a minute, finishes eighth.

LIGIER-MUGEN HONDA

Olivier Panis starts 15th and retires from 16th, lap seven, after hitting Irvine's Ferrari. Diniz qualifies 17th, collides with Hill whilst being lapped, lap 29, and finishes unimpressive 10th, one lap down.

JORDAN-PEUGEOT

Self-assured Barrichello qualifies excellent fifth with help of new undertray. Then has strong and impressive race. Passed by Coulthard at start but passes Alesi, Schumacher and Hill to lie third. Down to fifth at first stop, lap 24. Fourth behind Villeneuve, Schumacher and Coulthard for most of rest of race but passed by Hill, lap 58. Finishes fifth, only 0.2s behind Damon despite spongy brakes and losing time with fuel rig problems at both stops. Martin Brundle qualifies 11th after much post-Argentina testing to set up car. Has fine race. Gains four places first lap before being passed by Frentzen. Into points (sixth), lap 43, and finishes there to take first point with Jordan. Team delighted with double-points finish and with strength and reliability of Peugeot engine, which now seems the equal of anything.

SAUBER-FORD

Substantial revisions to Ford Zetec V10 enable it to race at 16,000 rpm with improved driveability - reportedly. Both drivers experience response problem as well as substantial understeer. Frentzen starts 10th and Herbert 12th, both over two seconds off pace. H-H benefits from bad Benetton starts to move up to eighth and then passes Brundle. Runs just behind five-car battle for second until lap 20 tyre/fuel stop. Into points, laps 23-31, and then fifth until lap 42 second stop. Thereafter car deteriorates and, running minimum wing to enhance straight line speed, Heinz spins out of 11th, lap 60. Herbert drives well despite poor second set of tyres and finishes seventh, 0.4s ahead of Mika Hakkinen.

TWR ARROWS-HART

First race as "TWR F1" (as team now fully controlled by Tom Walkinshaw's organisation), with all-new red and blue livery to emphasise change in ownership. Very noticeable difference in overall sharpness and cheerfulness of atmosphere. Brian Hart's organisation also understood to be working hard on engine development. Verstappen starts 13th despite being troubled by understeer, but excellent sixth fastest in warm-up after set-up changes. Loses two places at start but up to 10th, lap 5, and stays there behind Brundle/Herbert until pit stop, lap 21. Then gearchange deteriorates, obliging Jos to retire from 10th, lap 39. Ricardo Rosset starts 20th and last and races reliably to finish 11th, two laps down.

TYRRELL-YAMAHA

With new undertray and shrouded rear wishbones, designer Harvey Postlethwaite predicts the car will be good. But it isn't. Disappointed Mika Salo qualifies 14th, "and I don't know what's wrong." Katayama two places further back. Then it gets worse. Salo nerfed off track by delayed Alesi on second lap. Develops understeer, accompanied by misfire. Then loses two more places when Frentzen spins off in front of him. Lucky to finish 10th, one lap down, after being told to slow down with fluctuating oil pressure. Ukyo stalls at start, is push-started and loses lap but finishes 12th, two laps behind. Then both drivers excluded from results: Salo underweight at post-race check, Katayama had received forbidden push-start.

MINARDI-FORD

Giancarlo Fisichella back with team after Tarso Marques fails to raise enough money to continue. Does well to qualify 18th, a place ahead of far more experienced Pedro Lamy. In well balanced but underpowered cars, both race reliably with two routine pit stops to finish 12th (Lamy) and 13th (Fisichella), two laps down.

FORTI-FORD

Sadly, after beating the 107 per cent qualifying limit in Brazil and Argentina with their outmoded car, neither Andrea Montermini nor Luca Badoer succeed in doing so at the Nurburgring, where new car is revealed on raceday. Hope of better things to come.

RACE 4
FORMULA 1 WORLD CHAMPIONSHIP
EUROPE
28 April 1996

NÜRBURGRING – GRAND PRIX CIRCUIT

BIT KURVE
VEEDOL SCHIKANE
SHELL KURVE
CASTROL S
DUNLOP KEHRE
RÖHMER KURVE

CIRCUIT LENGTH: 2.831 MILES/4.556 KM

STARTING GRID

HILL 1m 18.941s	**VILLENEUVE** 1m 19.721s
SCHUMACHER 1m 20.149s	**ALESI** 1m 20.711s
BARRICHELLO 1m 20.818s	**COULTHARD** 1m 20.888s
IRVINE 1m 20.931s	**BERGER** 1m21.054s
HAKKINEN 1m21.078s	**FRENTZEN** 1m 21.113s
BRUNDLE 1m 21.177s	**HERBERT** 1m 21.210s
VERSTAPPEN 1m 21.367s	**SALO** 1m 21.458s
PANIS 1m21.509s	**KATAYAMA** 1m 21.812s
DINIZ 1m22.733s	**FISICHELLA** 1m 22.921s
LAMY 1m 23.139s	**ROSSET** 1m 23.620s

Did not qualify

MONTERMINI (Forti FG01B) 1m 25.053s	**BADOER** (Forti FG01B) 1m25.840s

RACE CLASSIFICATION

Pos	Driver	Nat	Car	Laps	Time
1	Jacques Villeneuve	CDN	Williams FW18-Renault V10	67	1h 33m26.473s
2	Michael Schumacher	D	Ferrari F310-Ferrari V10	67	+0.762s
3	David Coulthard	GB	McLaren MP4/11-Mercedes V10	67	+32.834s
4	Damon Hill	GB	Williams FW18-Renault V10	67	+33.511s
5	Rubens Barrichello	BR	Jordan 196-Peugeot V10	67	+33.713s
6	Martin Brundle	GB	Jordan 196-Peugeot V10	67	+55.567s
7	Johnny Herbert	GB	Sauber C15-Ford V10	67	+1m18.027s
8	Mika Hakkinen	SF	McLaren MP4/11-Mercedes V10	67	+1m18.438s
9	Gerhard Berger	A	Benetton B196-Renault V10	67	+1m21.061s
*Exc	Mika Salo	SF	Tyrrell 024-Yamaha V10		+1 lap
10	Pedro Diniz	BR	Ligier JS43-Mugen Honda V10		+1 lap
**Exc	Ukyo Katayama	J	Tyrrell 024-Yamaha V10		+2 laps
11	Ricardo Rosset	BR	Footwork FA17-Hart V8		+2 laps
12	Pedro Lamy	P	Minardi M195B-Ford V8		+2 laps
13	Giancarlo Fisichella	I	Minardi M195B-Ford V8		+2 laps

Retirements	Nat	Car	Lap	Reason
Heinz-Harald Frentzen	D	Sauber C15-Ford V10	59	Spin/handling
Jos Verstappen	NL	Footwork FA17-Hart V8	38	Gearbox
Eddie Irvine	GB	Ferrari F310-Ferrari V10	6	Electrics
Olivier Panis	F	Ligier JS43-Mugen Honda V10	6	Accident
Jean Alesi	F	Benetton B196 -Renault V10	1	Accident

Reasons for exclusion   * Underweight   **Push start

FASTEST LAP   Damon Hill 1m 21.363s lap 55 (125.265mph)

DRIVERS' CHAMPIONSHIP

Damon Hill	33
Jacques Villeneuve	22
Jean Alesi	10
Michael Schumacher	10
Eddie Irvine	6
Mika Hakkinen	5
Rubens Barrichello	3
David Coulthard	4
Gerhard Berger	3
Mika Salo	3
Olivier Panis	1
Jos Verstappen	1
Martin Brundle	1

CONSTRUCTORS' CUP

Williams-Renault	55
Ferrari	16
Benetton-Renault	13
McLaren-Mercedes	9
Jordan-Peugeot	6
Tyrrell-Yamaha	3
Ligier-Mugen Honda	1
Footwork-Hart	1

Results and Data © FIA 1996

Below. Ayrton Senna: revered
in Brazil, revered in Italy.
Main shot. The red berets.

They were getting at Damon Hill again. Having lost the European Grand Prix as the result of a bad start, he had been subjected to another outburst of unjustified criticism from the press. That's hard to take, and it might have agitated him in 1995. But not now. "I don't read it. I had some good fish and chips on Monday and caught a few glimpses!" He had exactly the right attitude, and his knockers would soon eat their harsh words.

Damon had won the 1995 San Marino Grand Prix in commanding style. Then, as now, his chief rival had been Michael Schumacher, but this year the German had got an extra boost to his performance - the whole of Italy.

Imola is just down the autostrada from the Ferrari factory at Maranello, and after Schumacher's fine performance at the Nurburgring the previous Sunday the fanatical tifosi were expecting great things from him at their home race. Not without reason, for Ferrari always produces something special in Italy and for Imola there was a "hand grenade' qualifying engine. This would give explosive performance for a short time, and if it could put Michael on the front row he would have a real chance of winning. It is hard to pass at Imola, and all the more so since chicanes were added in the wake of the tragic accidents which befell Ayrton Senna and Roland Ratzenberger in 1994. The circuit may no longer be as challenging, but it is still a fine venue, and it suited the Ferrari well.

Or at least, it suited Schumacher's.

Michael was fastest in the wet on Friday morning, and again in the afternoon when it was dry. The tifosi were ecstatic. But most people had been working on their race set-ups. The true test would be during Saturday afternoon's hour of qualifying...when the German was fastest again! His first pole posi-

SAN MARINO

tion for Ferrari and a genuine worry for Hill, who was 0.2s slower. Schumacher wasn't totally at ease, however. Almost as he crossed the line at the end of his pole lap his rear suspension broke, leaving the team with an all-nighter to strengthen the mounting points. Would the F310 hold together for the race?

No fewer than 130,000 people came to find out. It was a record crowd, for they could scent the first Ferrari win since Canada 1995 (Alesi) and the first at Imola since 1983 (Patrick Tambay). The weather was superb, the high banks overlooking the Tosa and Rivazza corners were jammed solid with scarlet anoraks topped by scarlet caps, the Prancing Horse banners were waving, the horns were blowing and the massed throats were yelling encouragement. It was a truly emotional scene, and you didn't need to be Pythagoras to work out that strategy was going to be all-im-portant.

The team's plans are secret before the race, of course, but we later discovered that Ferrari's was for Schumacher to make his usual lightning start, build up a lead and stop twice at the conventional intervals of roughly one third and two-thirds dis-

"The massed throats were yelling encouragement. It was a truly emotional scene"

Above. Red and blue alert: the potential dangers of mid-race pit stops were illustrated once again. Arrows mechanic Dave Lowe suffered a dislocated knee and shoulder seconds after this shot was taken, as Verstappen was given the 'go' signal prematurely.

tance. Sadly for Michael, two things went wrong. With a dodgy clutch he got away badly, and Williams had a better plan for Damon Hill.

Schumacher's misfortune was compounded by the fact that McLaren came good at Imola. Thus far the 1996 MP4/11 had been little better than the previous year's demeaning failure. But now, after minute examination of their sophisticated data acquisition system, the team claimed to have nailed the problem which had been caused by a flexing front wing, resulting in reduced downforce. With the benefit of the corrective tweaks Coulthard had taken fourth place on the grid and his start at Imola was, if anything, even better than his explosive getaway at the Nurburgring the previous weekend. As the lights went out he shot into the lead past Villeneuve, Hill and Schumacher as the tifosi's hearts sank. Michael's strategy had been blown already for not only was he stuck behind Coulthard, but Hill was keeping in touch. There had been a groan of dismay from the British contingent when Schumacher had

passed Damon on the second lap but in fact they needn't have worried.

Williams designer Adrian Newey had evolved a courageous and daring strategy for Damon. Start with a heavy fuel load, stop at roughly half-distance and then stop again near the end of the race for a top-up. For it to succeed, Hill had to stay within eight seconds of the leader until the first stops. Which he did. On lap 10 he was four seconds behind the battling Coulthard and Schumacher. On lap 19, when David came in, it was 3.5s and on lap 20 when the Ferrari stopped it was 2.7s. Brilliant!

For one glorious lap, as far as the tifosi were concerned, a Ferrari had led at Imola. But there had been plenty of other action for them to absorb. Such as Jean Alesi putting his foot in it. Between the European GP and Imola, Benetton boss Flavio Briatore had spoken freely and frankly with his not so merry men and told them that he was less than enchanted with the team's achievements so far, not least with Alesi's habit of departing the action prematurely. And Jean had done it again.

**Above.
No smoke without a flier: Damon Hill's strategy was perfect.**

Far left. David Coulthard makes the most of his feisty start to lead for McLaren. Hill and Schumacher follow; in the background, Jacques Villeneuve heads for the shops in Bologna.

Above. The world's most expensive truck stop? Note that the Forti cabs (yellow, near left) had a better record of getting to where they were supposed to, within the prescribed time limit, than the contents of their trailers...

Johnny Herbert has to wait to get into his Sauber as the team appears to be blocking his way with a roast turkey...

"McLaren had led a race on merit for the first time since Adelaide 1993"

Irvine, Brundle and Verstappen until the first round of stops.

When Coulthard and Schumacher stopped on laps 19 and 20, Hill took the lead and stayed out. And out. And out. It was nine laps after Michael's stop before he came in, emphasising how well he had been driving to stay in such close touch with the leaders. When he rejoined he was just ahead of Schumacher and, although there was still over half the race to run, it was effectively over.

Not that we knew that at the time. Schumacher was under a second behind the Williams, having passed Coulthard when he made his stop. Now the McLaren was dropping back, ahead of Berger,

Fifth on the grid he had tangled not once but twice with Villeneuve's Williams. The Canadian fell to last place with a first lap puncture; Alesi raced on with, unbeknown to him, a broken front wheel.

Mika Salo had been prominent, too, but in a more positive way. After a change in strategy by Tyrrell, he had at last succeeded in qualifying where he deserved to be - eighth. His start was as impressive as Coulthard's for he exploded past Berger, Irvine, Alesi and Villeneuve to lie a superb fourth for one lap, before Berger relegated him. He then stayed ahead of a terrific scrap for sixth between Barrichello, Alesi,

Barrichello and Irvine. On laps 39 and 40, two-thirds distance, the brilliance of Hill's strategy became clear as Schumacher and Coulthard, second and third, made their second stops and Damon stretched his lead. Yes, he too would have to stop later but by then he would have built an impregnable lead prior to only a short stop. No trouble for Schumacher at his second stop. In one second behind Hill, out 26 seconds down. But it was curtains for the unfortunate Coulthard, who stalled his engine and lost third place to Berger's Benetton. It hadn't been David's fault. His hydraulic system had been failing and, five laps later, it did so terminally. But McLaren had led a race on merit for the first time since Adelaide 1993. There was light at the end of a very long tunnel. At last.

It was now that a potentially cataclysmic incident occurred. When Jos Verstappen was waved out of the pit lane he was still attached to the fuel rig. He had been given the all-clear too soon and refueller Dave Lowe, tethered to the TWR-Arrows by the ponderously heavy nozzle and fuel pipe, didn't stand a chance. As he was sent flying by the Arrows' rear wheel it was a miracle that he received no more than a dislocated shoulder. But it was even more miraculous that only four litres of petrol were spilt. When we remembered the con-

flagration that two-and-a-half litres had caused in 1994 when, coincidentally, Verstappen's (Benetton) stop at Hockenheim had gone wrong, we breathed a massive sigh of relief that it hadn't ignited.

Any hope that Schumacher had of staying in touch with Hill when Damon made his final, short stop on lap 49 disappeared when he caught Mika Hakkinen, who was struggling to pass, of all things, Pedro Diniz's Ligier. It had been an awful Imola for Hakkinen. He had qualified 11th, had to race the spare McLaren after a problem with his race chassis in the warm-up, had started badly and had then been delayed by traffic. As he fought to get by the understandably unhelpful Diniz he was blocking Schumacher, for which both he and Pedro received a 10s stop-go penalty.

When Hill left the pits after his stop he was still 21s ahead of the Ferrari with only 14 laps to go. He hung on to win his second successive San Marino GP. His fourth victory from five starts extended his championship lead to a commanding 21 points over team-mate Villeneuve. Great for Damon, but no consolation for poor Jacques who, having superbly fought his way into the points in sixth place on lap 46, had to retire when his rear suspension broke.

Williams now led the constructors' championship by a daunting 40 points from Ferrari, but neither the team nor Hill were complacent. Of the 16s between Damon and Schumacher at the end of the race, nine had been caused by Michael's delay behind Diniz and Hakkinen and several more by the fact that he had covered the last third of a lap with a locked wheel after his right brake disc had exploded at the Acque Minerali chicane. He had been very lucky indeed to go the distance, but with Irvine having finished fourth Ferrari was very nearly there, as was McLaren. And Schumacher had won the next race, Monaco, on each of the last two years.

Me and my shadows.

FERRARI

To the delight of Ferrari-mad tifosi, Schumacher fastest in both wet and dry conditions on Friday. Then, with special qualifying engine, takes first pole position for Ferrari, immediately after which his left rear suspension collapses. Performance improvement is due to minor aerodynamic changes and superior engine driveability. Schumacher reverts to normal engine for race with strategy that depends on his taking lead at start. Clutch problem prevents him doing so and he is passed (and then delayed) by fast-starting Coulthard. Races immediately behind David until Coulthard's first stop, lap 19. Leads for one lap, then down to fifth after own stop. Back to second, lap 25, but now behind late-stopping Hill who rejoins track just ahead of the Ferrari following his lap 29 stop. Michael stops again, lap 39, and is then delayed by Diniz and Hakkinen. Finishes second, 16.5s down, and is lucky to do so after right front brake disc disintegrates on last lap. Completes race with wheel locked solid. Irvine starts sixth after spinning out on Friday due to major oversteer. Loses two places after bad start with same clutch problem as Schumacher but, with improved set-up, races strongly to finish fourth. An encouraging race, "But we must improve our clutch and starts," says team principal Jean Todt.

BENETTON-RENAULT

Unhappy atmosphere following Flavio Briatore pep talk. Car is difficult to drive with low fuel load, so Alesi and Berger qualify fifth and seventh, lacking grip and balance. Jean starts in spare car after heavy off during warm-up. Clashes twice with Villeneuve on first lap and breaks front wheel rim. Unknowingly races on in seventh place until first stop, lap 18. Takes 10s penalty for pit lane speeding (lap 27, as replacement steering wheel fitted at first stop has no speed limiter button). Drops to 14th. Charges hard after third stop lap 39 and, partly thanks to retirements, is lucky to finish sixth, one lap down. Berger passed by Salo at start but regains place and races fourth. To third during Coulthard's delayed stop, lap 41, and stays there for first Benetton podium.

WILLIAMS-RENAULT

Another great win amidst mutterings that Renault needs to raise its game to stay ahead of rivals. Hill wins pole by 0.2s to inspired Schumacher in closing minutes of qualifying but, with daring strategy, drives magnificent race, partly thanks to fact that Michael cannot pass outstanding Coulthard. Despite heavy fuel load, stays in touch with leaders. Takes lead on lap 21, stays out until lap 29 and rejoins just ahead of Schumacher. Then retains lead after second stop, on lap 49, to win fourth of five 1996 races and increase championship lead to 21 points, having set fastest lap (1m 28.931s, 123.057mph). Jacques Villeneuve starts third at first track on which he has both raced (in Italian F3) and tested for Williams, but is rudely assaulted twice by Alesi during first lap. Tours in with puncture and rejoins last. Races up to sixth, lap 46, after two more stops but retires, lap 58, with broken rear suspension. Williams now leads Ferrari in constructors' championship by massive 40 points.

McLAREN-MERCEDES

Minute examination of data identifies flexing front wing as cause of previous handling problem. With resultant changes David Coulthard qualifies fourth, 0.5s off pace and rips into lead with another Nurburgring-like start past Villeneuve, Hill and Schumacher. In McLaren's most impressive race since 1993, he superbly stays ahead of Schumacher until lap 19 stop. Down to third after first round of stops and races there until stalling at lap 40 stop due to failing hydraulics. Retires, lap 45, when hydraulics give up. Not so good for detuned Mika Hakkinen who desperately needs mental uplift. Starts 11th after spinning on fast lap. Races spare car and drops two places after bad start. Struggles with traffic and receives 10s penalty, lap 41, for blocking Schumacher whilst battling with Diniz (!). Running seventh when engine fails on penultimate lap but is classified eighth, two laps down. But, all in all, things are looking up.

LIGIER-MUGEN HONDA

After usual, inexplicable second day performance fall-off, Panis and Diniz start 13th and 17th. Amazingly, Pedro catches, passes and stays ahead of Olivier for first 13 laps whilst chasing Hakkinen. Panis delayed by brake problem during battle with recovering Alesi

and retires from eighth when gearbox breaks, lap 55. Diniz has best race yet in spite of 10s penalty, lap 41, for blocking Schumacher. After reliable and sensible drive finishes seventh, one lap down.

JORDAN-PEUGEOT

Barrichello looks good on Friday (second fastest), but starts disappointing ninth with Martin Brundle 12th after hydraulic, throttle and set-up problems. Rubens zaps up to sixth on lap one but loses time at both pit stops whilst team struggles to get fuel nozzle on to car. Mysterious inability to deliver fuel also thwarts Brundle who has to rejoin track after lap 21 stop and come in again next lap. Barrichello finishes fifth, in points for third successive race, after fine drive which should been far more rewarding. Brundle goes off and retires, lap 37 when 12th.

SAUBER-FORD

After four races of frustration, mainly caused by comparative lack of power from new Ford V10, Sauber needs to improve more than most, but fails to do so. Frentzen starts 10th but Herbert, a second slower, 15th on grid due to electronic throttle problem. Using conventional throttle mechanism H-H advances to seventh before lap 20 stop but then retires, lap 33, with brake problem. Herbert up to 12th, lap one, and races with Frentzen. Long stop with misfiring engine, lap 22, leads to lap 26 retirement. Worrying times at Sauber, especially amidst rumours that Frentzen will move in 1997.

TWR ARROWS-HART

At power circuit team suffers lack of horses from Hart V8. Verstappen happy to start 14th after going nose first into wall in Saturday morning session. Is ninth behind Brundle at second stop, lap 38, but leaves with fuel pipe still attached to car after being incorrectly waved out. Knocks over refueller Dave Lowe who dislocates his shoulder (very lucky it wasn't much worse). Jos retires immediately. Rosset uses new chassis to replace previous tub which was flexing after Brazil crash. Qualifies 20th after being confined by team to one set of tyres. Retires from 14th, lap 19, with tightening engine, when is unable to refuel from rig crippled by Verstappen incident.

TYRRELL-YAMAHA

In attempt to improve qualifying results team revises strategy by concentrating on set-up work during Friday, with excellent results. Salo qualifies highest-yet eighth and then makes sensational start to rocket up to fourth past Berger, Irvine, Alesi and Villeneuve. Loses place to Berger on lap two but up to third, lap 21, during first stops. After comfortably running fifth ahead of Barrichello, rejoins sixth but retires next lap when engine fails. Katayama has major engine problems on Friday and in qualifying and again has to use spare car set up for very differently shaped Salo. Starts 16th and drives well. Eighth at second stop, lap 38, and into points at sixth, lap 45, only for drive to fail and force retirement on next lap. Massive disappointments are tinged with hope.

MINARDI-FORD

Pedro Lamy starts 18th, outqualifying his less experienced teammate for the first time in 1996. Running towards rear he stays ahead of Fisichella until taking pit lane speeding penalty after lap 20 stop (speed limiter failure). Giancarlo retires from 17th, lap 31, with engine failure. With major understeer, Lamy carries on to finish ninth, two laps down. Team not unhappy in view of lack of power from Ford V8 ED customer engine, and looks forward to improved version from Monaco onwards.

FORTI-FORD

After dismal first four races with tubby and overweight FG01B, Forti arrives at Imola with one version of new FG03 which immediately establishes itself as vast improvement. Without previous testing, Luca Badoer qualifies 21st, 3.5s faster than old car and inside the 107 per cent limit which team had previously struggled to beat. Races at rear, not helped by two pit lane speeding penalties (the second for going too fast when he came in for the first!) and having gearbox jam in fifth for last 10 laps. Finishes 10th, four laps down. Montermini takes over sole new car in an attempt to qualify, but only has seven laps and fails. Appeal to let him race old car is turned down.

IMOLA – AUTODROMO DINO E ENZO FERRARI
CIRCUIT LENGTH: 3.040 MILES/4.892 KM

PIRATELLA
TOSA
VILLENEUVE
VARIANTE ALFA
ACQUE MINERALE
RIVAZZA
TRAGUARDO
TAMBURELLO
VARIANTE BASSA

FIA FORMULA 1 WORLD CHAMPIONSHIP

5

RACE

SAN MARINO

5 May 1996

STARTING GRID

SCHUMACHER 1m 26.890s	**HILL** 1m 27.105s
VILLENEUVE 1m 27.220s	**COULTHARD** 1m 27.688s
ALESI 1m 28.009s	**IRVINE** 1m 28.205s
BERGER 1m 28.336s	**SALO** 1m 28.423s
BARRICHELLO 1m 28.632s	**FRENTZEN** 1m 28.785s
HAKKINEN 1m 29.079s	**BRUNDLE** 1m 29.099s
PANIS 1m 29.472s	**VERSTAPPEN** 1m 29.539s
HERBERT 1m 29.541s	**KATAYAMA** 1m 29.892s
DINIZ 1m 29.989s	**LAMY** 1m 30.471s
FISICHELLA 1m 30.814s	**ROSSET** 1m 31.316s
BADOER 1m 32.037s	

Did not qualify
MONTERMINI
1m 33.685s

RACE CLASSIFICATION

Pos	Driver	Nat	Car	Laps	Time
1	Damon Hill	GB	Williams FW18-Renault V10	63	1h 35m 26.156s
2	Michael Schumacher	D	Ferrari F310-Ferrari V10	63	+16.460s
3	Gerhard Berger	A	Benetton B196-Renault V10	63	+46.891s
4	Eddie Irvine	GB	Ferrari F310-Ferrari V10	63	+1m01.583s
5	Rubens Barrichello	BR	Jordan 196-Peugeot V10	63	+1m18.490s
6	Jean Alesi	F	Benetton B196-Renault V10		+1 lap
7	Pedro Diniz	BR	Ligier JS43-Mugen Honda V10		+1 lap
8	Mika Hakinen	SF	McLaren MP4/11-Mercedes V10	61	DNF Engine
9	Pedro Lamy	P	Minardi M195B-Ford V8		+2 laps
10	Luca Badoer	I	Forti FG03-Ford V8		+4 laps
11	Jacques Villeneuve	CDN	Williams FW18-Renault V10	57	DNF Suspension

Retirements		Nat	Car	Lap	Reason
Olivier Panis		F	Ligier JS43-Mugen Honda	54	Gearbox
Ukyo Katayama		J	Tyrrell 024-Yamaha V10	45	Transmission
David Coulthard		GB	McLaren MP4/11-Mercedes V10	44	Hydraulics
Ricardo Rosset		BR	Footwork FA17-Hart V8	40	Misfire
Jos Verstappen		NL	Footwork FA17-Hart V8	38	Refuel incident
Martin Brundle		GB	Jordan 196-Peugeot V10	36	Spin
Heinz-Harald Frentzen		D	Sauber C15-Ford V10	32	Brakes
Giancarlo Fisichella		I	Minardi M195B-Ford V8	30	Engine
Johnny Herbert		GB	Sauber C15-Ford V10	25	Electrics
Mika Salo		SF	Tyrrell 024-Yamaha V10	23	Engine

FASTEST LAP Damon Hill 1m 28.931s lap 49 (123.057mph)

DRIVERS' CHAMPIONSHIP

Damon Hill	43
Jacques Villeneuve	22
Michael Schumacher	16
Jean Alesi	11
Eddie Irvine	9
Gerhard Berger	7
Rubens Barrichello	7
Mika Hakkinen	5
David Coulthard	4
Mika Salo	3
Olivier Panis	1
Jos Verstappen	1
Martin Brundle	1

CONSTRUCTORS' CUP

Williams-Renault	65
Ferrari	25
Benetton-Renault	18
McLaren-Mercedes	9
Jordan-Peugeot	8
Tyrrell-Yamaha	3
Ligier-Mugen Honda	1
Footwork-Hart	1

Results and Data © FIA 1996

ROUND 6

MONACO

Monaco is always a Formula One showbiz extravaganza, but this was something else. Of the 21 drivers who started, only three went the full distance. Seven of the top men went out. There were no points for Williams, Benetton or Ferrari. And, if you'd predicted the winner. you'd have been certified. A film script too far, in fact.

This was the one that Damon Hill really wanted to win. It was one of the few Grands Prix in which he had not been victorious, yet his famous father had won five times in Monte Carlo, becoming almost as much of a legend as the race itself.

Monaco is unique in motor racing. It may be a travesty of a Grand Prix circuit, because of its ridiculous working conditions and the near-impossibility for drivers to pass each other, but no other race has such a colourful setting and such charisma. The harbour, the yachts, the glamour, its money-soaked atmosphere and its glorious history allied to the fact that you can get so close to the stirring action make it an irresistible magnet.

Every driver hungers for a Monaco win on his CV and Damon's chances looked better than most. He had been second in 1993 and '95, had the best car and a burning ambition.

Only one thing seemed likely to stop him: Michael Schumacher. The world champion's Ferrari had been getting better and better and Schumacher had ruled supreme at Monaco. First in 1994, first in 1995, the lap record holder was now in a car which had taken him to second place in the previous two Grands Prix. Hill's passion to win was no greater than his rival's desire to complete a hat-trick - and to give Ferrari its first Monaco victory since Gilles Villeneuve triumphed in 1981.

On Saturday evening he looked more than capable of doing so. Thursday, traditionally the first day of practice at Monaco, had been fine and dry and Mika Hakkinen

had been fastest in his new, short-wheelbase McLaren, a mere 0.039s ahead of Hill. But it didn't mean a lot. With the first day's times no longer counting for the grid, it is mainly used for setting up the cars. Saturday afternoon counts. And that was Schumacher's.

Hill had been 0.6s faster than Michael in the morning and, with 10 minutes to go in the afternoon, he headed the times as he completed his maximum 12 laps. But he had gone too soon. In that last 10 minutes Schumacher reached deep down and produced two superb laps, each faster than Damon's best.

"It's disappointing," said Damon, but he won from second on the grid when I was in pole position last year, so maybe it'll be the same this time!"

It wouldn't.

Whatever strategy the teams had decided on was open to doubt after Sunday morning's warm-up, four hours before the race. For the first time since they'd arrived the heavens opened. There was a mandatory extra 15 minutes of practice, but by start time the rain had stopped and, although the track was wet, it looked as though it might dry out. Everyone bar Jos Verstappen started on rain tyres, and the Dutchman crashed

Left. Panis' people: yacht owners check the labels of their champagne bottles to question its strength. Why is the man who started from 14th on the grid looking so triumphant on that highly-fertilised TV set?

Above. Michael Schumacher's walk back lasted rather longer than his race...

Still searching for gold...but Martin Brundle's race ended against the Casino Square barriers.

within yards of the start.

Just as it had in Brazil, changeable weather was dramatically to affect the race. The first lap was sensational. Having worked so hard for pole, Schumacher blew it. With too much wheelspin he lost time as the starting lights went out and Hill surged into the lead with a magnificent getaway. Lamy and Fisichella drove their Minardis into each other at the first corner, yards after Verstappen's Armco-bashing, and Barrichello spun out at Rascasse. But, even before that, there was a gasp of amazement as Schumacher thumped nose-first into the barrier on the descent from Loews hairpin.

On lap one, the pole-sitter, hot favourite and double winner was out and only 16 of the 21 starters were left. More were to go, many more, but none more surprising than Schumacher who, typically, had no excuses. "I made a mistake. I am very sorry for the team and very angry with myself."

Meanwhile, Damon was revelling in the conditions. With the Benettons of Alesi and Berger behind him, he led by a whop-ping 4.2s at the end of the first lap. His advantage was 13s on the fifth and nearly 19s on the 10th.

He was in a class of his own.

Behind Berger, Eddie Irvine, seventh on the grid, was heading a nose-to-tail battle for fourth between himself, fast-starting Frentzen, David Coulthard (who, unusually, had made a bad start from fifth on the grid), Jacques Villeneuve and Mika Salo. On lap 11 this became a battle for third as Gerhard Berger drew in to the pits to retire (gearbox sensor). Irvine was delaying his pursuers. They could go faster if only they could get past; being Monaco, they couldn't. Frentzen was almost sawing the Ferrari in half with his Sauber front wing in his frustrated efforts to get by and, on lap 17, he overdid it. Entering the pits he wanted a fresh nose (granted) and slick tyres (refused, even though the track was drying). Out he went on another set of rain tyres, but Heinz had been right.

Eight laps later, with Hill now 22s ahead of Alesi and only eight seconds covering

Irvine, Coulthard, Villeneuve, Salo, Panis (remember that name!) and Herbert, Frentzen was in again. On slicks he immediately started going 10s a lap quicker and his rivals were quick to spot it on their sector-timing monitors. In came Hill, Irvine and Panis and, very significantly, Olivier took on next to no fuel. His Ligier team had daringly started him on full tanks and intermediate settings so all he needed was a top-up to last him the rest of the race which was clearly going to be one of two hours, rather than 78 laps. It was a brilliant decision that paid massive dividends.

When the stops had finished on lap 30, Hill was still very much in command, 31s ahead of Alesi. Significantly, Panis had passed Coulthard when the Scotsman had made his tyre stop (peculiarly after team-mate Hakkinen, who was four places behind him); the Frenchman was now reeling in Irvine at over three seconds per lap. Incredible. On lap 34 Panis was with the Ferrari and on lap 36 he dived inside it at

Loews and punted it aside to become third. Forceful and crude, but very effective and Irvine bore no grudge afterwards. Eddie's hope of a podium place was destroyed as he came into the pits in the belief that he would be excluded for having been push-started. He wasn't though, and he rejoined last but one, and lapped...after being given a new nosecone which he hadn't actually needed.

Every time the race looked as though it was settling down, it re-ignited. "I had a warning light for about a lap before the engine failed in the tunnel, so I knew there was a problem," said Hill. It was lap 41 when his Renault V10 spectacularly imploded with a burst of flame and a plume of smoke as he approached the chicane. Cruel luck. Damon was 26s ahead of Alesi; the race was in his pocket with 34 laps to go, but he was amazingly calm and cheerful about what was a truly bitter blow.

So now Alesi was in the lead of a race which he sorely needed to win to restore

**Below.
McLaren said
it would bring
a new, short
wheelbase
chassis to
Monaco.
Hakkinen
tries it out.**

**Below right.
Rumour has it
that Monaco's
funfair rides
cost millions
to build and
maintain.**

"Olivier took on next to no fuel. His Ligier team had daringly started him on full tanks. . . all he needed was a top-up to last him the rest of the race"

Right. Heinz-Harald Frentzen's novel front wing arrangement proved to be a minor handicap, though the extraordinary rate of attrition ensured that he would still be classified fourth.

"An awful day for Williams, Benetton, Ferrari and Jordan, but a great afternoon for spectators"

his tattered reputation. He wasn't to do so. On lap 60, after setting the fastest lap of the race, and with a lead almost as secure over Panis (19s) as Hill's had been over him, he limped into the pits to retire with a broken rear spring. Monaco was living up to its reputation for surprises.

Amazingly, Panis was now in the lead - and deservedly so. He had been driving brilliantly and his powerful Mugen-Honda engine hadn't missed a beat. All the Japanese top brass were there and, at a time when Ligier and TWR-Arrows were vying for use of the V10 in 1997, this wasn't doing the much-maligned French team any harm at all. The wet con-

ditions for the first 25 laps had slowed things down and now the two-hour limit was approaching.

Could Panis' limited fuel go the distance at the now faster speeds? And could he hold off the McLaren of David Coulthard, which was only three seconds behind him on lap 61 - and lapping faster? Yes, he could but it wasn't easy. "My problem was that the team had ordered me to ease off a bit or I might not make it to the finish. I was accelerating very carefully and I wasn't driving flat out in fifth, to try to hold back consumption," said Olivier. Coulthard closed to within 1.7s of the Ligier on lap 72, with three to go. "Having raced against Olivier in Formula 3000, I

knew he doesn't make many mistakes," explained David, "so it was just a case of getting the car home and picking up the points." Which he did, to finish 4.8s behind the euphoric Panis, who had superbly won his first Grand Prix in a French car in French-speaking Monaco and had given Ligier its first Grand Prix win since Jacques Laffite's victory in Canada, 1981 - and Mugen Honda its very first triumph.

That wasn't all the excitement at the end of this amazing race. On his 69th lap Eddie Irvine, back on the track but miles behind, lost control of his Ferrari at almost exactly the same place as Schumacher and spun to a standstill. Almost immediately the fierce battle for fourth between the two Mikas, Salo and Hakkinen, abruptly terminated as they ploughed into the back of his F310, letting Heinz-Harald Frentzen through to take fourth - behind team-mate Johnny Herbert who had driven an exemplary race.

So an awful day for Williams, Benetton, Ferrari and Jordan, but a great afternoon for spectators. It had been a race to remember, one to savour for a very long time.

Above. Olivier Panis: a first Grand Prix win for him, a first for Mugen Honda...and Ligier's first for 15 years.

Opposite page. Fashion statement courtesy of Bacofoil.

Left. Hard lines: Jacques Villeneuve found Monaco tough going. Particularly when Luca Badoer drove him off the road.

FERRARI

A meeting Michael Schumacher will not forget. Only 11th fastest on Thursday, with gear selection problem, and nose-first into St Devote barrier on Saturday morning. But brilliantly takes second successive pole position (Ferrari's first at Monaco since Jody Scheckter in 1979), over half a second faster than Hill. "I think we have the reliability for the race as the gearbox is less of a problem here and we have done a full race distance in testing at Imola." Maybe so, but of no avail as Michael surprisingly makes bad start, is out-dragged by Hill and goes into barrier at Loews. ``I made a mistake. I am very sorry for the team and very angry with myself." Eddie Irvine, still suffering from lack of testing and resultant lack of confidence in car, qualifies seventh. To fourth, lap one. Holds up Frentzen/Coulthard/Villeneuve/Salo battle as he races third after Berger's retirement, laps 10-27. Back to third after pit stop, but rammed by Panis at Loews and into pits with belts undone in belief that he would be disqualified after push start. Team unnecessarily changes nosecone. Eddie not excluded and rejoins after 80s, now lapped. Races on but spins lap 69 and is rammed by Salo and Hakkinen. Classified seventh, six laps down.

BENETTON-RENAULT

Tense atmosphere due to lack of success, and Berger under a cloud following allegations of sexual harassment in Australia. Alesi (third) and Gerhard (fourth) achieve best qualifying results yet. However, Berger angry at having to spin approaching chicane on fast lap to avoid delighted Schumacher, who is waving at crowd after pole lap. Both start well, and run second and third when Schumacher crashes. Berger retires, lap 10, when gearbox sensor fails. Alesi races second, over 20s behind Hill, until taking lead when Damon pits, lap 28. Back to second after own stop, lap 30, but then retakes lead when Damon retires, lap 41. With race seemingly in bag, nearly 20s ahead of Panis, retires, lap 60, when rear suspension breaks after he has set fastest lap (1m 25.205s, 87.37mph).

WILLIAMS-RENAULT

Damon Hill fastest by over half a second on Saturday morning, inside his own 1995 pole time. Concerned about grid position at time, goes too soon in qualifying and loses pole to Schumacher for second time running. However, makes brilliant start to outdrag Schumacher and lead by over four seconds on lap one after Michael crashes. Drives superb race in difficult wet/dry conditions to lead Alesi by over 22s at lap 28 pit stop. Regains lead lap 30 and is commanding 26s ahead of Jean on lap 41 when engine oil pump fails in tunnel. "I had a warning light for about a lap so I knew there was a problem. It was a shame because I thought I could hold Alesi at that gap. We have a lot of races to come but I could have done with some points today." A very gracious reaction. Villeneuve never really gets to grips with Monaco, finding it very hard to master with so little practice. Qualifies 10th and races sixth behind Frentzen and Coulthard, lap 10. Fifth when Frentzen damages wing, lap 18. Up to fourth behind Herbert, lap 60, but is nerfed off, lap 67, by lapped Badoer who is penalised for his inattentiveness. Teams fails to score points for first time in 1996.

McLAREN-MERCEDES

On 30th anniversary of its Grand Prix debut, McLaren reveals new MP4/11B with shorter wheelbase, revised rear suspension, high mid-wing and further-revised qualifying engine. All part of ceaseless quest to rejoin top teams. Hakkinen fastest on Thursday but qualifies disappointed eighth, blaming Schumacher for delaying him on his quick lap. Blots copybook by crashing in wet acclimatisation period one hour before race and has to start in spare car. Down to 10th after bad start and is still there following lap 29 stop. Passes Salo to fifth behind Villeneuve, lap 61, but repassed by the Finn lap 70. Crashes into Salo and stationary Irvine, lap 71. Classified sixth, five laps down. David Coulthard starts disappointed fifth (confusingly wearing borrowed spare helmet from Schumacher after his own misted up). This time he makes a bad start to be passed by Irvine and Frentzen. Loses potential win when passed by Panis at sole stop, lap 29, spending remaining 45 laps behind the Ligier. Closes to within 1.7s, lap 72, but finishes second 4.8s down. With both cars in points, team has best result yet of 1996 and closes to within two points of third-placed Benetton in constructors' championship.

LIGIER-MUGEN HONDA

Stunning success for French team which everyone thought was on the ropes. Olivier Panis sixth on Thursday but down to 14th on grid, after only driving three laps due to electrical problem. Bounces back by going fastest in warm-up (light fuel load). In wet conditions team makes daring decision to start Olivier on full tanks and intermediate settings and go for one-stop 'top-up' strategy, which is brilliantly successful. As track dries Panis climbs steadily through field and is amazing fourth, lap 30. To third lap 36 after pushing Irvine out of way at Loews. Second when Hill retires, lap 41. Despite spinning on Hill's oil, lap 42, takes lead, lap 60, when Alesi pulls in. Resists ceaseless Coulthard pressure to win first Grand Prix and Ligier's first in 15 years. ``At the end I had to ease off a bit because the fuel was running light and I might not make it to the finish, but it all worked out!" Pedro Diniz starts 17th and goes off on lap five.

JORDAN-PEUGEOT

Cars newly liveried in fetching gold to match B&H sponsor's true colour. Rubens Barrichello starts sixth, team's highest-ever Monaco position but out, lap one, after being hit on hill after St Devote and then spinning into armco at Rascasse. Martin Brundle a puzzled 16th on grid despite having been fastest in all three lap sectors. Spins out of seventh and race at Casino Square, lap 31.

SAUBER-FORD

Success at last. From ninth on grid, Frentzen passes Hakkinen and Coulthard and harries Irvine for fourth until overdoing it, lap 17. Down to 11th after stopping for new nose. Is refused slick tyres but in again, lap 25 to start rush for dry Goodyears. Rejoins 11th and immediately goes 10s per lap faster. Meantime Herbert, who started 13th, up to fine fourth prior to lap 29 stop. Rejoins sixth and, driving sensibly and patiently, profits from retirements to advance to third, lap 60. Stays there. H-H similarly progresses to finish fourth, one lap down.

TWR ARROWS-HART

Verstappen and Monaco first-timer Rosset destroy so many nosecones in qualifying 12th and 20th that neither is allowed out for Sunday warm-up or wet-weather acclimatisation. Jos boldly starts on slicks but crashes at first corner. Rosset lasts until lap four before he too crashes.

TYRRELL-YAMAHA

Yet another disappointing race, after dreadful Saturday when Katayama has electrical and tyre problems and Salo breaks engine and gearbox. Finn switches to spare (set up for Ukyo) and then has Verstappen spin in front of him. Result is Mika 11th on grid, Katayama 15th. Ukyo to swimming pool Armco on lap three. Salo makes fine start and is eighth lap one, having passed Hakkinen. Down to ninth from fifth after lap 28 stop but into points at sixth, lap 41. Passed by Hakkinen, lap 61, but repasses compatriot to fourth when Badoer takes out Villeneuve, lap 67. Collides with Irvine's stationary Ferrari, lap 71, and is then rammed by Hakkinen's McLaren. Still classified fifth, five laps down, for third points finish in six races.

MINARDI-FORD

A ghastly weekend for underfunded team. Lamy and perhaps overconfident Fisichella, who won 1993 Monaco F3 race and predicts he will qualify in top 12 for his first F1 race there, start 19th and 18th after repeated meetings with barriers. As if that isn't enough they then drive into each other at St Devote, first corner of race. After each blames the other Gian Carlo Minardi understandably apoplectic. ``In 12 years of Formula One I've never seen anything like this. After planning the race in detail it's annoying to see everything wasted by two unbelievable mistakes of our drivers." Who will be driving in Spain?

FORTI-FORD

Both Badoer and Montermini use new car. "It is another world," says Andrea. Luca still unimpressive, 4.7s off the pace but qualifies 21st. Andrea also gets in, 22nd, but crashes in wet acclimatisation period and does not start. Badoer lumbers round at back until taking out Villeneuve and himself, lap 60, for which he is fined and given two-race ban (suspended for three races).

RACE 6
MONACO
19 May 1996

MONACO – MONTE CARLO GRAND PRIX CIRCUIT

STE DEVOTE
MONTÉE DE BEAU RIVAGE
MIRABEAU
TABAC
NOUVELLE CHICANE
LOEWS
VIRAGE DU PORTIER
VIRAGE ANTHONY NOGHES
TUNNEL
LA RASCASSE

CIRCUIT LENGTH: 2.068 MILES/3.328 KM

STARTING GRID

	SCHUMACHER 1m 20.356s
HILL 1m 20.888s	
	ALESI 1m 20.918s
BERGER 1m 21.067s	
	COULTHARD 1m 21.460s
BARRICHELLO 1m 21.504s	
	IRVINE 1m 21.542s
HAKKINEN 1m 21.688s	
	FRENTZEN 1m 21.929s
VILLENEUVE 1m 21.963s	
	SALO 1m 22.235s
VERSTAPPEN 1m 22.327s	
	HERBERT 1m 22.346s
PANIS 1m 22.358s	
	KATAYAMA 1m 22.460s
BRUNDLE 1m 22.519s	
	DINIZ 1m 22.682s
FISICHELLA 1m 22.684s	
	LAMY 1m 23.350s
ROSSET 1m 24.970s	
	BADOER 1m 25.059s
MONTERMINI 1m 25.393s	

RACE CLASSIFICATION

Pos	Driver	Nat	Car	Laps	Time
1	Olivier Panis	F	Ligier JS43-Mugen Honda V10	75	2h 00m 45.629s
2	David Coulthard	GB	McLaren MP4/11-Mercedes V10	75	+4.828s
3	Johnny Herbert	GB	Sauber C15-Ford V10	75	+37.503s
4	Heinz-Harald Frentzen	D	Sauber C15-Ford V10		+1 DNF Pitted
5	Mika Salo	SF	Tyrrell 024-Yamaha V10		+5 DNF Accident
6	Mika Hakkinen	SF	McLaren MP4/11-Mercedes V10		+5 DNF Accident
7	Eddie Irvine	GB	Ferrari F310-Ferrari V10		+7 DNF Accident

Retirements	Nat	Car	Lap	Reason
Jacques Villeneuve	CDN	Williams FW18-Renault V10	66	Accident
Jean Alesi	F	Benetton B196-Renault V10	60	Suspension
Luca Badoer	I	Forti FG03-Ford V8	60	Accident
Damon Hill	GB	Williams FW18-Renault V10	40	Engine
Martin Brundle	GB	Jordan 196-Peugeot V10	30	Accident
Gerhard Berger	A	Benetton B196-Renault V10	9	Gearbox
Pedro Diniz	BR	Ligier JS43--Mugen Honda V10	5	Spin
Ricardo Rosset	BR	Footwork FA17-Hart V8	3	Accident
Ukyo Katayama	J	Tyrrell 024-Yamaha V10	2	Throttle/accident
Michael Schumacher	D	Ferrari F310-Ferrari V10	0	Accident
Jos Verstappen	NL	Footwork FA17-Hart V8	0	Accident
Rubens Barrichello	BR	Jordan 196-Peugeot V10	0	Spin
Pedro Lamy	P	Minardi M195B-Ford V8	0	Accident
Giancarlo Fisichella	I	Minardi M195B-Ford V8	0	Accident
Andrea Montermini	I	Minardi M195B-Ford V8	Warm-up accident	

FASTEST LAP Jean Alesi 1m 25.205s lap 59 (87.375mph)

DRIVERS' CHAMPIONSHIP

Damon Hill	43
Jacques Villeneuve	22
Michael Schumacher	16
Jean Alesi	11
Olivier Panis	11
David Coulthard	10
Eddie Irvine	9
Gerhard Berger	7
Rubens Barrichello	7
Mika Hakkinen	6
Mika Salo	5
Johnny Herbert	4
Heinz-Harald Frentzen	3
Jos Verstappen	1
Martin Brundle	1

CONSTRUCTORS' CUP

Williams-Renault	65
Ferrari	25
Benetton-Renault	18
McLaren-Mercedes	16
Ligier-Mugen Honda	11
Jordan-Peugeot	8
Sauber-Ford	7
Tyrrell-Yamaha	5
Footwork-Hart	1

Results and Data © FIA 1996

After Barcelona '96, I shall never again look at Michael Schumacher with anything other than admiration and awe. For at the Circuit de Catalunya his driving, in utterly appalling weather, was that of a towering genius. His victory was one of the most crushing I have ever seen, but it was something that even he had not expected. Third on the grid was the best he could do and he was not optimistic for the race. "Today I got the absolute maximum out of the car. Realistically the best I can hope for tomorrow is a podium position." Ever pragmatic, Michael acknowledged that the Barcelona track, which has a series of long, fast corners, did not suit his Ferrari with its lack of grip and handling problems. "The gap stems mainly from aerodynamic reasons and until we have the new parts we are developing it will be hard to close it."

On the outskirts of the great city of Barcelona, the 2.94-mile circuit is a good one, liked by drivers, teams and the media. It's just a pity the Spanish aren't so keen for, by usual standards, the crowds are thin. Yet, despite the raging torrent, some 53,000 turned up to watch on raceday, King Juan Carlos amongst them.

The weather on Friday and Saturday was superb: 25 degree temperatures, clear blue skies and not a cloud to be seen. Little did we know what we were in for. Jacques Villeneuve was fastest on Saturday morning, despite the fact that he lost half the session when his Renault engine blew. In the vital qualifying hour, Damon Hill was 0.4s faster than his Williams team-mate and a further 0.5s ahead of Schumacher. He had won at Barcelona in 1994, liked the track, had the best car, was quietly confident and meant to return to victory mode after the bitter disappointment of Monaco.

It looked like a Williams-Renault whitewash, particularly as the only drivers other than Schumacher who were likely to offer

any opposition, Alesi and Berger in their Benettons, were fourth and fifth, nearly 1.5s off the pace.

Barcelona is notoriously hard on tyres. The teams had been eking out the 28 Goodyears they are allowed per car, so that they had the maximum amount of fresh rubber for the race. Some of them had only used two sets, but they needn't have bothered. It wasn't just raining on Sunday, it was absolutely hosepiping down. Nor did it show the slightest sign of abating. The skies were black and low; everything and everybody was soaked and the carefully developed dry-weather set-ups and strategies were out of the window. There was just half an hour to try other settings in the final practice four hours before the race. It was virtually impossible to use all the alternatives in the time available, but Williams wasn't worried. A happy Damon Hill, delighted with his car, was comfortably fastest again,

"Your turn to get wet." Ferrari's sporting director Jean Todt emerges from the shelter of the pit wall canopy to discover that its raining corks and dogs. Left. Villeneuve heads Alesi, Hill, Berger and Barrichello. Further back, in the general direction of France, a man in a red car appears not to have noticed that it is, in fact, raining.

Far right. Jos Verstappen joins a group of trawlermen and the unfortunate JCB driver who had spun off earlier on.

Below. Herr Spray…Ferrari's team leader, breezes past Alesi into second place. Below right. Repeat performance: the HMS Schumacher glides past Villeneuve, taking part in a wet race for only the second time in his career.

ahead of Schumacher.

Then the weather got even worse. There was even talk of starting the race behind the safety car for the first time in the history of Formula One. It didn't happen because, with absolutely no let-up of the rain, when would its driver have pulled over to let battle commence?

Ferrari opted for a soft suspension/maximum downforce set-up to maximise grip on the waterlogged tarmac. Williams wrongly added only a little downforce to its previous set-up.

Ironically, Villeneuve hadn't had time to evaluate all the wet settings in the warm-up, because it was stopped short when Heinz-Harald Frentzen had a colossal accident. Even so, despite his lack of experience of racing in the rain, Jacques still rocketed away from the grid ahead of Alesi and Hill. Damon had got it wrong, and Schumacher was even worse. Once again his Ferrari clutch had failed to grip and he sat helplessly whilst the field streamed by. "I think even Diniz passed me."

It was time to knuckle down and go for it. And that he did.

Michael's progress was well-nigh unbelievable. Five drivers, including David Coulthard, went out through accidents brought on by near zero visibility on the first lap, and Eddie Irvine joined them on the second. By then, Schumacher was up to fifth, 7.4s behind Villeneuve who led Alesi, Hill and Berger.

On lap four Michael was fourth. Hill had slid off, to rejoin two places down. Not good. Schumacher made short work of Gerhard Berger - past the Benetton to third one lap later. Now he was five seconds behind Alesi, another wet-weather expert, but it took him a mere three laps not only to close the gap but to pass the Benetton and pull half a second clear. Next target was Jacques Villeneuve, now right in front of the Ferrari. The brilliant young Canadian did his best, but kept Schumacher behind him for only another two laps. At the same place where he had taken Alesi, Michael calmly slid inside the

Williams, powered ahead and was on his way.

"He simply flew by me," said Jacques. And now he flew away at the stupefying rate of some four seconds per lap. Schumacher wasn't just in another class at Barcelona. He was on another planet. No one could live with him. Certainly not Damon Hill.

Hill's set-up, which had been so good for the warm-up, was hopeless for the race. His off-track excursion on lap three was followed by another on lap eight and, finally, a third on lap 11 which took him into a gravel trap and out of the race. No points for the second Grand Prix in succession. "Today was a bad day for me. I made two mistakes and then a third. It was very, very dangerous, very difficult to see. I was in trouble right from the start."

So were plenty of others. On lap 12, only 12 of the 20 starters (neither of the Fortis had qualified) were left, and a lot more were to disappear. It would be untrue to say that the remaining 43 laps were excit-

"Five drivers, including David Coulthard, went out through accidents brought on by near zero visibility on the first lap"

ing. For the sodden and dispirited crowd and the worldwide millions watching TV, it must have been a literal turn-off. But, if you were a Formula One anorak, you knew that you were watching one of the great wet-weather drives of all time as Schumacher raced away, never putting a wheel wrong. On lap 14, with giant volumes of spray rearing up behind his Ferrari powerboat, he set the fastest lap of the race, over two seconds faster than anyone else.

Meantime, Villeneuve was a steadily receding second with Alesi close behind,

"I presume there will be those who say that I only owe my sixth place to the high attrition rate, but I know that I drove a perfectly respectable race"

Pedro Diniz

looking to polish his tarnished reputation by at least passing the Williams for six points. But no chance. "I was on the limit and could feel the car aquaplaning everywhere. I had problems on the straight, because when I got close behind Jacques I was getting water sprayed up into the airbox of my car. It is not just the tyres which aquaplane - it is the flat bottom of the car as well, so I was very happy not to hit the wall." They were all earning their high wages in Spain.

Schumacher was not only driving an inspired race. He was driving it to an inspired strategy. Where everyone else had one stop, he opted for two, and it worked to perfection. In on lap 24 and out again, still 23s ahead of Villeneuve. The others came in at about the halfway stage. Alesi first, to rejoin seventh; Berger next, down from third to fifth; and then Villeneuve, allowing the late-stopping Rubens

Above. Bitter irony: Benetton hadn't brought along models in swimsuits this time.

Left. Smart pitwork in the River Barcelona helped Alesi to overcome Villeneuve late in the afternoon.

Barrichello to move up to second in his Jordan-Peugeot.

It was about this time that Schumacher's Ferrari V10 became a V8. "It was an electrical problem and just got worse and worse. I lost about 10 kph on the straights, but it didn't seem to make much difference." Certainly not to his lead. Michael's second stop was on lap 42, when he was a massive 67s ahead of Barrichello, who came in on the same lap.

Poor Rubens rejoined fourth, but was sadly destined not to finish after another fine drive. Now Alesi was ahead of Villeneuve, having passed the Williams when Jacques made his sole pit stop on lap 36. And that was the way it was destined to stay, with Heinz-Harald Frentzen advancing to a lapped fourth as Gerhard Berger spun out trying to lap Pedro Diniz's Ligier.

The Spanish Grand Prix only just went the full 65-lap distance. It stopped 10.7s inside the two-hour limit, and only six of the 20 starters finished.

Frentzen was fourth, a depressed Mika Hakkinen, who had never been even remotely on the pace in his McLaren-Mercedes, was a lapped fifth and Pedro Diniz scored his first World Championship point by finishing sixth in his Ligier. "I presume there will be those who will say that I only owe my sixth place to the high attrition rate, but I know that I drove a perfectly respectable race".

He was right on both counts. Pedro may have been two laps down, but he had finished when 14 of his rivals had not.

So now Schumacher had won his first Grand Prix for Maranello, one race earlier than the halfway point of the season where he had predicted the team would be competitive. An absolutely brilliant victory, but was Ferrari now a championship-winning force? Team boss Jean Todt didn't think so, and nor did Michael.

"Here we were uncompetitive in the dry but dominant in the wet, while in Monaco the situation was the reverse. We must work very hard to really understand the problems with the car," said Schumacher.

A jubilant Todt was no less realistic. "This is not the time to talk of the dawning of a new age. We have won one race, just as we did in 1994 and 1995. We must continue with this positive trend and keep on improving."

FERRARI

Stunning Schumacher drive of awe-inspiring brilliance gives Ferrari its first win since Canada 1995. In dry qualifying F310's aerodynamic inadequacies result in Schumacher starting third, nearly a second slower than Hill. Irvine sixth, 1.7s off pole time. "This is not the best track for Ferrari," says Michael. "Realistically, my best finish is on the podium. We're too slow." Irvine is happier after two days testing at Mugello, but still concerned about instability. At wet (very wet!) warm-up, team tries various set-ups and opts for full-soft settings with a two-stop strategy, which turns out to be an inspired decision. Schumacher again has clutch problem at start and drops back to about 10th in appalling conditions. "I think even Diniz passed me. Now I know what it is like to be at the back and unable to see." But Michael stages incredible recovery and is sixth by end of lap one. Irvine spins out lap two and Schumacher moves up to fifth. To fourth, 8.5s behind race leader Villeneuve, lap four, when Hill spins. Then to third past Berger, lap five. Closes five-second gap to Alesi by lap eight and passes him to lie second, lap nine. Into lead past Villeneuve at same corner on lap 12. An absolutely incredible performance. With a clear track ahead, pulls away at an astounding four seconds per lap, including fastest lap of race (1m 45.517s, 100.216mph). Rejoins, still 23s ahead after first stop, lap 24. Despite misfire which reduces V10 engine to V8, rebuilds lead (over Barrichello) to 67s at second stop, lap 42, and rejoins 62s ahead of Alesi. Continues, wet and cold, to win his 20th GP and first for Ferrari by 45.3s. A great drive, by any standards.

BENETTON-RENAULT

Team reverts to rear springs in place of torsion bars in quest for greater suspension reliability, post-Monaco. Saving slicks for expected dry race, Jean and Gerhard Berger qualify contented fourth and fifth. Neither able to try all alternative wet set-ups in warm-up, but Alesi past faltering Hill and Schumacher to take second at start, with Berger fourth. Incredible Schumacher passes Gerhard lap five and Alesi lap nine. JA/GB run third and fourth behind Villeneuve/Schumacher until pit stops, laps 32 and 33 respectively. Alesi back to second, lap 43 (62s behind Schumacher), but Berger spins out from fifth, lap 45, whilst trying to lap Diniz. Jean finishes second, 45s down after major aquaplaning problems, and advances to fourth in championship.

WILLIAMS-RENAULT

Hill and Villeneuve dominate qualifying to give team third front row monopoly of season (and Damon his 15th career pole). Hill a confident fastest in wet warm-up, but leaves suspension settings the same for much wetter race conditions four hours later. Villeneuve makes superb start and takes lead as Hill drops to third behind Alesi. Whilst Jacques continues to lead (with Schumacher rapidly gaining), Hill slides off on laps three, seven and 11 - out of the race. Jacques caught and passed by sensational Schumacher, lap 12. Loses second to Alesi at lap 36 stop. Finishes third to stay second in championship, now equal with Schumacher and 17 points behind Hill.

McLAREN-MERCEDES

Back to 'long' wheelbase chassis...and Monaco feelgood factor melts. Hakkinen and Coulthard demoralising 10th and 14th on grid, 2.5s off pace due to acute handling problems. Coulthard loses front wheel in attack from unknown assailant before first corner. Hakkinen does best he can, following Verstappen for much of the race, in "very difficult to drive" car. Finishes lapped fifth. "At no stage this weekend did we ever come to grips with the car's set-up," says Ron Dennis.

LIGIER-MUGEN HONDA

Cesare Fiorio returns from Forti as Sporting Director, with team spirits high after Monaco victory. Panis does well to qualify career-best eighth; Diniz 17th. Olivier maintains improved form with third-fastest time in warm-up, but is punted off during shambolic first lap. This was Pedro's happiest day, though. Drives steadily round at the back to finish last, two laps down, but still scores his first-ever point. "I pre-

sume there will be those who will say that I only owe my sixth place to the high attrition rate (true), but I know that I drove a perfectly respectable race." Also true. Pedro finished where 14 did not.

JORDAN-PEUGEOT

Amidst dramatic team expansion plans thanks to Benson & Hedges money, Barrichello qualifies respectable seventh with Brundle down in disappointing 15th ("traffic") on his 37th birthday. Sadly, Jordan reliability problems recur during race. Barrichello opts for late-stop strategy. Drives excellent race to advance to second, lap 36, prior to lap 42 stop. Rejoins fourth but car develops clutch problem. In again, lap 45, to retire. Climbs out after another praiseworthy drive, but team gets it going. Rubens back in race but retires on first lap out when differential fails. Brundle also opts for heavy fuel load/late stop strategy. After fine start, shoots up five places to 10th during first lap fracas but, despite coping with severe aquaplaning, retires from ninth, lap 18, when his differential also fails.

SAUBER-FORD

Delighted Johnny Herbert (ninth) outqualifies Frentzen (11th) for the first time since joining Sauber. Team enjoys highest-yet grid position of 1996, although both drivers still grappling with ever-present understeer. H-H has gigantic crash exiting last corner in wet warm-up, and wipes rear end off car. Is pronounced fit to race and bravely starts in spare car although, amazingly, team has his crash remains rebuilt in time. Herbert's set-up unsuitable for wet and has major aquaplaning-problems. Slides off, recovers, then falls off again on lap 21, into gravel trap. Frentzen is superb after morning accident. Sensibly concentrates on staying on track and finishes fourth (one lap down) for second race in succession.

TWR ARROWS-HART

Good news is that Castrol signs as sponsor. Bad news is that new TWR engineers are finding it difficult to master the Alan Jenkins-designed FA17. Verstappen 13th on grid; Rosset 20th. Ricardo out at start when, unable to see through spray, rams Lamy's stationary Minardi. Jos 12th, lap one. Then zaps up to eighth behind Frentzen, lap three. Races strong seventh, laps 8-44, and then to excellent fifth, laps 45-47 between Frentzen and Hakkinen, only to aquaplane off, lap 48.

TYRRELL-YAMAHA

Buzz in pit lane when team reveals carbon fibre-shrouded front suspension. Is it structural (legal)? Or aerodynamic (illegal)? "It's structural," says team. FIA Technical Delegate Charlie Whiting agrees. But it doesn't seem to help. Salo qualifies 12th, Katayama 16th. Ukyo zonks into Fisichella's Minardi at the start. Carries on but retires from 13th, lap nine, with engine electrical failure. Salo even worse. Yamaha engine cuts out at start of formation lap. Tries to start from pits, but has same problem. Switches to spare car and is black-flagged for illegally using spare after start of race.

MINARDI-FORD

Using much-revised Ford ED V8, Lamy qualifies 1.5s faster than 1995. But, of course, everyone else has made progress too. Pedro still only 18th, 0.6s faster than team-mate Giancarlo Fisichella (19th). Having collided with each other at start of Monaco GP, the team-mates amazingly do so again on first lap. To compound the agony, Rosset also thumps into stationary Lamy. Fisichella completes a lap but is then biffed into retirement by Katayama's Tyrrell.

FORTI-FORD

More changes to hard-trying, slowly-evolving team as Cesare Fiorio leaves to join Ligier, ex-Ferrari drawing office chief George Ryton joins as chief designer and cars take on green and white livery of mysterious backer Shannon, which is also supporting 13 F3 cars and two F3000 runners. Neither Luca Badoer nor Andrea Montermini is able to qualify. George Ryton says he has already initiated a much-needed weight reduction and aerodynamic development programme.

FIA FORMULA 1 WORLD CHAMPIONSHIP

7

RACE
SPAIN
2 June 1996

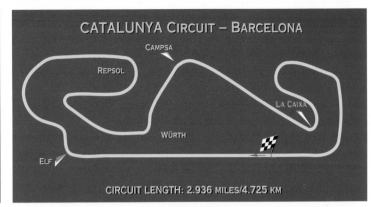

CATALUNYA CIRCUIT – BARCELONA

CAMPSA
REPSOL
LA CAIXA
WÜRTH
ELF

CIRCUIT LENGTH: 2.936 MILES/4.725 KM

STARTING GRID

HILL 1m 20.650s	**VILLENEUVE** 1m 21.084s
SCHUMACHER 1m 21.587s	**ALESI** 1m 22.061s
BERGER 1m 22.125s	IRVINE 1m 22.333s
BARRICHELLO 1m 22.379s	**PANIS** 1m 22.685s
HERBERT 1m 23.027s	**HAKKINEN** 1m 23.070s
FRENTZEN 1m 23.195s	**SALO** 1m 23.224s
VERSTAPPEN 1m 23.371s	**COULTHARD** 1m 23.416s
BRUNDLE 1m 23.348s	**KATAYAMA** 1m 24.401s
DINIZ 1m 24.468s	**LAMY** 1m 25.274s
FISICHELLA 1m 25.531s	**ROSSET** 1m 25.621s

Did not qualify

BADOER (Forti FG03) 1m 26.615s	**MONTERMINI** (Forti FG03) 1m 27.358s

RACE CLASSIFICATION

Pos	Driver	Nat	Car	Laps	Time
1	Michael Schumacher	D	Ferrari F310-Ferrari V10	65	1h 59m 49.307s
2	Jean Alesi	F	Benetton B196-Renault V10	65	+45.302s
3	Jacques Villeneuve	CDN	Williams FW18-Renault V10	65	+48.388s
4	Heinz-Harald Frentzen	D	Sauber C15-Ford V10		+1 lap
5	Mika Hakkinen	SF	McLaren MP4/11-Mercedes V10		+1 lap
6	Pedro Diniz	BR	Ligier JS43-Mugen Honda V10		+ 2 laps

Retirements	Nat	Car	Lap	Reason
Jos Verstappen	NL	Footwork FA17-Hart V8	47	Spin
Rubens Barrichello	BR	Jordan 196-Peugeot V10	45	Differential
Gerhard Berger	A	Benetton B196-Renault V10	44	Spin
Johnny Herbert	GB	Sauber C15-Ford V10	20	Spin
Martin Brundle	GB	Jordan 196-Peugeot V10	17	Differential
Mika Salo	SF	Tyrrell 024-Yamaha V10	16	Black flag*
Damon Hill	GB	Williams FW18-Renault V10	10	Accident
Ukyo Katayama	J	Tyrrell 024-Yamaha V10	8	Electrics
Eddie Irvine	GB	Ferrari F310-Ferrari V10	1	Spin
Olivier Panis	F	Ligier JS43-Mugen Honda V10	1	Accident damage
Giancarlo Fisichella	I	Minardi M195B-Ford V8	1	Accident damage
David Coulthard	GB	McLaren MP4/11-Mercedes V10	0	Accident
Ricardo Rosset	BR	Footwork FA17-Hart V8	0	Accident
Pedro Lamy	P	Minardi M195B-Ford V8	0	Accident

*Excluded for taking over spare car after race had started

FASTEST LAP Michael Schumacher 1m 45.517 lap 14 (100.249mph)

DRIVERS' CHAMPIONSHIP

Damon Hill	43
Jacques Villeneuve	26
Michael Schumacher	26
Jean Alesi	17
Olivier Panis	11
David Coulthard	10
Eddie Irvine	9
Mika Hakkinen	8
Gerhard Berger	7
Rubens Barrichello	7
Heinz-Harald Frentzen	6
Mika Salo	5
Johnny Herbert	4
Jos Verstappen	1
Martin Brundle	1
Pedro Diniz	1

CONSTRUCTORS' CUP

Williams-Renault	69
Ferrari	35
Benetton-Renault	24
McLaren-Mercedes	18
Ligier-Mugen Honda	12
Sauber-Ford	10
Jordan-Peugeot	8
Tyrrell-Yamaha	5
Footwork-Hart	1

Results and Data © FIA 1996

Synchronised
grinning:
Villeneuve,
Hill and Alesi.

Damon Hill was worried. No points at Monaco; no points in Spain; Ferrari getting stronger. And now there was massive support for team-mate Jacques Villeneuve in his native Canada. Although he was 17 points ahead in the champi- onship, with nine races still to go, Hill needed to do well. No reason why he shouldn't, of course. His Williams-Renault was the class of the field and, although he had yet to win there, this would be his fourth race on the unique island circuit.

Montreal interrupted the run of European

Synchronised grinning: Villeneuve, Hill and Alesi.

CANADA

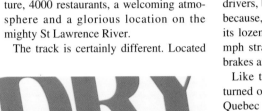

events, and was more than worth the trip. The lively French-Canadian city is popular, with its blend of old and new architecture, 4000 restaurants, a welcoming atmosphere and a glorious location on the mighty St Lawrence River.

The track is certainly different. Located on a man-made island, created for Expo '67 and also used for the 1976 Olympic Games, it is not particularly demanding for the drivers, but is traditionally hard on their cars because, with hairpin bends at each end of its lozenge shape, both approached by 180 mph straights, it places great demands on brakes and transmissions.

Like the USA, Canada as a whole isn't turned on by Formula One. But the State of Quebec most certainly is. Quebec was the home of national hero Gilles Villeneuve, and he scored his first GP win at Montreal, in 1978.

The return of the Villeneuve name to F1 set Montreal aflame with enthusiasm. The pressure on the calm and phlegmatic Jacques was immense.

In 1993 he had won a Formula Atlantic race at the circuit named after his father; driving an F1 car here was very different. "The speeds are so much higher and the car is so much wider that my experience is no use," he said.

With the expectation of Canada weighing heavily on him, Jacques was fastest on Saturday morning, In the vital afternoon qualifying session he was quickest of all until almost the end of the session. He had gone out early and set a time which no one could do anything about, not even team-mate Damon Hill. But, as he always does in conditions of adversity, Damon dug really deep. With seconds to go he went a wafer-thin 0.02s faster than Jacques. Close, but enough to secure his fifth pole position of the year and put both Williams-Renaults on the front row.

Only Michael Schumacher was close to them, in a Ferrari with a new high nose which improved its performance. "It's not a giant leap, about a tenth of a second better, but every little helps." This was the race that Schumacher had been predicting would see the new Ferrari in a position to win. Team-mate Eddie Irvine, in the other F310, was fifth on the grid, sandwiched between Jean Alesi's Benetton-Renault and Mika

"Stand by for some fantastic action," I said. "Just remember how Schumacher started 16th in Belgium last year and still won the race" Wrong again!"

**Above.
It was vital for
Villeneuve
(left), on a one-
stop strategy,
to get ahead of
Hill at the start.
To his chagrin,
he didn't quite
pull it off.**

**Right. Dodgem
City: Rubens
Barrichello finds
something that
handles to
his liking. Why
is everyone else
facing the
other way..?**

Hakkinen's McLaren-Mercedes. Truth be told, Schumacher looked as though he was the only one likely to offer any real opposition to another Williams walkover. Situation normal.

What about race strategies? Unlike most of today's restrictive circuits, it is possible to pass at several places in Montreal, which also has a very short pit lane approach. Both characteristics would affect the team's strategies, as would the elimination of a tight new chicane, which had marred the return straight the previous

year. Now there was a long, flat-out blast from the East Hairpin to the 90-deg right/left at the pits.

Virtually everyone had stopped only once in 1995, but in 1994 race-winner Schumacher had stopped twice. What to choose?

One of the many things that have always enthused me about Formula One is its unpredictability. Who would ever have thought that Ferrari couldn't start Schumacher's engine? But they couldn't. As everyone rocketed away on the formation lap, Michael sat motionless on the grid. When his V10 eventually fired up, he had to obey the rules and line up last. "Stand by for some fantastic action," I said in the commentary. "Just remember how Schumacher started 16th in Belgium last year and still won the race." Wrong again! Michael was 13th by lap 11, but then he bogged down. He was at least going though. Team-mate Eddie Irvine had been out of the race for 11 laps. Up to fourth on lap one, Eddie had alarmingly seen his right front suspension break.

A pretty grisly race for Ferrari already, but worse was to come. Up front, Hill was looking good. We didn't know it at the time but it was absolutely vital that he beat Villeneuve into the first corner, because Hill was on a two-stop strategy whereas Jacques had decided to stop only once. So Damon had to start fast and build up enough of a lead to compensate for the extra time that two stops would take. On lap five he was 4.1s ahead of Villeneuve. On lap 15, the gap was seven seconds and, on lap 27, when he came in for his first stop, it was 11. With Villeneuve now in the lead, Hill rejoined the track seven seconds down and started to charge again.

Meantime Jean Alesi, lucky to be in the race after a colossal off the previous day when one of his Benetton brake pipes fractured, had been a consistent third ahead of team-mate Gerhard Berger. Full of pain, he was achieving the best he could hope for, drawing away from Berger, who was being pursued by both Jordans.

Martin Brundle had been struggling all year with a car which he couldn't set up to suit his style but now, with the help of new engineer Andy Tilley, he had got it to his liking and was flying. Up to seventh past team-mate Barrichello on lap one, from ninth on the grid, he soon passed Mika Hakkinen and closed on Berger. When Rubens took Mika on lap 11, both Jordans were in the top six. But would they finish the race?

By half distance, we had the strategy

Below. Canvas to canvas, dust to dust. Frentzen and Barrichello do damage to tyres and herbaceous borders respectively.

Left. Giancarlo Fisichella finished eighth - albeit last - for Minardi, but the team's faith in youth was being jeopardised by its need for cash.

Schumacher trails forlornly after Salo, Herbert and Panis. His Ferrari's reluctance to start meant he had to start at the back of the grid; progress was not the work of a moment.

Below. Penalty Scot: Coulthard loses his way during qualifying.

Bottom. Disjointed colours of Benetton, courtesy Gerhard Berger.

answers. Virtually everyone was stopping once, as they had done the year before. Villeneuve came in on lap 35, 6.4s ahead of Hill. Damon regained the lead, but still had his second stop to come. Berger stopped on lap 34, Alesi on lap 36. But Brundle was stopping twice, and poor Barrichello was out with clutch failure, his fifth retirement from eight races.

Now, could Hill build up enough of a lead over Villeneuve to make his second stop and retain his lead? If he couldn't, Jacques was going to be mighty hard to pass. There had been nothing between them all weekend, and he would be leading at home spurred on by the fervent support of a record 107,000 crowd. Intelligent observation said that Damon would pit around lap 49, and that by then he would need to be at least 25 seconds ahead of Villeneuve.

On lap 45 it was 24s; on lap 49, when he swept into the pit lane, it was 29.9. It was more than enough. After an 8.6s stop, Hill led Villeneuve by 13.6s at the end of lap 50. What had happened to Jacques? As he was lapping Johnny Herbert's Sauber, he saw a flurry of yellow flags and wisely backed off to avoid being penalised. Wise, but expensive. His action cost him some five seconds. Now all Damon had to do was stay cool and maintain the gap.

> "There had been nothing between them all weekend, and he (Villeneuve) would be leading at home spurred on by the fervent support of a record 107,000 crowd"

Ferrari's cup of misery was full to overflowing. Schumacher's lack of progress, his failure to get past Mika Salo's Tyrrell and his inability even to draw away from Pedro Diniz's Ligier was caused by a brake imbalance which he could not correct because of a broken control bar. On lap 40 he came in for a late stop, and when he blasted away, his left-hand driveshaft broke and went bouncing down the pit lane for all to see. Embarrassing. "The championship is nearly decided," said Schumacher. "It's clearly Damon's year." With eight races to go, I certainly wouldn't have agreed with him, but he had every reason to feel despondent after a poor showing by his team.

Gerhard Berger was the next to go when he spun out. It was his second off in two days in the hard-to-drive Benetton. Now David Coulthard was fourth, with a lapped Mika Hakkinen fifth after spinning whilst trying to lap Giancarlo Fisichella's Minardi.

But Villeneuve wasn't giving up. "I knew Damon was far ahead, but I kept pushing just in case he had some backmarkers or made a mistake." Down came the gap, to 7.9s on lap 67 when Jacques set the fastest lap (1m 21.916s, 120.732mph). It was further reduced to 6.8s with one lap to go, but Damon knew the score and took his 18th Grand Prix victory and the 10 points he so wanted.

It was Williams' fourth one-two of 1996, increasing its constructors' championship lead over Ferrari to a monumental 50 points and lifting Hill's advantage over Villeneuve to 21. Comfortable, but by no means a foregone conclusion. A great race for Williams, a reasonable race for Benetton (with Alesi third), but no great joy for McLaren, even though Coulthard was fourth and Hakkinen a lapped fifth. There was a happy outcome for Martin Brundle though, back in the points (sixth) despite ramming Pedro Lamy's Minardi after his pit stop.

After another great race for Renault, the marque would announce its withdrawal from Formula One at the end of 1997. Interesting times ahead!

Above. "He's spending too much at the funfair." Eddie Jordan, Martin Brundle and engineer Andy Tilley contemplate their other driver's malaise.

FERRARI

Steady forward progress lurches to demoralising halt. Schumacher uses new high nose and reports that it benefits top speed, downforce and stability. Qualifies third, 0.14s slower than Hill and intends to have one-stop race. So he does, but not in the way he intended. Low fuel pressure prevents team firing car up for formation lap, so Michael has to start from back. Advances five places to 15th on first lap, then past Diniz to 14th. But then, with brake balance problem, is unable either to pull away from Pedro or pass Mika Salo's Tyrrell. Up to seventh out of 12, 73s behind Hill, at late pit stop, lap 41. Left driveshaft breaks as he rejoins, forcing retirement. Even worse for Irvine who qualifies fifth, also using high nose, after Friday problems with fuel pressure and set-up. Front suspension push-rod breaks on lap two. An appalling day of misfortune for team. Schumacher says, "I think the championship is nearly decided. It's clearly Damon's year."

BENETTON-RENAULT

New floor, diffuser, front wing and damper settings, but car unstable under hard braking as a result of which Berger goes off in qualifying. Alesi also has heavy crash in qualifying when front brake pipe fractures. Despite this Jean, starts fourth, 0.47s off Hill's time. Berger is seventh. In considerable pain, Alesi runs close third to Villeneuve for opening laps but is 10s behind Jacques by lap 20, wrestling with rear tyre problem. Races on to finish contented third to dominant Williams duo. Berger non-threatening fourth to Alesi until lap 34. Down to sixth after pit stop and back to fourth, lap 41. Spins out, lap 43. "My fault. I was trying to catch Jean and braked too late."

WILLIAMS-RENAULT

An idyllic weekend amidst patriotic Canadian fervour in support of Jacques Villeneuve (who is, typically, totally cool about it). Hill, concerned about failure to score at Monaco and in Spain, has thrilling battle for pole position with team-mate Villeneuve and takes it by mere 0.02s in final two minutes of qualifying. Team rivals decide on different strategies. One stop for Jacques, two for Damon. That means Hill must take lead at start and build a lead. He does so and is 11s ahead of Villeneuve at first stop, lap 27. Loses lead but regains it when Jacques stops, lap 35. Needs to build lead of some 25s to be sure of getting out of pit lane ahead of Jacques after second stop and is 30s ahead when he comes in, lap 49. Rejoins 13.6s ahead. Villeneuve drives magnificently to maintain constant pressure. Loses some five seconds by not passing Herbert's Sauber on seeing yellow flags but sets fastest lap of race and closes gap to 4.2s at finish as Hill backs off. Damon increases lead over Villeneuve to 21 points; Williams now a massive 50 points ahead of Ferrari in constructors' contest. Renault lifts GP win tally to 80, but later announces that it will pull out of Formula One at the end of 1997.

McLAREN-MERCEDES

Disappointed and, no doubt, increasingly frustrated Mika Hakkinen qualifies sixth, 0.75s off the pace. Coulthard loses valuable setting-up time with hydraulic problem on Friday afternoon; spins on fast qualifying lap and starts 10th after having enormous engine blow-up in warm-up and then going off in spare car. Mika fourth after good start but, with heavy fuel load for late stop, is passed by Berger and both Jordans. Spins out of fourth on lap 36 whilst trying to lap Fisichella who finishes fifth, a lap down. Coulthard drives steady and reliable race with late, lap 40, stop to finish full-distance fourth. "We lapped as fast as everybody except the Williams," says Ron Dennis but Coulthard pragmatically expects no real progress before 1997. "We have a fundamental aerodynamic problem."

LIGIER MUGEN-HONDA

After myriad practice problems, Panis qualifies 11h using B-spec Mugen-Honda engine but unhappy with set-up. Diniz has electronic throttle problem and starts 10th. After overnight set-up changes, and switch to A-spec engine for race, Panis up to eighth, lap 21. Down to 11th after lap 23 stop but climbs to seventh, lap 39, only for engine to cut out, lap 40. Diniz has to switch to spare car with unfamiliar brakes after electrical problem. Runs 12th out of 15, grappling with

brake problem, until his engine also fails, lap 39.

JORDAN-PEUGEOT

With new race engineer Andy Tilley plus set-up progress at Silverstone test, Martin Brundle has best 1996 pre-race performance (ninth on grid, fourth in warm-up) for his 150th GP. Up to sixth behind Berger on lap two and then fifth past Hakkinen, lap six. Passed by both late-stopping McLarens at lap 24 stop but regains fifth, lap 41, only to collide with Lamy's pit-exiting Minardi, lap 44. To pits for new nose and finishes lapped sixth for single point. Barrichello qualifies eighth but has clutch problem at start and drops to ninth. In points (sixth), lap 11, until stop, lap 20, when clutch fails.

SAUBER-FORD

Ford V10 cleared for up to 16,500 rpm in race, but only "slightly better" says Frentzen, who has much-revised seating position to prevent helmet obstructing airbox. H-H qualifies 12th, three places ahead of despondent Johnny Herbert, fed up with lack of power and brakes. Heinz-Harald up to excellent seventh, lap two, but passed by Barrichello and Hakkinen. Retires from eighth, lap 20 (gearbox). Phlegmatic Herbert has "uneventful race, really" to finish lapped eighth. Sauber still two seconds off the pace of the front-running Williams and a second slower than the Benettons, McLarens and Jordans.

TWR ARROWS-HART

Front suspension changes benefit car (less understeer, better behaviour over bumps and under braking). Jos Verstappen qualifies 13th, two seconds off pace; Ricardo Rosset 21st, 4.1s down, after having to switch to spare car with different seating and brake balance. Ricardo makes good start, but is punted into retirement by over-optimistic Ukyo Katayama, lap seven. Verstappen drives carefully to preserve brakes but out from 11th, lap 11 when engine fails.

TYRRELL-YAMAHA

Team's miserable 1996 continues to disappoint. Salo does only five laps on Friday morning before gearbox fails. Same again after eight laps in afternoon and six on Saturday morning. So does well to qualify 14th, two seconds off pace, after mechanical fault diagnosed and fixed. Starts in spare car (water leak) and races up to 10th, keeping ahead of Schumacher, until lap 23 stop. Rejoins 12th behind Panis and regains 10th before retiring, lap 40, with blown engine. Katayama loses places at start with clutch problem and spends five laps trying to pass Rosset. Overdoes it on lap seven, removes Arrows' front suspension and is given one-race ban, suspended for two races, for "causing an avoidable collision."

MINARDI-FORD

Lamy blows one of limited number of improved-spec Ford ED3 V8s on Saturday morning before qualifying 19th, three places behind quietly impressive but sponsorless Giancarlo Fisichella (who is still being supported by Gian Carlo Minardi). "We need more horsepower," says Fisichella (Minardi is trying to negotiate for 1995 Ferrari V12s to use in '97). Lamy down to 20th and last at start. Runs last for most of time until being rammed by Brundle's Jordan during short but sharp altercation at turn one after exiting pits on lap 45. Fisichella drives reliable race to finish eighth and last, two laps down.

FORTI-FORD

With new wings, diffuser and revised front suspension, Saturday is red-letter day for Forti when one of its drivers out-qualifies an opponent for the first time in 1996 (Luca Badoer beats Ricardo Rosset to 20th on grid). Montermini maintains tradition, however, by qualifying 22nd and last, with gearbox trouble. Neither finishes. Badoer steadily improves to 14th, laps 21/22 stop and stays there until retiring from 10th, lap 45, with broken gearbox. Montermini out from last but one, lap 23, with bizarre problem - loose ballast, which dangerously sloshes about cockpit and causes Andrea to spin on lap 19.

RESULTS AND STATISTICS

FIA FORMULA 1 WORLD CHAMPIONSHIP

8

RACE

CANADA

16 June 1996

MONTREAL – GILLES VILLENEUVE CIRCUIT

PITS HAIRPIN

ISLAND HAIRPIN

CIRCUIT LENGTH: 2.747 MILES/4.421 KM

STARTING GRID

HILL	VILLENEUVE
1m 21.059s	1m 21.079s
SCHUMACHER	**ALESI**
1m 21.198s	1m 21.529s
IRVINE	**HAKKINEN**
1m 21.657s	1m 21.807s
BERGER	**BARRICHELLO**
1m 21.926s	1m 21.982s
BRUNDLE	**COULTHARD**
1m 22.321s	1m 22.332s
PANIS	**FRENTZEN**
1m 22.481s	1m 22.875s
VERSTAPPEN	**SALO**
1m 23.067s	1m 23.118s
HERBERT	**FISICHELLA**
1m 23.201s	1m 23.519s
KATAYAMA	**DINIZ**
1m 23.599s	1m 23.959s
LAMY	**BADOER**
1m 24.262s	1m 25.012s
ROSSET	**MONTERMINI**
1m 25.193s	1m 26.109s

RACE CLASSIFICATION

Pos	Driver	Nat	Car	Laps	Time
1	Damon Hill	GB	Williams FW18-Renault V10	69	1h 36m03.465s
2	Jacques Villeneuve	CDN	Williams FW18-Renault V10	69	+4.183s
3	Jean Alesi	F	Benetton B196-Renault V10	69	+54.656s
4	David Coulthard	GB	McLaren MP4/11-Mercedes V10	69	+1m 03.673s
5	Mika Hakkinen	SF	McLaren MP4/11-Mercedes V10		+1 lap
6	Martin Brundle	GB	Jordan 196-Peugeot V10		+1 lap
7	Johnny Herbert	GB	Sauber C15-Ford V10		+1 lap
8	Giancarlo Fisichella	I	Minardi M195B-Ford V8		+2 laps

Retirements	Nat	Car	Lap	Reason
Pedro Lamy	P	Minardi M195B-Ford V8	44	Accident
Luca Badoer	I	Forti FG03-Ford V8	44	Gearbox
Gerhard Berger	A	Benetton B196-Renault V10	42	Spin
Michael Schumacher	D	Ferrari F310-Ferrari V10	41	Driveshaft
Olivier Panis	F	Ligier JS43-Mugen Honda V10	39	Engine
Mika Salo	SF	Tyrrell 024-Yamaha V10	39	Engine
Pedro Diniz	BR	Ligier JS43-Mugen Honda V10	38	Engine
Rubens Barrichello	BR	Jordan 196-Peugeot V10	22	Clutch
Andrea Montermini	I	Forti FG03-Ford V8	22	Loose ballast
Heinz-Harald Frentzen	D	Sauber C15-Ford V10	19	Gearbox
Jos Verstappen	NL	Footwork FA17-Hart V8	10	Engine
Ricardo Rosset	BR	Footwork FA17-Hart V8	6	Accident
Ukyo Katayama	J	Tyrrell 024-Yamaha V10	6	Accident
Eddie Irvine	GB	Ferrari F310-Ferrari V10	1	Broken pushrod

FASTEST LAP Jacques Villeneuve 1m 21.916s lap 67 (120.713mph)

DRIVERS' CHAMPIONSHIP

Damon Hill	53
Jacques Villeneuve	32
Michael Schumacher	26
Jean Alesi	17
David Coulthard	13
Olivier Panis	11
Mika Hakkinen	10
Eddie Irvine	9
Gerhard Berger	7
Rubens Barrichello	7
Heinz-Harald Frentzen	6
Mika Salo	5
Johnny Herbert	4
Martin Brundle	2
Jos Verstappen	1

CONSTRUCTORS' CUP

Pedro Diniz	1
Williams-Renault	85
Ferrari	35
Benetton-Renault	28
McLaren-Mercedes	23
Ligier-Mugen Honda	12
Sauber-Ford	10
Jordan-Peugeot	9
Tyrrell-Yamaha	5

Results and Data © FIA 1996

France 1996 was bad news for Formula One. With Williams-Renault having steam-rolled the opposition in the first half of the season, it seemed likely that the year was going to be almost as much of a one-team walkover as it had been with McLaren in 1988. The much-vaunted dream team of Alesi, Berger, Benetton and Renault hadn't really looked like winning; McLaren was doing little better than it had in 1995; Jordan hadn't even had a podium finish. Only Ferrari had seemed capable - sometimes - of challenging Williams, but for the proud Maranello team France was to be an even more hideous experience than Canada.

No one deserved success more than Damon Hill and Williams, but variety is the spice of life and the world (outside Britain!) was beginning to yearn for something different at the front. It wasn't to get it in France...

Magny-Cours is a circuit which struggles to stir the emotions. Situated in the scenic Nevers region of central France, it was built, regardless of cost by the state, to be a motor racing showpiece. Its layout embraces really fast bends, quick straights, two 40 mph corners, a bit of gradient and a billiard-smooth

Below left. Damon Hill had never failed to win pole position at the French GP, and he'd never won. In 1996, he managed both.

Main pic. With both Benetton drivers aware that getting to the finish was a priority, they weren't about to drive into each other. Berger follows Alesi dutifully.

surface. Its grandstands are huge, its pit garages excellent, its facilities superb and its paddock features green carpet, potted plants and shrubs. But, having said that, the place is completely devoid of atmosphere.

It has a curiously remote, clinical and soulless feel and it seldom hosts close or exciting racing. Sadly, 1996 was no exception.

The track is incredibly responsive to temperature changes, of which there are usually a lot at Grand Prix time. On Friday it varied between 23 and 28 degrees. On Saturday morning, when it was also wet, it was 15 degrees. During the afternoon qualifying session, it was 20. As the teams struggled to get the right set-up, they would find lap times varying enormously.

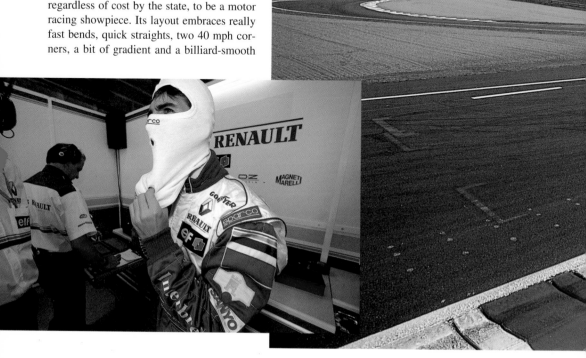

FRANCE

It was the same for everyone, but that didn't make it any easier.

Olivier Panis was fastest on Friday morning, but that was no great surprise. Magny-Cours is Ligier's base and the team had probably done more miles there than all the others put together. But when Mika Hakkinen was quickest in the afternoon, it marked a pleasant change. A new front wing, successfully tested at Silverstone, had worked wonders for the car's balance.

Barrichello's Peugeot-powered Jordan was fastest during Saturday morning's wet/dry/wet session, so there was a buzz about qualifying.

With the apparent prospect of rain, everyone was out quickly at the start of the session. Schumacher had been moaning about the balance of his Ferrari in the morning,

when he had only been fifth, but halfway through the hour he rocketed round in a searing 1m 15.989s - 1.3s faster than Damon Hill's 1995 pole time.

Then Jacques Villeneuve went off. It was a colossal accident, taking him into the tyre wall at the exit of the 150 mph Estoril corner, but he was unharmed. He calmly climbed out of his wrecked Williams, trotted back to the pits, took over the spare car and qualified sixth.

It took half an hour to clear up the debris, and by then the temperature had risen. The track was slower and the best that Damon Hill could manage was 0.07s slower than Schumacher. In pole position for the last three years, the Englishman would be starting alongside his arch-rival, with Alesi, Berger, Hakkinen, Villeneuve, Coulthard

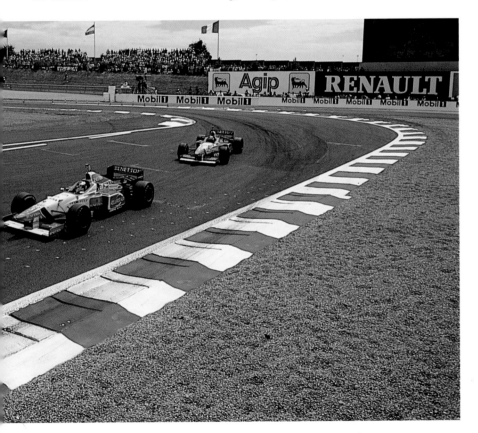

"Opposite, top. Battle of the fags: Mr Brundle was not destined to score today, but ensured that Coulthard would have to start smoking rubber to earn his single digit."

Below. Life ending at Forti? Luca Badoer pulls over as escalating rumours hint that the team's future is rockier than Everest.

and Martin Brundle next up, the latter having out-qualified his Jordan team-mate Rubens Barrichello for the first time.

Sunday was sunny, thank heavens. Just as in Canada, a Ferrari was at the back of the grid. This time, it was Eddie Irvine's. He had qualified 10th before being demoted for having his aerodynamic 'barge boards' mounted too high.

In front of an 86,000 crowd, the field surged away for the formation lap. Before it was complete, there was a gigantic plume of oily smoke from the rear of Schumacher's Ferrari. With Hill right behind him, his engine had blown apart before he had even reached the grid. "I was worried," said Damon. "I had to back off, because his car was spraying a lot of oil onto the track and over my visor. It changed my thinking for the race a bit but I still had to make a good start."

His concern was unnecessary. Whilst a stunned world audiencewas aghast at Schumacher's failure, Damon made a perfect start. He led by 1.5s at the end of the first lap and, effectively, that was the last

that any of his rivals saw of him.

Hakkinen and Brundle got it right at the start, too. Mika moved past Berger to chase second-placed Jean Alesi; and Martin was up to sixth, past David Coulthard. With a sore, muscle-stretched Villeneuve fourth and Berger fifth, the points-scoring places were settled for 20 laps.

Long before that, Ferrari's woe was complete as Irvine toured in to retire on lap six with a failed gearbox selector valve: four retirements for four different reasons from two successive races, enough to appal anyone. "At first I was very angry but I have calmed down now," said Michael. "I expected reliability problems from the moment I started working for Ferrari. However, I thought we would have them at the start of the season. We must grit our teeth and continue to push on." For Jean Todt, who had worked so hard to revive Ferrari's lost fortunes, it was "the blackest day of my long career in motor sport."

It was a glorious day for Hill, as it would be, ultimately, for his team-mate

For Jean Todt, who worked so hard to revive Ferrari's lost fortunes, it was "the blackest day in my long career in motor sport"

Michael Schumacher enjoys a rare opportunity to drive something which doesn't come with a plume of trailing smoke as standard.

Peugeot had reliability. Now where does one start to look for a bit more speed?

Villeneuve. On lap 21, when Alesi came in, the first of the front runners to stop for tyres and fuel, Hill was 9.4s ahead. When Damon stopped, six laps later, he lost the lead to Villeneuve for three laps. When Jacques rejoined after his stop (lap 30) he was up to third, ahead of Hakkinen and behind Alesi.

In fact, Hakkinen was struggling. He had lost first and second gears after his lap 27 stop, and was having to take the Adelaide hairpin in third. His handicap would cost him another place before the race was over.

It was at this time, too, that the much-maligned Pedro Diniz retired - from sixth place! Pedro had taken some stick during 1995 for his mobile-chicane antics in the awful Forti but, in the Ligier-Mugen seat which his supermarket millions had bought him, he was steadily improving. After qualifying a best-ever 12th, he blasted past team-mate Panis and Barrichello's Jordan and stayed ahead of both of them. During the first round of stops, he was promoted to sixth for two laps, only to pull

Face of
concentration:
Jacques
Villeneuve
dismissed his
150 mph
qualifying
accident as a
minor setback.
He'd had far
worse in
Indycars,
he insisted.

off on lap 29 when his engine failed.

With 41 laps to go, and the first stops completed, Hill was back in the lead he was to keep until the end of the race. Jean Alesi was 10.7s behind him, with Villeneuve another 3.7s further back - and charging. In four laps he was tight up behind the Benetton and on lap 37 he pulled out of Alesi's slipstream at Adelaide and took second place. "I didn't give him any opposition," said Jean "I had a problem with my brakes. I tried to stay with him after he had passed but it was impossible."

Behind Alesi, Hakkinen was doing very well indeed to stave off Berger. Further back, David Coulthard had got past Martin Brundle to take sixth after the Jordan's first stop. Having been pincered behind Martin for the first 22 laps, the Scot was relieved

to stay ahead of him following his own stop.

Now, with nearly 50s covering the top six, it was a case of waiting to see whether the second round of stops made any difference.

They did, but only to fourth place. When the stops were over, Damon led Jacques by 9.4s with 19 laps to go. All over? Yes, but Villeneuve didn't seem to realise. Despite the pain from his neck muscles, he really went for it, having already set the fastest lap of the race. "My second set of tyres was really good, but the third set wasn't and I spent a lot of time lapping Panis."

Once he had got past the Ligier on lap 66, with the gap to Hill now up to 13.8s, Jacques charged. To make up that much time and pass Damon was a forlorn hope, but he kept up the pressure. All his closing

laps were faster than those of Hill, but Damon was in charge, knew the score and drove accordingly, being very careful about where and when he lapped people. It was much closer for third, though. On lap 52, Alesi and Berger had moved back to third and fourth when the gallant Hakkinen made his second stop. In third gear, his automatic speed limiter didn't work, so he had to be told what revs to use in the pits.

Jean and Gerhard were less than second apart in identical cars and both were after a place on the podium. For the whole of the rest of the race they were together, each mindful of the fact that above all else they had to bring both the Benettons home.

Driving into each other would have earned them no points, and certainly no brownie points.

Villeneuve closed to within 8.13s of Hill at the end of the race, but Damon was the justifiable victor. After three successive second places at Magny-Cours, he had

No smoke without tyres: Goodyear's monopoly looked likely to be short-lived, with Bridgestone anticipated to arrive in 1997.

Left. Minardi's Pedro Lamy just cannot see a way to out-qualifying his very rapid team-mate Fisichella.

"It was Williams' fourth one-two of the year, and it now led the shattered Ferrari team by a gigantic 66 points in the constructors' contest"

won his first French GP to increase his championship advantage to 25 points. It was Williams' fourth one-two of the year, and it now led the shattered Ferrari team by an gigantic 66 points in the constructors' contest.

McLaren was not dissatisfied with fifth and sixth for Hakkinen and Coulthard, but the happiest contestant of all in France was Renault. Only a week after announcing its withdrawal from Formula One at the end of 1997, it had powered the first four cars to finish at its home Grand Prix.

FERRARI

A thoroughly demeaning weekend compounds the embarrassment of Canada. "We still have a long way to go with the car and right now we're fighting just to keep up," says Eddie Irvine. Further aerodynamic changes and an all-new clutch introduced, but both drivers still unhappy with inconsistent handling...until Schumacher benefits from major set-up changes to take his third pole position for the marque. "The car was fantastic, but there will be a problem in the race because the tyres go off very quickly." Michael into gravel trap in warm-up with brake problem and returns with car on truck. Worse to come when a piston collapses on the formation lap. "I was aware of the fact that we would have reliability problems from the moment I started working for Ferrari, but I thought we would have them at the start of the season," he sighs. Irvine qualifies 10th (understeer) but is demoted to rear of grid after scrutineering when his turning vanes are discovered to be 15mm too high. Pole-holder Schumacher's are hastily repositioned behind closed doors! Eddie races up six places to 16th, lap one, but retires from 14th, lap six, when gearbox selector valve fails. So no points for Ferrari for the second successive race and a storm of furious wounded pride in Italy. "This was the blackest day of my long career in motor sport. If they want my head they can have it," says shattered sporting director Jean Todt.

BENETTON-RENAULT

First use of upgraded Renault RS8B engine enables Alesi to qualify third, equalling his best grid position of 1996. Stops in warm-up with lack of gearchange hydraulic pressure, but has good race against dominant Williams-Renaults. Second to Hill until lap 21 pit stop (9.3s down). Back to second after first round of stops, but caught and passed by Villeneuve, lap 37. Finishes contented third, 46.4s behind Hill, for first French GP podium. Berger admits that first half of season was difficult but "I'm not going to run away." Qualifies fourth, despite unsuitable tyre pressures, and has error-free race to finish fourth, 0.4s behind Alesi after challenging Jean for the last 19 laps. "I did not feel threatened by Gerhard," says Alesi. "I knew he could not pass so I was able to slow down and play games with him at some places!" Benetton now equal second with Ferrari in constructors' championship.

WILLIAMS-RENAULT

Another stunning success. After taking pole position for the last three French Grands Prix, Hill qualifies second to Schumacher (only 0.07s slower) to retain unbroken 1996 front-row record. Has "warm-up from hell" in which he collides with Frentzen whilst "fiddling about with the brake balance," and then goes off in spare car. But nothing goes wrong in race. Damon commandingly wins his first French Grand Prix after leading all way except for three laps after first pit stop. Villeneuve has colossal off during qualifying but calmly runs back for spare car and qualifies sixth. "It was not the biggest crash I've had." But it was mighty big. Benefiting from neck massage from team trainer, Jacques runs fourth behind Hakkinen for 20 laps but moves ahead at Mika's lap 27 stop and stays there. Closes 3.7s gap to second-placed Alesi in four laps and passes Jean, lap 37. Is 9.4s behind Hill after Damon's second stop, lap 53, and charges hard. Sets fastest lap (1m 18.610s, 120.944 mph) and finishes excellent second, 8.13s down. Using new RS8B V10, this is Williams' 50th win with Renault and, with Benetton third and fourth, gives euphoric French manufacturer the first four places at its home race. Hill and Williams now lead their championships by 25 and 66 points.

McLAREN-MERCEDES

Team insiders pleasantly surprised after predicting "disastrous" race. Following successful Silverstone test, Hakkinen fastest on Friday and qualifies fifth. Two places adrift, David Coulthard loses valuable set-up time after going off on both Friday and Saturday (he only just missed Villeneuve's wrecked Williams in middle of track). "We have never got to grips with Magny-Cours," confesses Ron Dennis, but Mika and David third and fourth fastest in warm-up. Hakkinen to third past Berger at start and stays there, although always losing time to Alesi ahead. Passed by Villeneuve at lap 27 stop. Runs fourth despite losing first and second gears, lap 29. Passed by Berger, lap 43, and has to be push-started after second pit stop, but finishes well-pleased fifth. Coulthard makes bad start and loses place to Martin Brundle. They race together until Martin's lap 23 stop. David gets ahead and stays there after his own first stop to finish sixth. Team well pleased with progress.

LIGIER-MUGEN HONDA

At team's home track, using evolution Mugen Honda Panis qualifies disappointed ninth. Conversely, Pedro Diniz a best-ever 12th, 1.7s off pole and 0.3s slower than Olivier. Much-maligned Diniz, with heavy fuel load for one-stop strategy, has inspired start, passing Panis and moving up four places. Races eighth between Coulthard and Barrichello, and is in points (sixth), laps 26/27, during first pit stops. Retires from that position, lap 29, when engine breaks. Panis switches to three-stop strategy after fuel rig problem during early first halt, lap 18, and sets second fastest lap of race before finishing frustrated seventh.

JORDAN-PEUGEOT

Evolution Peugeot V10 for French manufacturer's home race, but only in qualifying. Martin Brundle outpaces team-mate Rubens Barrichello for first time, and starts eighth. Rubens is 11th. Brundle up to sixth at start, but loses place to Coulthard at lap 23 stop. Despite substantial understeer, finishes eighth, one lap down. Barrichello also has reliable, understeery race and finishes ninth, 17s behind Brundle.

SAUBER-FORD

Amidst a semi-despondent team atmosphere (long-term budget security, but neither engine nor chassis good enough in the short term, and no real sign of improvement), Frentzen and brake-troubled Herbert start 13th and 17th. Heinz-Harald driven into by Hill during warm-up and has to race spare. Does his best with tricky combination of no grip/sticking throttle before retiring from 10th, lap 57, when he goes off. Despondent Herbert "just couldn't keep up" in car with wrong set-up which causes heavy tyre wear. Finishes 11th, two laps down, only to be excluded for illegally high (by 150 mm) turning vanes.

TWR ARROWS-HART

Jos Verstappen goes off twice on Friday ("heavy oversteer, and the car gets worse if we change it!"). Does so again on wet Saturday morning, losing almost the whole session. Qualifies 16th. Up five places lap one. Stays 11th, between Panis and Frentzen, until lap 11 when front right steering arm pulls out of upright. Ricardo Rosset, on track he knows and in car with improved braking system, starts much-happier 18th and is pleased to finish first race since Nurburgring in 11th place, three laps down.

TYRRELL-YAMAHA

Team concentrates on reliability at post-Canada testing but increasingly frustrated with too small a budget Yamaha power deficiencies and failures. Mika Salo loses whole of Saturday morning session with water leak but starts 14th, happy with improved balance. Ukyo Katayama has new stiffer chassis with much-improved seating position and is delighted to qualify 15th, within 0.2s of Mika. "I am comfortable for the first time this year!" But Yamaha fails again. Katayama brought in to retire from 12th, lap 33, with fading power. Salo finishes 10th, two laps down, running in cruise mode for the last 21 laps due to falling oil pressure.

MINARDI-FORD

Using Ford ED3 evolution engine for qualifying, Giancarlo Fisichella again quicker than Pedro Lamy to start 18th, one place ahead of his team-mate. His time is nearly three seconds faster than Minardi's best in 1995. But Giancarlo's fuel pump fails on lap three. Lamy finishes 12th and last, three laps down, with "something wrong with the engine, which was unnaturally slow." A very tough and fruitless weekend. "Being the only Italian team that finished this race is very pale satisfaction," says Gian Carlo Minardi.

FORTI-FORD

Grim signs that the struggling Italian team is suffering inadequate sponsorship. Badoer's car equipped with new wings and diffusor, but no accompanying turning vanes due to incomplete research programme. Neither car appears during Sunday warm-up (engines too close to needing financially crippling rebuilds), after Luca qualified 21st and Andrea Montermini 22nd. Montermini pulls out on lap three, allegedly with electrical failure, whilst Badoer retires from last but one on lap 30 with "fuel feed failure." Inside story is that both cars are withdrawn because of engine mileage situation. Silverstone looks unlikely...

FIA FORMULA 1 WORLD CHAMPIONSHIP

RACE 9

FRANCE

30 June 1996

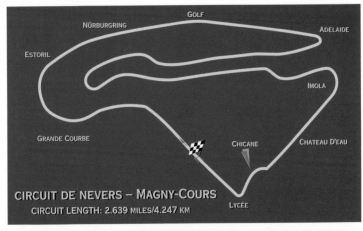

CIRCUIT DE NEVERS – MAGNY-COURS
CIRCUIT LENGTH: 2.639 MILES/4.247 KM

STARTING GRID

	SCHUMACHER 1m 15.989s
HILL 1m 16.058s	
	ALESI 1m 16.310s
BERGER 1m 16.592s	
	HAKKINEN 1m 16.634s
VILLENEUVE 1m 16.905s	
	COULTHARD 1m 17.007s
BRUNDLE 1m 17.187s	
	PANIS 1m 17.390s
BARRICHELLO 1m 17.665s	
	DINIZ 1m 17.676s
FRENTZEN 1m 17.739s	
	SALO 1m 18.021s
KATAYAMA 1m 18.242s	
	VERSTAPPEN 1m 18.324s
HERBERT 1m 18.556s	
	FISICHELLA 1m 18.604s
LAMY 1m 19.210s	
	ROSSET 1m 19.242s
BADOER 1m 20.562s	
	MONTERMINI 1m 20.647s

IRVINE
1m 17.443s
**time disallowed for
technical infringement

RACE CLASSIFICATION

Pos	Driver	Nat	Car	Laps	Time
1	Damon Hill	GB	Williams FW18-Renault V10	72	1h 36m 28.765s
2	Jacques Villeneuve	CDN	Williams FW18-Renault V10	72	+8.127s
3	Jean Alesi	F	Benetton B196-Renault V10	72	+46.442s
4	Gerhard Berger	A	Benetton B196-Renault V10	72	+46.859s
5	Mika Hakkinen	SF	McLaren MP4/11-Mercedes V10	72	+1m 02.774s
6	David Coulthard	GB	McLaren MP4/11-Mercedes V10		+1 lap
7	Olivier Panis	F	Ligier JS43-Mugen Honda V10		+1 lap
8	Martin Brundle	GB	Jordan 196-Peugeot V10		+1 lap
9	Rubens Barrichello	BR	Jordan 196-Peugeot V10		+1 lap
10	Mika Salo	SF	Tyrrell 024-Yamaha V10		+2 laps
*EX	Johnny Herbert	GB	Sauber C15-Ford V10		+2 laps
11	Ricardo Rosset	BR	Footwork FA17-Hart V8		+3 laps
12	Pedro Lamy	P	Minardi M195B-Ford V8		+3 laps

Retirements	Nat	Car	Lap	Reason
Heinz-Harald Frentzen	D	Sauber C15-Ford V10	56	Stuck throttle
Ukyo Katayama	J	Tyrrell 024-Yamaha V10	33	Engine
Luca Badoer	I	Forti FG03-Ford V8	29	Engine mileage
Pedro Diniz	BR	Ligier JS43-Mugen Honda V10	28	Engine
Jos Verstappen	NL	Footwork FA17-Hart V8	10	Steering arm
Eddie Irvine	GB	Ferrari F310-Ferrari V10	5	Gearbox
Giancarlo Fisichella	I	Minardi M195B-Ford V8	2	Fuel pump
Andrea Montermini	I	Forti FG03-Ford V8	2	Engine mileage
Michael Schumacher	D	Ferrari F310-Ferrari V10	0	Engine

*Excluded for technical infringement

FASTEST LAP   Jacques Villeneuve 1m 18.610s lap 48 (120.944mph)

DRIVERS' CHAMPIONSHIP

Damon Hill	63
Jacques Villeneuve	38
Michael Schumacher	26
Jean Alesi	25
David Coulthard	14
Mika Hakkinen	12
Olivier Panis	11
Gerhard Berger	10
Eddie Irvine	9
Rubens Barrichello	7
Heinz-Harald Frentzen	6
Mika Salo	5
Johnny Herbert	4
Martin Brundle	2
Jos Verstappen	1
Pedro Diniz	1

CONSTRUCTORS' CUP

Williams-Renault	101
Ferrari	35
Benetton-Renault	35
McLaren-Mercedes	26
Ligier-Mugen Honda	12
Sauber-Ford	10
Jordan-Peugeot	9
Tyrrell-Yamaha	5
Footwork-Hart	1

Results and Data © FIA 1996

Unlike Frank
Williams, the
Silverstone
spectators were
quite keen to
ask Damon to
sign on the
dotted line.

Opposite,
Villeneuve
receives the
plaudits for his
second win of
the year (top);
Williams tries a
new system for
getting Hill off
the startline
more efficiently
(below).

ROUND **10**

BRITAIN

There was an all-ticket, sell-out, 90,000 crowd at Silverstone for the British Grand Prix. Fewer than that memorable day in 1992, when 120,000 Nigel Mansell-crazy fans crammed the circuit to bursting point but, frankly, all the better for it. The British Racing Drivers' Club, which owns the enormously popular venue, had again limited ticket sales to make things more enjoyable for those who did get in, and it worked. Perfect weather, the usual friendly and relaxed atmosphere and the traditional support races, parades and demonstrations contributed to an enjoyable day. Pity the main race wasn't more exciting, but the crowd witnessed a great drive by a great driver, even if he wasn't the one they were chiefly rooting for.

Damon Hill was the people's choice. It had taken a long time for the likeable, quiet and deep-thinking Englishman to replace the extrovert, crowd-pleasing Mansell in the affections of British race fans, but there was no doubt that he had done so at Silverstone. I had the great privilege of riding with Hill and Jacques Villeneuve in a magnificent Rolls-Royce Silver Ghost open tourer during the drivers' parade, and it was an incredible experience as tens of thousands of people cheered, waved their Union Flags, blew their horns and enthusiastically made it very clear who their favourite was.

Jacques sat quietly beside me, focusing on beating Hill at his home circuit just as Damon had beaten him at Montreal a month earlier. He wasn't to be disappointed.

Amidst confident expectations that Hill would virtually sew up the 1996 World Championship with a third successive victory, the main speculation revolved around Ferrari. After four humiliating retirements at the last two Grands Prix, surely the Maranello team would bounce back at Silverstone? Fiat President Giovanni Agnelli, one of the most powerful men in Italy, and Ferrari boss Luca di Montezemolo certainly expected an improvement, and visited the team on Friday to show support in public.

It wasn't going to be easy. Ferrari, like all the continental teams, had not tested at Silverstone, where their nervous and under-developed car was a long way from being right. It handled badly over the bumps. Williams knew the place like the back of its hand though, and had done thousands of miles of testing. For Villeneuve, at last, here was a track he really knew. Instead of having to spend Friday learning where it went before he could set up his car, he could concentrate on getting a good grid position from the start. He did what he had not been able to do before, practising for the next day's qualifying session with a low fuel load and new tyres. It paid off. Jacques was

Below. Mika Hakkinen (left) tries out his new Gerhard Berger glove-puppet. Third and second respectively, the two notched up their best results of the season to date.

fastest on Friday. Faster than Hill's 1995 pole time (since which Stowe Corner had been made faster) and a very impressive 0.7s faster than Damon. Time for the favourite to get his act together.

Saturday's crowd was a record for a qualifying day. Those who hadn't been able to get tickets for the race made sure they were there for the qualifying and they weren't disappointed. There were 54,000 to witness a thrilling battle for the vital pole position, which is just as important at Silverstone as it is anywhere else. The track may be wider than others, but over-taking remains a tricky art.

It was between the two Williams men, and Villeneuve headed the list until Hill scorched round in 1m 26.875s, just 0.195s faster than his team-mate's best. It was the fifth Williams front row monopoly of the season, Damon's sixth pole position and Villeneuve was 0.7s faster than third-placed Michael Schumacher, who had never expected to be better than third. Even that was a tribute to his skill. Colleague Eddie Irvine was only 10th, 2.3s slower than Hill. Only Villeneuve, Schumacher and Hakkinen, in his short-wheelbase McLaren, were within a second of Hill. Alesi and Barrichello, fifth and sixth, were some 1.5s off the pace. The British Grand Prix looked like being a Williams-Renault benefit, but which driver?

There were no team orders, Hill meant to win at home and Villeneuve intended to

Left. With
Villeneuve
already in
another strato-
sphere, Alesi,
Hakkinen and
Schumacher
lead the first lap
pursuit (left).

Frustrated by
a sequence of
disappointing
results, Jordan
diversifies with
the creation of a
four-man bob
team (below).

stop him.

Damon was destined to fail, the rot starting as the race began. He bogged down and, in a flash, was passed by Villeneuve, Alesi (an astounding start), Hakkinen and Schumacher. Slipping from first to fifth before the first corner, Hill's work in qualifying had been for nothing. What's more, he was behind traditional rival Michael Schumacher, who certainly wouldn't make it easy to pass. Until lap three, that is. Astoundingly, he pulled over and slowed to touring pace. Three retirements in three successive races!

Worse was to come for Ferrari, and not much further on, either. Irvine, with a grey plume of smoke behind him, rolled equally disconsolately into the pit lane. Three races. Six starts. Six failures. Maranello's shame was complete. Schumacher's car had stuck in sixth gear; Irvine had suffered a failed differential. It scarcely mattered; the Prancing Horse looked fit for the knacker's yard.

Meantime, Villeneuve was making the most of the clear track ahead of him. By lap 20 (of 61), Jacques had lapped Panis,

Fisichella and Lamy and was 18s ahead of Alesi. Only 3.6s separated Alesi, Hakkinen and Hill, but so difficult is it to pass in Formula One these days that second to fourth places looked static.

Something dramatic had to happen to change things; on lap 27 it did. Damon Hill went off. In what looked to be a mirror-image of his 1995 Hockenheim departure, the back of his Williams stepped out as he entered the 120 mph Copse Corner and Damon was gone. For the second British Grand Prix in succession his race had ended in the gravel trap; this time it wasn't his fault. "I had a sensation at the front of the car for three or four laps and got on the radio to say I had a problem. As I was going into Copse something seized at the front." A loose wheel nut had stopped the left-side brakes from working. A bitterly disappointed Damon was out.

Clearly, only some similar misfortune was going to prevent Villeneuve winning his second Grand Prix. He lost the lead to Alesi when he came in for fuel and tyres on lap 26, but after dropping down to fourth he was in the lead again by lap 31 after his rivals had made their stops.

Would things have been better for Benetton if Michael Schumacher had been at the wheel? The German had won nine races for the Enstone team the previous year, and now even the talented Alesi could do nothing about the flying Villeneuve. The Canadian continued to pull away and, in doing so, had set the fastest lap of the race (1m 29.288s, 127.07mph).

On lap 35, with the first stops completed, Mika Hakkinen was a heartening second, albeit a very disheartening 30s behind Villeneuve. It was also a false position, because Mika would be in again for fuel and tyres whereas Alesi had

"Something dramatic had to happen to change things; on lap 27 it did. Damon went off."

Katayama
(opposite top)
outqualified
team-mate Salo
for once, but
failed to outlast
him in the race.

It was a dismal
weekend for
Ligier, with
both cars
(Diniz, below)
retiring.

made what was to be his sole stop. When Mika came in on lap 44, however, it was Gerhard Berger who usurped him. "Jean was pushing very hard and I could see dust from his rear brakes. I rebalanced mine and took care." Gerhard's experience and tactical thinking reaped its reward as Alesi moved over and let his team-mate through. Jean's brakes were shot and he was out. "I am hugely disappointed because I was on course for a podium position which would have put me into third place in the championship."

To be honest the last 17 laps were interesting rather than exciting. For me Formula One, is never boring because I am mindful of the facts that I am watching supermen in supercars and that anything can happen to change the order. But at Silverstone nothing did. Villeneuve won a brilliant victory by 19s, never having put a wheel wrong. In

so doing, he transformed the World Championship from an apparent racing certainty for Damon Hill to an unpredictable battle. What had been a 25-point lead for Hill was now reduced to 15, with 60 still to be won. Damon was still looking good, but less so than before. Williams, however, was nigh on impregnable, now a massive 70 points ahead of Benetton in the constructors' contest.

But if Williams went home to its Grove headquarters wreathed in smiles, McLaren and Jordan were quietly satisfied too. McLaren really had made progress with its short-wheelbase chassis powered by the reliable and powerful Mercedes-Benz V10. Mika Hakkinen was delighted with his third place, his first podium finish of the year, whilst David Coulthard had brought the second MP4/11B home fifth after a poor start and a race-long struggle with a

"Jean was pushing very hard and I could see dust from his rear brakes. I rebalanced mine and took care"

"Smoke gets in
your eyes..."
or at least it
gets into every-
one else's.
Irvine does
his familiar
Red Arrows
impression.

holiday to ease up after years of overwork, caused raised eyebrows. And the presence of 3000 guests from sponsor Benson & Hedges didn't alleviate the pressure. But Rubens Barrichello and Martin Brundle rose to the occasion superbly with fourth and sixth places in cars that had given no hint of trouble. Which is more than the downcast Ferrari team could say as it prepared for another early start for the long trip back to Italy.

It had been another demeaning race for Ferrari, but at least it had made the start. There is always someone worse off, no matter how bad things appear. In this case it was the Forti team who, strapped for cash to pay its Cosworth rebuild bills, had only done a combined total of six laps during the whole weekend and had come nowhere near qualifying. Was it going the way of Pacific and Simtek the year before? We would know at Hockenheim, where Jacques Villeneuve would renewed his far from futile attempt to become a rookie world champion.

car he had never been able to balance properly.

The biggest sigh of relief must have come from Jordan, though. The Silverstone-based team was under terrific pressure with the knowledge that Renault's withdrawal from Formula One at the end of 1997 was going to make the now-excellent Peugeot V10 even more desirable to the opposition - especially Williams and Benetton. The fact that Eddie Jordan had told Gary Anderson, the team's much respected chief designer, to take a long

FERRARI

After France, Ferrari had thought things couldn't get worse. Incorrect. Team arrives with cars in Magny-Cours specification, and has disadvantage of no Silverstone testing. Fiat President Giovanni Agnelli and Ferrari boss Luca di Montezemolo visit track on Friday to demonstrate solidarity with their beleaguered Maranello colleagues. Sporting director Jean Todt defines objective as being to finish with one driver on podium and the other in the points. Schumacher demonstrates validity of the aim by qualifying third, albeit over 0.8s off Damon Hill's pole time. Eddie Irvine 10th, troubled by inability to achieve satisfactory set-up. Sunday's race even worse than Canada and France. Schumacher passed by super-starting Alesi and Hakkinen, but passes Hill to run fourth, laps one and two. Then, to general consternation, slows and tours in, lap three, jammed in sixth gear due to total loss of hydraulic pressure. Irvine up to sixth, laps three to five, but similarly limps in amidst plume of smoke, lap six, with failed differential bearing. Everyone makes now usual statements of concern and stresses need to maintain morale and work harder, hoping that already-tested aerodynamic, rear suspension and gearbox changes will revive fortunes at Hockenheim.

BENETTON-RENAULT

Team optimistic that "10 more horsepower" from airbox modifications will help at Silverstone. Alesi "really, really happy" with third fastest on Friday but slumps to fifth in qualifying, over 1.4s slower than Hill despite several set-up changes. Berger experiments with electronic differential on Friday before qualifying seventh with standard unit. Alesi makes sensational start to pass Hakkinen, Schumacher and Hill and challenge Villeneuve for lead at first corner. Runs increasingly distant second and is 22s down when Villeneuve pits, lap 23. Holds lead until own stop, lap 31, when passed by Villeneuve, Berger and Hakkinen. After Berger's stop Jean runs increasingly distant third with failing brakes. Passed by Berger, lap 44, and retires, lap 45, when brakes give up. Berger opts for one-stop strategy and drives carefully to preserve tyres and brakes. Down to fourth from second at late, lap 33, stop but passes Hakkinen to regain second at Mika's second stop, lap 45. Despite tired brakes, stays there for best-yet finish of 1996 with second fastest lap of race. Benetton breaks tie with Ferrari to become sole second in constructors' championship (70 points behind Williams). Team protests Williams front-wing end plates but rejected by stewards following lengthy deliberation.

WILLIAMS-RENAULT

Hill and Villeneuve again dominate pre-race sessions to monopolise front row of grid for fifth time, with Hill 0.2s faster than thrilling battle. Damon then blows it by dropping to fifth at start, passed by Villeneuve, Alesi, Hakkinen and Schumacher. Presses third-placed Hakkinen hard but cannot pass. To third when Villeneuve pits but spins out, lap 27, when loose front wheel nut 'disconnects' left-side brake. "I am really, really disappointed. All was not lost because I could have done a one-stop strategy but it was not to be." Villeneuve drives superb, dominant race. Records fastest lap (1m 29.288s, 127.07mph) and leads Alesi by 22s at first stop, lap 23. Regains lead, lap 31, and retains it at second stop, lap 42. Wins second GP from 10 starts by 19 seconds, gets revenge on Damon for his defeat in Canada and closes championship gap to Hill to 15 points. Benetton submits protest against Williams' allegedly illegal front wing end plates but this is rejected by stewards.

McLAREN-MERCEDES

Team continues progress with short wheelbase car, revised head-rest and improved-spec Mercedes-Benz V10 for qualifying. "Best package yet," says delighted Mika Hakkinen, who qualifies fourth, 0.96s off pole time. Is fastest in damp/dry warm-up and makes superb start to pass Hill for third. Stays ahead of thrusting Damon and up to second, laps 24-26, when Villeneuve stops. Back to second, lap 34 (30s behind Jacques), after first round of stops but loses place to Berger at second stop (lap 44). Finishes well-pleased third for first podium of year. David Coulthard, unable to balance car, starts ninth. After poor start pushes hard in reliable car and finishes full-distance fifth. "We are getting closer," says Ron Dennis, after both cars score points for the third successive race.

LIGIER-MUGEN HONDA

With no prior testing at Silverstone, team all at sea in setting-up cars. Panis starts unhappy 16th with Diniz 18th after crashing on Saturday. Olivier improves to seventh in warm-up, following car

changes, but still off pace and handicapped by low grid position. Stops three times before retiring from last, lap 41, with continued handling problems. Diniz retires lap 39 with gearbox-induced engine failure.

JORDAN-PEUGEOT

Major pit lane buzz when team announces that much-respected designer Gary Anderson "has been instructed to take a six-week holiday due to overwork." After using new evolution engine and new set-ups, Barrichello and Brundle start sixth and eighth. Crucial race in front of 3000 B&H guests, and with vital need to reassure Peugeot that it has chosen the right team for its powerful and envied V10. Both drive excellent race to finish in top six, returning team to fifth place in constructors' championship. Barrichello takes fault-free fourth with Brundle sixth (one lap down), despite having to make unplanned third stop due to puncture.

SAUBER-FORD

Like Ferrari, Ligier, Minardi and Forti, Sauber arrives at Silverstone with no testing experience at a track where it is difficult to find the ideal balance (fast straights/several slow corners). Like all their continental rivals, they suffer for it. Ford again allows up to 16,500 rpm for qualifying but "we are in deep trouble here" says one team insider after Frentzen and Herbert qualify 11th and 13th, 2.7s and 3.1s respectively off the pace. Behind the scenes the "deep trouble" is attributed to the engine rather than the car, and Ford later announces that an all-new V10 will be produced for 1997 "incorporating lessons we (Cosworth) have learned from this configuration, which is new to us." Since Jackie Stewart's new team expected to have exclusive use, this is cold comfort to Sauber. Frentzen opts for one-stop strategy with Herbert stopping twice. It makes little difference. Team-mates race each other most of way, and only 0.8s separates them at end of race. Frentzen is eighth, Herbert ninth, both one lap down. Despondency reigns.

TWR ARROWS-HART

Team delighted to introduce substantially-revised Hart V8, featuring air-valves and all-new cylinder heads. After only brief bench testing, major gamble succeeds with over 1000 extra revs and no reliability problems. Team also uses new front wing. Usual understeer inhibits Verstappen, but Jos qualifies 15th, well pleased with engine. Uses normal spring-valve motor for race to achieve only second finish of season (10th), despite losing time with underpressured tyres after first stop. Ricardo Rosset qualifies 17th, but starts from back of grid as penalty for missing red light and failing to stop for scrutineering checks. On track he knows, is more confident. Passes Lamy and Fisichella to 16th, lap eight, and closes on Salo and Diniz but retires with electrical failure, lap 14.

TYRRELL-YAMAHA

Team delighted - and very relieved - to have trouble-free qualifying. Ukyo Katayama happily beats Salo to start 15th, one place and 0.04s ahead. "But we are too slow and we don't know why." Speculation suggests that Yamaha has detuned its V10 for reliability. Ukyo has phenomenal avoidance of spinning Diniz on lap two before being called in to retire from 15th, lap 13, with rising water temperature. Salo has much happier time. Is fine seventh at sole pit stop, lap 31, and regains place on lap 45. Finishes seventh but "we need to be quicker on the straights to fight with the leaders." Ken Tyrrell takes up Mika's option for 1997.

MINARDI-FORD

With no Silverstone testing and inadequate power from Ford V8 ED customer engine, Minardi does not expect to do well - and doesn't. Fisichella and Lamy qualify 19th and 20th, both some 4.5s off pole time. However, both start ahead of penalised Ricardo Rosset. Ricardo passes both Minardis which race at tail of field, with Fisichella ahead, until Lamy retires, lap 22 (clutch failure). Fisichella soldiers on to finish 11th and last, two laps down in what sadly looks like being his last appearance, for financial reasons.

FORTI-FORD

In an unhappy situation for Formula One, and the team, both Badoer and Montermini make only token qualifying appearances on Saturday due to Forti's reported failure to meet Cosworth engine bills. Both drivers well outside the 107 per cent qualifying limit. However, team stoutly maintains it will have sorted its affairs in time for the German GP.

RACE 10
BRITAIN
14 July 1996

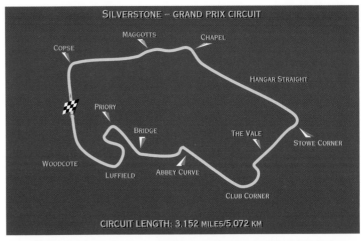

SILVERSTONE – GRAND PRIX CIRCUIT

MAGGOTTS CHAPEL COPSE HANGAR STRAIGHT PRIORY BRIDGE THE VALE STOWE CORNER WOODCOTE LUFFIELD ABBEY CURVE CLUB CORNER

CIRCUIT LENGTH: 3.152 MILES/5.072 KM

STARTING GRID

HILL 1m 26.875s	**VILLENEUVE** 1m 27.070s
SCHUMACHER 1m 27.707s	**HAKKINEN** 1m 27.856s
ALESI 1m 28.307s	**BARRICHELLO** 1m 28.409s
BERGER 1m 28.653s	**BRUNDLE** 1m 28.946s
COULTHARD 1m 28.966s	**IRVINE** 1m 29.186s
FRENTZEN 1m 29.591s	**KATAYAMA** 1m 29.913s
HERBERT 1m 29.947s	**SALO** 1m 29.949s
VERSTAPPEN 1m 30.102s	**PANIS** 1m 30.167s
DINIZ 1m 31.076s	**FISICHELLA** 1m 31.365s
LAMY 1m 31.454s	**ROSSET** 1m 30.529s*

*time disallowed for failing to stop for
scrutineering check

Did not qualify

MONTERMINI (Forti FG03) 1m 35.206s	**BADOER** (Forti FG03) 1m 35.304s

RACE CLASSIFICATION

Pos	Driver	Nat	Car	Laps	Time
1	Jacques Villeneuve	CDN	Williams FW18-Renault V10	61	1h 33m 00.874s
2	Gerhard Berger	A	Benetton B196-Renault V10	61	+19.026s
3	Mika Hakkinen	SF	McLaren MP4/11-Mercedes V10	61	+50.830s
4	Rubens Barrichello	BR	Jordan 196-Peugeot V10	61	+1m 06.716s
5	David Coulthard	GB	McLaren MP4/11-Mercedes V10	61	+1m 22.507s
6	Martin Brundle	GB	Jordan 196-Peugeot V10		+1 lap
7	Mika Salo	SF	Tyrrell 024-Yamaha V10		+1 lap
8	Heinz-Harald Frentzen	D	Sauber C15-Ford V10		+1 lap
9	Johnny Herbert	GB	Sauber C15-Ford V10		+1 lap
10	Jos Verstappen	NL	Footwork FA17-Hart V8		+1 lap
11	Giancarlo Fisichella	I	Minardi M195B-Ford V8		+2 laps

Retirements	Nat	Car	Lap	Reason
Jean Alesi	F	Benetton B196-Renault V10	44	Brakes
Olivier Panis	F	Ligier JS43-Mugen Honda V10	40	Handling
Pedro Diniz	BR	Ligier JS43-Mugen Honda V10	38	Engine
Damon Hill	GB	Williams FW18-Renault V10	26	Wheel nut
Pedro Lamy	P	Minardi M195B-Ford V8	21	Gearbox
Ricardo Rosset	BR	Footwork FA17-Hart V8	13	Electrics
Ukyo Katayama	J	Tyrrell 024-Yamaha V10	12	Engine
Eddie Irvine	GB	Ferrari F310-Ferrari V10	5	Diff bearing
Michael Schumacher	D	Ferrari F310-Ferrari V10	2	Hydraulics

FASTEST LAP	Jacques Villeneuve 1m 29.288s lap 21 (127.074 mph)

DRIVERS' CHAMPIONSHIP

Damon Hill	63
Jacques Villeneuve	48
Michael Schumacher	26
Jean Alesi	25
David Coulthard	16
Gerhard Berger	16
Mika Hakkinen	16
Olivier Panis	11
Rubens Barrichello	10
Eddie Irvine	9
Heinz-Harald Frentzen	6
Mika Salo	5
Johnny Herbert	4
Martin Brundle	3
Jos Verstappen	1
Pedro Diniz	1

CONSTRUCTORS' CUP

Williams-Renault	111
Benetton-Renault	41
Ferrari	35
McLaren-Mercedes	32
Jordan-Peugeot	13
Ligier-Mugen Honda	12
Sauber-Ford	10
Tyrrell-Yamaha	5
Footwork-Hart	1

Results and Data © FIA 1996

GERMANY

Pressure point: Gerhard Berger resolutely holds off Damon Hill's clearly faster Williams. The strain told: one Renault V10 went bang, the other didn't...

Two weeks after Silverstone came Hockenheim, where the thousands of Union Flag-waving Damon Hill supporters were replaced by even more, equally biased, German tricolour-bearing aficionados of Michael Schumacher. The nationalistic atmosphere may have been the same, but the surroundings were very different.

Where Silverstone is essentially a highly developed, open, flat and wide airfield perimeter road with temporary-looking scaffolding grandstands, Hockenheim, close to the university city of Heidelberg, is very Teutonic. Purpose-built, its spectator appeal comes not from its two curved 'straights' which slash their chicane-bisected way through dense and gloomy pine forest, but from its stadium section, ringed with gigantic concrete grandstands, where 100,000 fans shout, cheer, drink their beer, wave their flags and fire their rockets. When the weather is good the buzz is terrific, and it was very good as the fervent thousands began their four-day vigil at the shrine of St Michael.

Not that they had any right to expect a scintillating race. Hockenheim is a car-breaker, where the combined effects of heat and the stresses of accelerating up to 200 mph and then braking down to 60, four times every lap, make terrific demands on engines and brakes. The 1995 GP had been dull and processional, with only nine of the 22 starters finishing. This year, by sharp contrast, would be worth every pfennig of the admission ticket.

There were 48,000 people on Friday and another 76,000 on Saturday, hoping against hope that 'Schumi' would put his Ferrari on pole position. Where 1995 had been a sea of Benetton blue in the stadium, 1996 was an uninterrupted blanket of Ferrari red. The clothes stalls must have made a killing. Amazingly, Germany's hopes were almost fulfilled. Ferrari's dogged non-stop development of the fragile F310, which had failed to finish at the last three Grands Prix, had produced new aerodynamics, a new rear suspension and other changes which, according to Schumacher, made the car more user-friendly.

The proof of the pudding was in the eating. At 14.00 on Saturday, Michael was in pole position, where he had been for more or less the whole session. The uproar in the stands was deafening. Schumi had apparently done it for them...but they failed to realise that Hill and, more surprisingly, Gerhard Berger were still on their last laps, which had begun just one minute before the chequered flag had gone out.

When Damon crossed the line and brandished an exultant fist, he was over half a second quicker than Schumacher after a brilliant effort. The crowd's dejection was immense.

And Berger had yet to finish his lap, which was also a very quick one. He had been unhappy with the Benetton all season, but post-Silverstone testing had got it much more to his liking and he was flying. Not quite high enough though: nearly 0.4s slower than Hill's mega lap, but faster than Schumacher's. The Ferrari wasn't even on

the front row of the grid. It had been a great session, with the fourth-placed Mercedes-powered McLaren of Mika Hakkinen throwing a sop to the locals, Jean Alesi's Benetton fifth, a very disappointed Jacques Villeneuve sixth for Williams and only 0.9s covering the top three rows of the grid.

Jacques had reduced Hill's championship lead to 15 points at Silverstone, and was looking to narrow it still further, even though he had never raced at Hockenheim before. But a blown engine on Saturday morning, the resultant loss of track time and a less powerful replacement Renault V10 had hindered him.

There was rain on Sunday after the warm-up, but the track was dry when the five red lights went out to signal the start of the 45-lap German Grand Prix. And Damon blew it again. Pole position at Silverstone but fifth into the first corner. Pole again in Hockenheim - "the best of my career" - but he needn't have bothered.

With too few revs, his Williams bogged down and Berger shot by into the lead. Incredibly, from the third row, Alesi rock-

Fed up with rumours that his place at Benetton was under threat, Alesi contemplates switching to the mini-cab business. Post-explosion, Berger gives the service a trial run.

"Schumi had apparently done it for them...
but they failed to realise that Hill and, more surprisingly,
Berger were still on their last laps"

eted past Damon too. Jean's start was sensational, taking him past Hakkinen and Schumacher as well as Hill, and at the first forest chicane, the Jim Clark Kurve, Benettons were first and second for the first time in 1996. David Coulthard had done well, too. Seventh on the grid, he took Hakkinen as Mika was rudely chopped by Schumacher and then passed Villeneuve to take fifth on the run up to the chicane.

We didn't know it at the time, but Hill's start could have cost him the race. He was on a two-stop strategy, whereas the two Benettons ahead of him were only coming in once. With his lighter fuel load, Damon needed to be ahead and pulling away to compensate for his extra stop, but he was bottled up behind Gerhard and Jean with no hope of passing them.

By lap 10 the three leaders were nine seconds ahead of a close battle for fourth between Schumacher, Coulthard, Villeneuve, Irvine and Hakkinen, with Schumacher obviously holding up his pursuers. The Ferrari certainly didn't look as though it was going to repeat its qualifying form, but maybe something dramatic would happen at the pit stops.

Those stopping twice would be coming in from about lap 20, maybe before. Mika Hakkinen came in from his eighth place at the end of the snake on lap 13; but on lap

Martin Brundle (above) finds that mice have developed a taste for Goodyear's finest.

The reigning - but soon to be outgoing - world champion searches vainly for Top of the Pops (left), so that he can practise his Spice Girls dance routine...

Italian aristocrat Giovanni Lavaggi (right) brought more finance to Minardi than he did prowess at the wheel.

David Coulthard (below) bounces with health. The sole surviving McLaren finished fifth, hot on Schumacher's heels.

14 he was out. Just as in France, his gearbox was playing up and he needed a shove from his mechanics to get going. A few hundred yards further on he was out.

Hill was the first of the leaders to stop, on lap 20. In third; out fifth. Then Alesi, Schumacher and Villeneuve came in on lap 22, Berger on lap 23. Schumacher and Villeneuve came in together and left together with a slightly slower Schumacher only just getting under way ahead of the Williams. He certainly didn't expect to be passed by Jacques on the approach to the first chicane, but he was. "My brakes gave me a lot of problems and when Villeneuve passed me I could not defend my position." One place nearer to Hill for Jacques!

Now Damon was where he should have been at the start. In front, with a clear track. Time to get the hammer down and build the lead of 18s he needed to exit the pits still ahead after his second stop. And how he flew. On lap 24, after Berger's stop, he led by 3.2s. On lap 25 it was 4.7s.

On lap 26 he set the fastest lap of the race in 1m 46.504s (143.312mph) to increase the gap to 6.3s. But he would have to go even faster to create the cushion he needed. And he didn't. On lap 34, when he peeled off the track into the long pit approach, he was 15.9s ahead of Berger, who was 4.4s clear of Alesi.

With Schumacher now another 30s down the road fighting for fifth with Coulthard's McLaren, the partisan crowd was rooting for Berger. Austrian he may be, but at least he spoke the right language. As Gerhard and Alesi entered the main straight, Hill was motoring down the pit lane at the

mandatory 75 mph. As he shot on to the track, his Williams slotted between the two Benettons.

With 11 laps to go, he was 2.2s behind Berger. It didn't take long for Damon to catch Gerhard. In two laps he was tucked behind the Benetton but, as ever, catching is one thing, passing another. This was Berger's 191st Grand Prix, he hadn't won one for exactly two years and he wasn't about to make it easy for Damon. For six laps he used all his accumulated experience and skill to stay ahead, matching Hill's every attempt to pass by legitimately blocking the Williams.

"It would have taken an error by Gerhard for me to have passed him," confirmed Damon. "We had the same engines, we were doing the same speed down the straight and I never got a sufficiently good tow to be alongside him. Every time I tried to draw level he pulled across in front of me - which he was entitled to do." But then the cruel fate which had denied Damon several wins in the past struck Gerhard. As he approached the stadium on his 43rd lap, with only two to go, his engine belched a vast plume of oily grey smoke and disintegrated - just as Villeneuve's had done at the same place the day before. Bitter, bitter luck. Gerhard's race was over and Hill had only to cruise home to win his first German GP, his 20th in all, equalling the tally of Michael Schumacher and stretching his championship lead over Villeneuve to 21 points.

"Bloody good!" he said. "Was it lucky? Absolutely no way! I have had my share of bad luck here at Hockenheim: I have been leading by 30s and had a puncture on the penultimate lap. Unfortunately these things happen in motor racing." Damon deserved his win after a fine drive but so, just as much, did Gerhard, who was typically phlegmatic. "I was confident I could have held off Hill, as I had done for the previous laps. I had no warning that anything was wrong until suddenly the engine blew. What more can I say? C'est la vie..."

Seeing what had happened to Berger, Jean Alesi sensibly backed off to preserve

"But then the cruel fate which had denied Damon several wins in the past struck Gerhard... Bitter, bitter luck"

his engine and finished second for the third time in 1996. Berger's departure cleared the way for Jacques Villeneuve's eighth podium finish from his first 11 Grands Prix, a fine achievement but not wholly what he had wanted. The World Championship in his rookie year was his objective, but the gap he had reduced at Silverstone had now been increased.

Schumacher was just relieved to have finished after three successive failures. "It was important to see the chequered flag again. I am disappointed to have finished so far behind the leaders (41.5s) but the car was better here than in the last few races." It needed to be, and only the talent of Schumacher kept it ahead of a very determined David Coulthard, who had been harrying Michael for the last seven laps and who finished a mere 0.7s behind the Ferrari.

Formula One had unexpectedly come alive again at Hockenheim. Williams was now within two points of its eighth constructors' championship but, with five races still to run, the drivers' contest was still very much alive. Roll on Hungary!

Pre-race rumours linked Heinz-Harald Frentzen with a Williams seat in 1997: for now, he had to make do with one of Switzerland's less precise creations...

FERRARI

Another inadequate performance, although nothing like as bad as Canada, France and Britain. Previously tested modifications used for race - new diffusor, rear suspension, six-speed gearbox, stronger wheel bearings and improved hydraulics. "A big improvement," says Schumacher, who is nevertheless slower than Irvine on Friday. "The car's all over the place and we don't know why." After beneficial overnight changes, Schumacher holds pole position to delight of home crowd until 42 seconds after chequered flag goes out, when both Hill and Berger are already on their last, and faster, laps. Starts third, 0.5s slower than Hill, with Irvine eighth, another second slower. Schumacher passed by meteoric Alesi at start, chops off charging Hakkinen and runs increasingly distant fourth behind Hill, holding up Coulthard, Villeneuve, Irvine and Hakkinen. Pits on lap 22 at same time as Villeneuve, who boldly passes brake-troubled Schumacher at chicane, demoting Michael to sixth. Battles for fifth with Coulthard after David's second stop, lap 32, but profits from Berger's retirement to finish fourth, 41.5s down, his first full race distance since Spain. But with fastest lap 2.1s slower than Hill's, not a very encouraging drive. Irvine, also with brake problems, races seventh behind Villeneuve until first of two stops, lap 14. Back to seventh, lap 22, until second stop, lap 30. Retains place but retires, lap 35, when gearbox loses its oil.

BENETTON-RENAULT

Team's best 1996 race to date with encouraging improvement in performance. Using new wings and brakes, Berger fastest on Friday with Alesi fourth. Gerhard much happier with new chassis and very nearly takes pole position on exciting last lap; misses it by 0.38s after inspired drive by Damon Hill. Nevertheless Berger starts second - the first time a Benetton has appeared on the front row this season. It's also the first time he has outqualified Alesi in '96. Disappointed Jean fifth, unhappy with set-up. Both make superb starts, Berger taking lead from Hill and Alesi sensationally blasting up to second past Hakkinen, Schumacher and Hill. Gerhard, Jean and Damon race in close formation until Alesi pits, lap 22, followed by Gerhard one lap later. Berger regains lead when Hill has second stop, lap 34, but Damon rejoins just ahead of Alesi. Hill eliminates 2.2s gap and catches Berger, lap 37, but is unable to pass. Gerhard resists non-stop pressure for six laps only for engine to blow spectacularly with two laps to go. Classified 13th, three laps down. Alesi backs off to preserve engine, finishes second, 1.5s down, and moves ahead of Schumacher to third in championship.

WILLIAMS-RENAULT

Hill only eighth fastest on Friday but unconcerned as did not use new tyres. Then, using four sets, is fastest when it matters on Saturday, taking pole position from Schumacher on his last lap. Is overjoyed to do so at Michael's home track in front of 90,000 less than euphoric Germans. Villeneuve unhappy for first race at Hockenheim. Finds track easy to learn, but has major engine blow-up on Saturday. Loses valuable set-up time. Qualifies disappointed sixth after having to use less powerful replacement engine. Minardi protests Hill for allegedly passing red scrutineering light, but this is rejected by stewards. All Damon's good work nullified when he makes another poor start and is passed by Berger and Alesi. Races behind two Benettons until first stop, lap 21. Down to fifth but takes lead, lap 24, following Alesi, Schumacher, Villeneuve and Berger stops. Charges hard and builds 16s lead by lap 33 but rejoins track between Berger and Alesi after second stop, lap 34. Closes 2.2s gap to Gerhard in three laps, but unable to pass despite unremitting pressure. Takes lead, lap 43, when Berger's engine disintegrates and wins first German GP by 11.5s. Extends championship lead over Villeneuve to 21 points. Jacques races sixth behind Coulthard until David's first stop, lap 16. Pits behind Schumacher, lap 22, but outbrakes Michael at chicane and up to fifth. To fourth at Coulthard's second stop, lap 33, and finishes third after Berger retirement. Williams now only two points off eighth constructors' championship.

McLAREN-MERCEDES

Short wheelbase cars with new-spec Mercedes-Benz engines. Hakkinen excellent fastest at Mercedes' home track on Friday and Saturday mornings, but Coulthard unable to balance car (nevertheless fastest on straight at breathtaking 212mph). Hakkinen qualifies fourth with Coulthard seventh. Mika then fastest in warm-up; David

second. Hakkinen chopped by Schumacher at start and down to eighth. In for early stop, 15s down, lap 13. Mechanics have to push for him to rejoin and he retires moments later with gearbox problem. Coulthard up two places to fifth at start. Harries Schumacher until first stop, lap 16. Up to fourth, lap 23, but passed by Villeneuve and Schumacher at second stop, lap 32. Closes six second gap to Michael in six laps but is then unable to pass. Finishes fifth.

LIGIER-MUGEN HONDA

Delighted team announces renewal of Mugen-Honda engine deal for 1997, with option for 1998. But good news ends there. Pedro Diniz laudably out-qualifies Panis for first time to start career-best 11th, one place ahead of Olivier. Both drivers inhibited by brake problems. Diniz down to 13th on lap one but up to 10th, lap 15, before lap 20 retirement when engine stops with suspected electronic throttle problem. Panis flat-spots tyres and into pits, lap four, when 12th. Rejoins 18th and last. Up to eighth at sole scheduled stop, lap 24, and finishes praiseworthy full-distance seventh.

JORDAN-PEUGEOT

Sadly another unfulfilled race. Barrichello and Brundle ninth and 10th on grid. Rubens drives hard to finish sixth, "but we were pretty slow compared to the others." Brundle races with Barrichello until lap 22 puncture when eighth. Loses a lap and finishes 10th, one lap down. Only team other than Williams to finish both cars, but not much consolation. An unsettled atmosphere at Jordan with Gary Anderson "on long holiday", team manager John Walton tipped to be leaving to join Arrows and some personnel feeling that drivers could do better.

SAUBER-FORD

Angry Frentzen qualifies 13th, 3.0s off pace and slower than 1995. Herbert 14th, 0.8s slower after engine blow-up and gearbox problems. Johnny has downshift and engine response problems and retires from 15th and last, lap 26. Frentzen "did the best I could" and races to eighth, one lap down. "The most exciting thing was being on television when Berger and Hill lapped me!"

TWR ARROWS-HART

Both drivers complain about lack of balance during pre-race runs, primarily caused by running with minimum downforce to compensate for comparative lack of power from V8. Verstappen has problem with air-valve engine and uses spring-valve Hart to qualify 17th. Runs into back of Katayama's Tyrrell on first lap, breaks front wing and retires. Rosset starts 19th. On one-stop strategy (lap 22) races last but one, ahead of Lamy, and finishes 11th, one lap down.

TYRRELL-YAMAHA

Always willing to try something different (like six-wheel cars in 1976/77), team fits narrower front tyres to reduce drag on long, fast straights during qualifying. Katayama does his fastest lap thus equipped, but Salo has to switch to spare when engine develops water leak. Ukyo starts 16th, 0.2s and one place behind Mika, but blots copybook by spinning out at first chicane when 14th, lap 20, seven seconds behind Salo. Mika races on to finish ninth, one lap down, downcast at inability to keep up due to lack of power. Yamaha just relieved not to have had problems during race at circuit notoriously hard on engines.

MINARDI-FORD

Team protests Hill's pole time. Had the appeal been successful, then seasonal debutant Giovanni Lavaggi, a source of financial relief, would have qualified with the 107 per cent limit. It isn't, so the Italian aristocrat doesn't. Pedro Lamy hampered by lack of straightline grunt from Cosworth V8. Starts 18th; finishes 12th.

FORTI-FORD

As at Silverstone, both cars forlornly sit on garage stands, unable to run. Forti issues statement that it will not be competing due to lack of funds, but promises to return in Hungary with a new sponsor. Subsequently, erstwhile sponsor Shannon states that it possesses a 51 per cent majority shareholding in the team and is "determined to solve the financial and economic problems of the company". It also implies that it will replace team founder Guido Forti! A messy, unhappy and very undesirable situation.

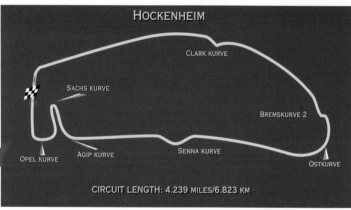

Results and Data © FIA 1996

FORMULA 1 WORLD CHAMPIONSHIP

11

RACE
GERMANY
28 July 1996

HOCKENHEIM

CLARK KURVE

SACHS KURVE

BREMSKURVE 2

OPEL KURVE · AGIP KURVE · SENNA KURVE · OSTKURVE

CIRCUIT LENGTH: 4.239 MILES/6.823 KM

STARTING GRID

HILL 1m 43.912s	
	BERGER 1m 44.299s
SCHUMACHER 1m 44.477s	
	HAKKINEN 1m 44.644s
ALESI 1m 44.670s	
	VILLENEUVE 1m 44.842s
COULTHARD 1m 44.951s	
	IRVINE 1m 45.389s
BARRICHELLO 1m 45.452s	
	BRUNDLE 1m 45.876s
DINIZ 1m 46.575s	
	PANIS 1m 46.746s
FRENTZEN 1m 46.899s	
	HERBERT 1m 47.711s
SALO 1m 48.139s	
	KATAYAMA 1m 48.381s
VERSTAPPEN 1m 48.512s	
	LAMY 1m 49.461s
ROSSET 1m 49.551s	

Did not qualify
LAVAGGI
(Minardi M195B)
1m 51.357s

RACE CLASSIFICATION

Pos	Driver	Nat	Car	Laps	Time
1	Damon Hill	GB	Williams FW18-Renault V10	45	1h 21m 43.417s
2	Jean Alesi	F	Benetton B196-Renault V10	45	+11.452s
3	Jacques Villeneuve	CDN	Williams FW18-Renault V10	45	+33.926s
4	Michael Schumacher	D	Ferrari F310-Ferrari V10	45	+41.517s
5	David Coulthard	GB	McLaren MP4/11-Mercedes V10	45	+42.196s
6	Rubens Barrichello	BR	Jordan 196-Peugeot V10	45	+1m 42.099s
7	Olivier Panis	F	Ligier JS43-Mugen Honda V10	45	+1m 43.912s
8	Heinz-Harald Frentzen	D	Sauber C15-Ford V10		+1 lap
9	Mika Salo	SF	Tyrrell 024-Yamaha V10		+1 lap
10	Martin Brundle	GB	Jordan 196-Peugeot V10		+1 lap
11	Ricardo Rosset	BR	Footwork FA17-Hart V8		+1 lap
12	Pedro Lamy	P	Minardi M195B-Ford V8		+2 laps
13	Gerhard Berger	A	Benetton B196-Renault V10		+3 laps DNF/Eng

Retirements	Nat	Car	Lap	Reason
Eddie Irvine	GB	Ferrari F310-Ferrari V10	34	Gearbox
Johnny Herbert	GB	Sauber C15-Ford V10	25	Handling
Pedro Diniz	BR	Ligier JS43-Mugen Honda V10	19	Hydraulics
Ukyo Katayama	J	Tyrrell 024-Yamaha V10	19	Accident
Mika Hakkinen	SF	McLaren MP4/11-Mercedes V10	13	Gearbox
Jos Verstappen	NL	Footwork FA17-Hart V8	0	Accident

FASTEST LAP Damon Hill 1m 46.504s lap 26 (143.12mph)

DRIVERS' CHAMPIONSHIP

Damon Hill	73
Jacques Villeneuve	52
Jean Alesi	31
Michael Schumacher	29
David Coulthard	18
Gerhard Berger	16
Mika Hakkinen	16
Olivier Panis	11
Rubens Barrichello	11
Eddie Irvine	9
Heinz-Harald Frentzen	6
Mika Salo	5
Johnny Herbert	4
Martin Brundle	3
Jos Verstappen	1
Pedro Diniz	1

CONSTRUCTORS' CUP

Williams-Renault	125
Benetton-Renault	47
Ferrari	38
McLaren-Mercedes	34
Jordan-Peugeot	14
Ligier-Mugen Honda	12
Sauber-Ford	10
Tyrrell-Yamaha	5
Footwork-Hart	1

ROUND 12

HUNGARY

t was 11 years since our first visit to Hungary. Then, it was an Iron Curtain country, there were 20,000 Russian troops in Budapest ready to quell any repeat of the bloody 1956 insurrection, there hadn't been a Grand Prix there since 1936 (won by the legendary Tazio Nuvolari in an 8C Alfa Romeo) and we didn't know what to expect. What we found was a glorious city, a modern circuit, unbounded enthusiasm and wonderful weather.

And ever since, it has got better and better and is now one of Formula One's favourite countries, so there was great sadness at the thought that this could be Hungary's swansong, and that it might be replaced by a revived Austrian GP. It turned out during the meeting that there could be a change of heart, so it was a case of fingers crossed and hope for the best. Eastern Europe deserves a Grand Prix.

This year was as good as ever. Blue skies, 26-degree heat, Budapest and the mighty River Danube absolutely pulsating with life after another year of economic improvement, the biggest crowds since the record 200,000-plus attendance in 1986 and a totally absorbing race which changed the face of the World Championship.

Damon Hill was going to win, wasn't he? With the best car and engine he arrived at the Hungaroring as a double-winner (1993 and '95), back on top form after his lucky, but confidence-building, victory at Hockenheim. The only person who seemed to have the slightest chance of challenging him was his team-mate Jacques Villeneuve, but he had never raced at the Hungaroring, which was reckoned to be hard to learn. Damon, then, held all the cards. If he got pole position, as he had done seven times already this year, he'd have it made.

The Hungaroring is notoriously difficult to pass at, and Hill at the front in a Williams-Renault would surely be a racing cert for another 10 championship-nearing points? Fine in theory but, as is so often the case, it wasn't practised. Damon didn't get pole position, he had another rotten start and Villeneuve won. Disheartening for Hill, but great for Formula One, which now envisaged the championship going down to the wire.

But first things first. After seven demeaning retirements from its last eight starts, Ferrari appeared to have got its act together. The aerodynamic changes which hadn't worked at Hockenheim did so at the high-downforce Hungaroring; both Schumacher and Irvine were flying. Second and fourth on Friday, first and fifth on Saturday morning and then their best qualifying performance yet, with Schumacher in his fourth pole position of the season and Irvine fourth. Both were delighted, Irvine "because I'm the best of the second division", Schumacher "because I thought the car would be a disaster over the bumps here but it works. The good thing is that we can keep the tyres together." Wrong, Michael, as the next day would show.

It was mighty close for pole, with just 0.130s covering Schumacher, Hill and Villeneuve. A superb achievement by Jacques who hadn't found the Hungaroring as hard to learn as he had expected, who had been on the pace as early as Friday afternoon and who could have been starting at the front if he hadn't had a slightly down-on-power engine. Being second on the front row wasn't going to be much use to Damon, though. It was on the dirty right-hand side of the little-used Hungaroring whereas Schumacher immediately in front of him and Villeneuve just behind him were on the well-scrubbed, grippier left-hand side. Damon did his best to clean it up during the morning warm-up, but he lost out again at the start. "The way the clutch works doesn't suit me. The start was going OK but then I got a bit of wheelspin and when I used the clutch to modulate it, it suddenly gripped." By then he was down to fourth, passed by Villeneuve and super-starting Jean Alesi from fifth on the grid.

Jacques Villeneuve finds Irvine's stray Ferrari slicing across his bows (inset), but the Canadian overcame all potential hazards to send the maple-leaf flag to the top of the highest pole for the third time.

101

For the first 18 laps there were two races at the front. Schumacher and Villeneuve battling for the lead, Alesi and Hill fighting for third an ever-increasing distance behind. Alesi was over a second a lap slower than the two leaders, and Hill couldn't get past him. "I lost the race in the first 10 laps," said Damon. On lap 10 he was over 12s behind the Ferrari and on lap 19, when Schumacher made his first stop, the gap was more than 20s. Hungary is always about strategy and pit stops, the trick being to time them right to avoid the traffic. Hill had started the race intending to stop twice, but when he fluffed the start his minders decided that three stops would be better.

Somehow, the change of plan didn't get through to Damon though. "It was a bit confusing. They were looking ahead to Michael with a view to getting me out in front of him but whatever happened I was pushing as hard as I could to make up time."

Hill led for three laps after Schumacher, Villeneuve and Alesi had made their first stops but on lap 26 of 77, after his own stop, he was down to fifth with Villeneuve now in the lead. The Canadian's stop had been faster than Schumacher's, and from then on he never looked back. When Hill rejoined he was, frustratingly, right behind Alesi's Benetton again. Only a mistake by Jean could elevate Damon to third, and that is exactly what happened. On lap 31 Alesi slid wide at the first corner and locked up. In a flash Hill was past, now some 32s behind Villeneuve and 22s behind Schumacher with 44 laps to go.

Meanwhile, the slippery Hungaroring was taking its toll. Salo, Diniz and Jos Verstappen were out as the result of a multiple collision on the first lap. Martin Brundle was out after losing control of his Jordan at the 110 mph Turn Four. David Coulthard, never really in the running after starting ninth, spun out on lap 23 when his Mercedes-Benz V10 seized. Pedro Lamy retired with a collapsed rear suspension as a result of clipping Diniz's Ligier on lap one and, sadly, Eddie Irvine dropped out from sixth on lap 32 when his Ferrari gear-box gave up. Again. For four laps Johnny Herbert's Sauber, going well, took his place but then he too retired (engine).

The top runners were all planning three stops, and when their second visits had been concluded on lap 42 the race looked set. Villeneuve was leading Schumacher by over 14s with Hill a further 12 behind. The Benettons of Alesi and Berger, separated by six seconds, were fourth and fifth, with Hakkinen a distant sixth. Everyone else had been lapped. The only excitement was that Alesi, caught by Berger after their second stops, refused to let his team-mate pass. After being instructed from the pit lane to move over, he did so in a fury, though he was to beat an unfortunate Gerhard in the end.

With the prospect of a fine win for Villeneuve but a dull finish to the race, it turned out to be quite the reverse. Schumacher was in trouble. His tyres which he had optimistically thought would hold up, were not doing so. "The F310 wears them out quite quickly in high temperatures like these, which made it impossible to match the pace of the Williams," said team boss Jean Todt after the race. When Michael made his last stop, from second place on lap 52, a charging Hill had reduced the gap from nearly 12s to virtually nothing. As Schumacher pulled into the pits, Hill shot past him and now the Williams men were first and second,

30s apart with a stop each to make. Schumacher would have to settle for third.

Villeneuve's last stop very nearly cost him the race. Yet again, Williams had a wheel nut problem and Jacques lost 10s as a result of it. When Hill raced out of the pit lane he was 6.6s behind Jacques, with 14 laps to go. If he could catch and pass his team-mate, he would increase his championship lead to 25 points.

The last 14 laps were anything but dull. First of all, poor Berger went out with a

"Poor Berger went out with a repetition of the gigantic Renault engine eruption which had cost him victory in Germany"

Schumacher (left) found that Ferrari's new aerodynamics worked far better than he had dared anticipate while Hill was getting pretty cheesed off with the view facing him for most of the day: Alesi's rear wing (below).

Pedro Diniz
(left) had left his
Budapest A-Z at
home; Mika
Salo heads for
the gravel, and
retirement.
Everyone else
gets on with
the race.

heartbreaking repetition of the gigantic Renault engine eruption which had cost him victory in Germany.

At the time he was fourth, but six laps later he would have been third because that was when Schumacher registered Ferrari's ninth retirement from 10 starts. "The throttle was getting stiff and tended to stick open. Then the gearbox began to play up on downshifts. Approaching the slower corners the only way I could slow down was by using the cut-out switch to kill the engine but I made a mistake, hit the neutral selector switch and the engine would not fire up again. But I am not frustrated because I did not expect to fight for the title this year." I respect Michael, and would not doubt him, but he had to be a man of iron not to be disheartened by his constant misfortune.

With only three men now on the same lap and Alesi a massive 78s behind, it was a question of which Williams would win. Both Villeneuve and Hill meant it to be them. Damon recorded the fastest lap of the race on lap 67 (1m 20.093s, 110.829 mph). On lap 75, with two to go, he was right under Villeneuve's rear wing having taken six seconds out of the Canadian's

"Whatever happened, the championship would not be decided before the penultimate race in Portugal"

Hard times (above). Herbert and Salo compare retirements.

His engine having seized (below), David Coulthard demonstrates his suitability for the GB Armco-vaulting team.

lead. But that was it. Push as he might, he could not pass and this time the Renault engine ahead of him went the distance to give Villeneuve a third Grand Prix victory in his first year of Formula One. His winning margin was a mere 0.771s and it closed the championship gap to 17 points, with 40 still to be won. Whatever happened, the title would not be decided before the penultimate race in Portugal and it seemed more likely to be settled in Japan. That would at least give us all a motivation for going there!

"When Damon came up behind me I started pushing again," said Villeneuve, "but he was a bit quicker and that meant a tough race all the way to the end." Tough, and immensely enjoyable for everyone who was watching. Confirmation, too, that Villeneuve in a Williams was indeed a star. The next Grand Prix on the world's finest circuit, at Spa in Belgium, would be an especially demanding test for Jacques. He had never raced there and it would be harder to learn than the Hungaroring. "It should suit me better, because I like fast corners and I'm told that Spa has got plenty of them," he predicted.

Despite their proliferation of wings, the McLarens weren't exactly flying: Hakkinen eventually got fourth a lap adrift, thanks to others' problems.

FERRARI

A very encouraging Friday/Saturday at the Hungaroring, where good grid positions are as important as at Monaco. Schumacher and Irvine second and fourth fastest on Friday: "I think pole is possible," says Schumacher who finds, to his surprise, that aerodynamic changes for low-downforce Hockenheim work better at high-downforce Hungaroring. "The car is not the disaster over the bumps that I expected." Schumacher fastest on Saturday morning and then takes fourth 1996 pole position, 0.053s faster than Hill. Irvine's excellent fourth place gives Ferrari best '96 grid so far. Although concerned about possible clutch problem at start, Schumacher has excellent getaway and leads for 18 laps, closely followed by Villeneuve and pulling away from Alesi/Hill battle for third. Down to fifth at lap 19 stop but second behind Villeneuve from lap 26 until second stop, lap 39. Regains second when Hill stops, lap 41, but down to third again at third stop, lap 52. Cannot match Villeneuve/Hill times on worn tyres and, clearly in trouble, retires with faulty throttle control, lap 71. "The throttle was getting stiff and tended to stick open. Then the gearbox began to play up. Approaching slow corners the only way I could slow down was to kill the engine then switch it on again." Classified ninth, seven laps down. Irvine passed by Alesi at start and runs fifth until taken by Berger when runs off course, lap 15. Pits from fourth, lap 25, and retires from sixth, lap 32, with another gearbox failure.

BENETTON-RENAULT

Neither driver goes out on Friday morning (dirty track) and both struggle in afternoon with set-up and downforce problems. Saturday not much better with Alesi and Berger fifth and sixth on grid, over 1.6s off Schumacher's pole time. Alesi hopes for another start like Hockenheim and Silverstone and gets it, shooting past Irvine and Hill to third. But cannot match Schumacher/Villeneuve pace and holds up frustrated Hill until first stop, lap 22, when 18s behind leaders. Back to third by passing Hill in pits, lap 26, but runs wide, lap 31, and taken by Damon. Drops back and caught by Berger after second stops, laps 46 (JA) and 49 (GB). Holds up faster team-mate for five laps until angrily yielding following pits command. Berger now fourth, 20s behind Schumacher but retires, lap 66, after another explosive engine failure, just like Hockenheim. Alesi to third when Schumacher retires, but almost a lap behind Villeneuve and Hill.

WILLIAMS-RENAULT

Yet another magnificent Hungary for Williams, who clinch eighth constructors' World Championship with four races still to go. Hill misses pole position by 0.053s and has to start on dirty side of track; Villeneuve third, on clean side. A superb effort by Jacques, who had never even seen Hungaroring before Thursday of race week and who, significantly, had been allowed to follow his own distinctive ideas on car set-up for the first time. With combination of dusty track and clutch problem, Hill makes third successive bad start and drops to fourth, passed by Villeneuve and Alesi. Jacques harries Schumacher as both race away from Alesi/Hill battle with Alesi unable to hold leaders and Hill unable to pass. "I lost the race in the first 10 laps," says Damon, who is 20s down when Schumacher makes first stop on lap 19. Villeneuve takes lead during first round of stops, lap 25, and retains it to end of race, including his second and third stops, laps 40 and 58. But long third stop wheel-nut problem loses some 10s and Hill is only 6.6s down after his final stop, lap 63. Damon charges magnificently, to close within 0.784s of Villeneuve on lap 72 with five to go. Pushes hard but cool Villeneuve makes no mistakes, and wins his third GP in his first year of F1 by 0.771s. Championship gap between Hill and Villeneuve now down to 17 points with 40 still to be won from remaining four races.

McLAREN-MERCEDES

Another disappointing race. Hakkinen and Coulthard qualify seventh and ninth, some two seconds off the pace, both unable to overcome balance and grip problems. Coulthard initially hampered by heavy fuel load for one-stop strategy but to eighth, eight seconds behind seventh-placed Hakkinen on lap 18. Then well placed to benefit from risky strategy, but retires lap 24 when water pump drive fails. Hakkinen happy to finish fourth, albeit a lap down. "We never got the potential performance out of the car," admits Ron Dennis.

LIGIER-MUGEN HONDA

Olivier Panis re-signs for fourth year with Ligier after receiving 1997 offers from other teams, notably Jordan. Seventh fastest on Friday but starts 11th, 2.4s off pace with balance problems. Adopts unusual strategy by opting for two relatively close stops on laps 29 and 44. Down to 14th after bad start but benefits from strategy, non-stop attack and reliable car to finish contented fifth (one lap down). Diniz starts 15th after losing Friday set-up time with burnt-out wiring loom, but retires on first lap after colliding with Salo's Tyrrell.

JORDAN-PEUGEOT

Team's worst-yet qualifying of year. "The car doesn't want to go round corners," says Martin Brundle, who proves it by starting 12th, one place ahead of Barrichello. But both are nearly three seconds slower than Schumacher's pole time, despite high extra mid-wing and new front wing endplates. Barrichello races to unimpressed sixth after "fighting more to keep the car on the track than for a position." Brundle goes off on lap six and breaks front suspension. Talk persists of both drivers being dropped in 1997.

SAUBER-FORD

Cosworth produces upgrade of Ford Zetec V10 with 20 more bhp and better top-end performance plus, more importantly, much-improved driveability with resultant benefits (notably greater driver confidence and no downshift problems). Delighted Johnny Herbert goes fifth fastest on Saturday morning, only one second off race. Drops to eighth on grid in afternoon but still outqualifies Heinz-Harald Frentzen, who starts 10th, 2.3s slower than poleman Schumacher. Still a long way to go. Herbert runs eighth "held up by Hakkinen" until lap 17 stop, when he drops to 10th. Promisingly into points at sixth, laps 32-35, but retires, lap 36, when engine tightens up. Frentzen starts well but stuck in 11th behind Barrichello. Stops early, on lap 14, and up to 10th past Barrichello when Rubens stops, lap 24. Improves to eighth (behind Rubens again), lap 45, but retires immediately after third stop, lap 49, when engine fails. More to do for Cosworth, criticised for cautiousness, but some consolation from sixth fastest lap of race for Frentzen (1.8s slower than Hill's).

TWR ARROWS-HART

With team concentrating on 1997 car at new Leafield base (and Tom Walkinshaw beavering away at getting free works engines), only two cars at Hungaroring. New rear wing for more downforce but both Verstappen and Rosset continue to moan about understeer. "It needs a new front end to put it right and there isn't going to be one," says Walkinshaw. Verstappen starts 17th, with Rosset 18th for first F1 race in Hungary. Verstappen gets away well, passes Diniz and Salo as both involved in multiple collisions with both of them. Carries on but spins out from 14th on lap 11, a likely after-effect of impact damage. Rosset races at rear to finish eighth of 10, three laps down but pleased with best Formula One finish to date.

TYRRELL-YAMAHA

Lacklustre meeting for Tyrrell. Katayama pleased to outqualify Salo (14th to 16th) after Salo loses valuable set-up time on Friday morning when engine blows on out-lap. Both concerned by understeer and lack of balance. Mika's race ends seconds after start. "I was hit by Verstappen at the second corner, then Diniz lost his car and pushed me off the track after breaking my left front suspension." Katayama drives solid and reliable race to finish seventh with two stops on laps 22 and 48. It's his highest placing of year so far despite being told to slow down at mid-distance, with overheating engine as a result of stone from Brundle's course-departing Jordan puncturing radiator.

MINARDI-FORD

Both Lamy and Lavaggi qualify within 107 per cent of pole time limit. Lamy 4.6s off pace (19th) and Lavaggi 5.34s off (20th). Lavaggi not worthy of F1 but, in fairness to both, car is underpowered with Ford V8 and money-strapped team is unable to keep up in development race with well-funded top teams. Lamy just fails to avoid Diniz/Salo collision on first lap and damages left-rear suspension. Carries on but is withdrawn by team at lap 24 pit stop, when gravity of damage realised. Lavaggi motors round at back and, over five seconds off the pace, is lapped by lap 15. Ironically receives 10s penalty for speeding...but only in the pits, during lap 27 stop. Spins out on lap 74 of 77 but classified 10th and last, eight laps down.

FORTI-FORD

Team fails to appear and now seems to be out of series as result of financial problems.

FIA FORMULA 1 WORLD CHAMPIONSHIP

RACE 12
HUNGARY
11 August 1996

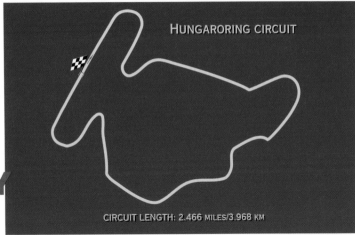

HUNGARORING CIRCUIT

CIRCUIT LENGTH: 2.466 MILES/3.968 KM

STARTING GRID

SCHUMACHER 1m 17.129s	HILL 1m 17.182s
VILLENEUVE 1m 17.259s	IRVINE 1m 18.617s
ALESI 1m 18.754s	BERGER 1m 18.794s
HAKKINEN 1m 19.116s	HERBERT 1m 19.292s
COULTHARD 1m 19.384s	FRENTZEN 1m 19.463s
PANIS 1m 19.538s	BRUNDLE 1m 19.828s
BARRICHELLO 1m 19.966s	KATAYMA 1m 20.499s
DINIZ 1m 20.665s	SALO 1m 20.678s
VERSTAPPEN 1m 20.781s	ROSSET 1m 21.590s
LAMY 1m 21.713s	LAVAGGI 1m 22.468s

RACE CLASSIFICATION

Pos	Driver	Nat	Car	Laps	Time
1	Jacques Villeneuve	CDN	Williams FW18-Renault V10	77	1h 46m 21.134s
2	Damon Hill	GB	Williams FW18-Renault V10	77	+0.771s
3	Jean Alesi	F	Benetton B196-Renault V10	77	+1m 24.212s
4	Mika Hakkinen	SF	McLaren MP4/11B-Mercedes V10		+1 lap
5	Olivier Panis	F	Ligier JS43-Mugen Honda V10		+1 lap
6	Rubens Barrichello	BR	Jordan 196-Peugeot V10		+2 laps
7	Ukyo Katayama	J	Tyrrell 024-Yamaha V10		+3 laps
8	Ricardo Rosset	BR	Footwork FA17-Hart V8		+3 laps
9	Michael Schumacher	D	Ferrari F310-Ferrari V10		+7 laps DNF
10	Giovanni Lavaggi	I	Minardi M195B-Ford V8		+8 laps DNF spin

Retirements	Nat	Car	Lap	Reason
Gerhard Berger	A	Benetton B196-Renault V10	64	Engine
Heinz-Harald Frentzen	D	Sauber C15-Ford V10	50	Engine
Johnny Herbert	GB	Sauber C15-Ford V10	35	Engine
Eddie Irvine	GB	Ferrari F310-Ferrari V10	31	Gearbox
Pedro Lamy	P	Minardi M195B-Ford V8	24	Suspension
David Coulthard	GB	McLaren MP4/11B-Mercedes V10	23	Engine
Jos Verstappen	NL	Footwork FA17-Hart V8	10	Accident
Martin Brundle	GB	Jordan 196-Peugeot V10	5	Accident
Pedro Diniz	BR	Ligier JS43-Mugen Honda V10	1	Suspension
Mika Salo	SF	Tyrrell 024-Yamaha V10	0	Accident

FASTEST LAP Damon Hill 1m 20.093s lap 67 (110.810mph)

DRIVERS' CHAMPIONSHIP

Damon Hill	79
Jacques Villeneuve	62
Jean Alesi	35
Michael Schumacher	29
Mika Hakkinen	19
David Coulthard	18
Gerhard Berger	16
Olivier Panis	13
Rubens Barrichello	12
Eddie Irvine	9
Heinz-Harald Frentzen	6
Mika Salo	5
Johnny Herbert	4
Martin Brundle	3
Jos Verstappen	1
Pedro Diniz	1

CONSTRUCTORS' CUP

Williams-Renault	141
Benetton-Renault	51
Ferrari	38
McLaren-Mercedes	37
Jordan-Peugeot	15
Ligier-Mugen Honda	14
Sauber-Ford	10
Tyrrell-Yamaha	5
Footwork-Hart	1

Results and Data © FIA 1996

Every year the glorious Spa-Francorchamps circuit shows us what Grand Prix racing ought to be like. Not for Spa the safety-minded succession of second and third gear corners which dominate so many of today's circuits. Not for Spa the boring flatness which sometimes makes you wonder where you are.

Spa is uniquely different. It is a fabulous throwback to the days when motor races were held on closed public roads and when long, flat-out corners were a daunting challenge. A place which emphasises that Grand Prix drivers are a breed apart, as they straddle the razor's edge which separates success and disaster.

Set amongst pine-clad hills in the picturesque Ardennes, it is a half-size cutdown of a breathtaking 8.8-mile circuit which began its career in 1924, and where the legendary Rudolf Caracciola and

Hermann Lang drove their Mercedes-Benz Silver Arrows to victory in the late 1930s.

The 'mini-Spa' was first used in 1984 and, although some 4.5 miles shorter than the original, has lost none of its character. The drivers love it, and it makes a magnificent spectacle.

So, with heightened interest in the World Championship after Jacques Villeneuve's brilliant victory in Hungary, there were great expectations for round 13 of the 1996 series. Damon Hill had already won twice at Spa (1993/94), but although it was new to Villeneuve, the need to master a new track quickly hadn't prevented the brilliant young Canadian from nearly winning his first Grand Prix, in Australia, or from actually doing so at the Nurburgring and in Hungary.

In just 17 laps he was on the pace, revelling in the challenge. "It's not an easy track. It's tough to learn but there are lots

With the benefit of useful pre-Spa practice on a computer game, Jacques Villeneuve converts fantasy into reality and leads away from pole position at one of the world's most demanding circuits. But he couldn't prevent Schumacher (right) from taking Ferrari's second win of the season.

of demanding high-speed turns so it's fun. I really enjoy it."

Significantly, Williams was giving Villeneuve much more freedom in implementing his unusual ideas on car set-up, and the proof of the pudding was in the eating. Jacques was fastest by an electrifying 1.7s on Saturday morning, and he went on to take his second pole position. Faster than Hill, second on the grid; faster than the Benettons; faster than the McLarens; and faster than Michael Schumacher, who had won three times in Belgium (although he was disqualified in 1994). An amazing achievement, assisted by some practice on a computer simulation of the circuit, but both Hill and Schumacher had other reasons for being beaten.

One of Spa's characteristics is that its weather can change incredibly quickly from clear blue skies and blazing sunshine to black clouds and lashing rain; and that's

what happened 40 minutes into the one-hour qualifying session. With Villeneuve heading the times, Hill's last run had to be aborted. And it was amazing that Schumacher was able to go out at all. On Friday morning he lost the Ferrari exiting the downhill Fagnes corner, smashing into the Armco backwards at over 100 mph. It was a miracle that he did no more than bruise his knee. It was a gigantic tribute both to his fitness and the expertise of the Ferrari mechanics, who built him a new car, that he was able to start third on the grid ahead of Coulthard's McLaren, Berger's Benetton and Hakkinen's McLaren.

What was the weather going to be like on race day? How would it affect strategies, especially considering the long lap length? And would Hill, who had been practising his starts at Spain's Barcelona circuit, get away well this time?

It was just Damon's luck that, after morning rain, there were damp patches on his side of the road. The approach to Spa's first corner, the notoriously tight La Source hairpin, is only about 200 metres from the front of the grid and, just as at Monaco, collisions after the start are by no means unusual as everyone jostles for position before the 160 mph run down to Grand Prix racing's most demanding corner complex, Eau Rouge.

And 1996 was no exception. The 19-car field (Giovanni Lavaggi had failed to qualify) was down to 16 immediately as Panis, Herbert and Frentzen drove into each other, whilst Rubens Barrichello had to stop for a new track rod. Damon Hill faltered again and, as Schumacher and Coulthard rocketed past him, Villeneuve was in the lead. And that was within a few hundred yards of the start.

The battle for the lead was superb. For 13 laps there was never more than a second or so between Villeneuve and Schumacher, with the Ferrari looking much more stable than hitherto. For the first time it was fitted with the new seven-speed gearbox that Michael had asked for, and it was clearly helping.

At Spa, the German's genius was spellbinding, but even he was having a hard time keeping up with the magnificent Villeneuve as they drew away from Coulthard, Hill, Hakkinen and Berger. Then, on lap 12, all hell broke loose. Holland's Jos Verstappen lost control of his TWR-Arrows as he accelerated out of Stavelot corner and had a gigantic accident. He was little more than concussed, but with debris all over the track the Safety Car emerged. And that was when Michael Schumacher won the Belgian Grand Prix for the third time in five years (and for the fourth time on the road).

With the Safety Car on the track but the field yet to bunch up behind it, in came Schumacher for his first stop. An inspired decision by Ferrari? "No, it wasn't,

"At Spa, the German's genius was spellbinding, but even he was having a hard time keeping up with the magnificent Villeneuve"

actually," said a truthful Michael, "it was the decision of my fuel tank. I had to stop."

It was accidentally perfect timing. Williams tried to get Villeneuve in too, by screaming at him over the radio, but Jacques didn't understand and drove on. So his stop was a lap late, which made it even worse for Hill. Realising that it had missed Villeneuve, Williams then tried to prevent Hill from coming in, as all Villeneuve's kit was still in place, but Damon didn't get the message until he was on his way into the pits.

"Stay out! Stay out!" Damon heard. He only managed to do so by threading his way between the polystyrene marker boards and actually stopping by a marshal until the track was clear to resume. When he finally stopped on lap 16, he had slipped to 12th out of 15 behind the Safety Car. A management shambles? Yes, of course it was, but it is easy to criticise when you're not the one who is under pressure.

Hill's cause looked lost. He had started the race in the spare car, because in the morning warm-up he had spun and run backwards in a forward gear. What could that have done to his Renault engine? Better to take the other car than risk the original breaking. Trouble was, the spare had substantial understeer which Damon just had to contend with.

When the Safety Car pulled off, he was

Perpetuating a legend (above).

Villeneuve waits in vain for the traditional Ferrari breakdown (far right).

Schumacher always insists on taking his life-size Jean Todt teddy bear everywhere with him (below right).

last but one with 13 cars between him and the race leader - who was David Coulthard! McLaren had opted for a daring one-stop strategy, so Coulthard and Hakkinen stayed out whilst everyone else was stopping. For eight intoxicating laps it was a McLaren one/two, but they knew their strategy had been compromised. When Mika and David rejoined after their stops they were down to fifth and eighth, and now it was Schumacher leading with Villeneuve second, Alesi third, a superb Mika Salo fourth in his Tyrrell-Yamaha and Damon Hill up to a forceful sixth after gaining seven places in eight laps. Who says you can't pass in modern Grand Prix racing?

Schumacher's fortuitous good timing had got him ahead of Villeneuve, but it was a close thing. Jacques was right behind the Ferrari when Michael made his second stop on lap 30, and he led for three laps until he too came in. As he exited the pit lane once more, Schumacher swept past into the spine-chilling drop to Eau Rouge and the race was on again with a vengeance. But, deservedly, this was Michael's day.

Whilst chasing Hakkinen's McLaren earlier on, he had deranged his Ferrari's steering by hammering over the kerbs and he was a touch fearful as he tackled the blindingly fast corners. "I spoke to the team over the radio and they told me that if I stayed away from the kerbs I wouldn't have any further problems. So I did!" Yet more confirmation that Grand Prix drivers are no ordinary mortals.

Jos Verstappen (below): going off at Stavelot at 140 mph destroys a) his car and b) Williams' chances of winning the race.

Villeneuve was in trouble too. "On each new set of tyres the car was very good for two or three laps and then it pushed (understeered) like a pig, so I drove really hard on the first laps but then I just lost my front end and couldn't turn into the corners any more. At the end I was hearing some noise from the exhaust so I preferred just to lay back." Which enabled Schumacher to extend his lead until he took the chequered flag 5.6s ahead of Villeneuve's Williams and 15.7s ahead of Hakkinen's McLaren.

It was only McLaren's third podium place of the year, but if it hadn't been for the safety car Mika could have won. 'If' is a big word in Formula One though.

Jean Alesi was fourth after a comparatively uneventful race, but who was going to be fifth? Hill had been there since lap 35, but Berger was catching him. Gerhard had sunk down to last but one on lap 19, whilst trying to pass Irvine's Ferrari following a delayed pit stop. Like Hill, he made a wonderful charging comeback and on lap 38 he was sixth, with eight laps to go. His 42nd lap was the fastest of the race (1m 53.067s, 137.86 mph) and closed him to within 1.4s of the Williams but, as I always say, catching is one thing, passing quite another. Damon stayed ahead by 0.7s to take fifth place and two valuable points. Not nearly as bad as it might have been, for at one time he had been convinced that Villeneuve was going to win while he scored no points.

Well done Michael, though! He had now

Johnny Herbert (right) got all the way to the first corner before his team-mate hit him. Gerhard Berger (below) engaged in an energetic late-race pursuit of Damon Hill (bottom). To his chagrin, the Austrian just failed to catch the World Championship leader.

"Even if we were not quicker than the Williams, we were able to keep at their pace and won by doing everything right"

Michael Schumacher

won as many races for Ferrari in 1996 as Berger and Alesi combined over the past two years, and he had single-handedly achieved the team's modest but realistic target for the season. "Even if we were not quicker than the Williams, we were able to keep at their pace and won by doing everything right - the set-up, the strategy and the pit stops."

Ferrari's home race at Monza was next, and with genuine prospects of a third win the atmosphere would be even more frenetic than usual. Especially as Damon Hill could clinch his first World Championship there, even though Villeneuve's Belgian victory had reduced his lead to 13 points. But before then he was to suffer a devastating blow delivered, of all people, by Frank Williams.

FERRARI

Is this the long-awaited revival at last? Using new seven-speed gearbox for first time, Schumacher second fastest on Friday morning despite colossal off at Fagnes corner at over 100 mph. This virtually destroys car and badly bruises Michael's right knee (very lucky it wasn't much worse). Benefiting from supreme fitness, is OK on Saturday and qualifies third, 1.2s off pace, coping with "understeer into corners and oversteer out." But is happy to have out-qualified the Benettons and McLarens. Passes Hill at start and fights for lead with Villeneuve until first stop on lap 14, which coincides with appearance of Safety Car following Verstappen crash. Down to third, but ahead of Villeneuve after Jacques' stop, lap 15. Into lead after completion of first pit stops, lap 24. Loses it to Villeneuve at second stop, lap 30, but excitingly regains it by passing Jacques, lap 33, as he exits pits after his second stop. Enthralling battle continues until lap 40, when Villeneuve settles for second. A superb third Belgian GP win for Schumacher, who has now won as many races for Ferrari in 1996 as both its drivers did in the previous two seasons. Irvine continues to struggle with the F310 (not helped by his continued lack of testing). Qualifies ninth and retires from 13th, lap 30, after second pit stop, when gearbox again gives up - Eddie's ninth DNF from 13 races. Nevertheless a very important victory for Maranello for, unlike Spain, it was not all down to Schumacher's brilliance. "Today we were at the same level as Williams," says team boss Jean Todt. "Now we must do all we can to win some more."

BENETTON-RENAULT

Gerhard Berger fastest in both Friday sessions on circuit he loves, but unhappy with set-up on Saturday and qualifies fifth after rain ruins what would have been his quickest lap. Passed by Hakkinen at start, and runs sixth until lap 13. Loses time when Safety Car exit compromises his planned first stop. Spins down to 14th and last but one, when trying to pass Irvine, lap 19. Recovers brilliantly with a series of fastest laps including best of race (1m 53.067s, 137.76 mph). Gains seven places and catches fifth-placed Damon Hill on last lap. Finishes sixth, 0.7s behind. Alesi has to switch to spare car in qualifying after fuel system problem stops race car. Starts seventh. Benefits from Safety Car appearance to pass Berger at Gerhard's first pit stop. Fourth after second round of stops and stays there until end, dropping to fourth in championship, one point behind Schumacher.

WILLIAMS-RENAULT

Jacques Villeneuve vastly impressed by Spa-Francorchamps circuit which is new to him but which he has learned on computer game! Again demonstrates ability to master new tracks quickly by being on pace after only 17 laps. On new tyres is fastest by astounding 1.7s on Saturday morning, and then brilliantly achieves second F1 pole of his career. Takes lead at start and battles with Schumacher for 14 laps. Misunderstands crucial radio call into pits when Safety Car comes out, stops a lap late and is passed by Schumacher. Back into lead, lap 30, at Schumacher's second stop, but loses it as rejoins track after own second stop, lap 33. Pushes hard, but unable to pass Schumacher and settles for second. Hill thwarted by rain on best qualifying lap and starts second, beaten by Villeneuve for the first time since Melbourne. On damp side of track, has another poor start in spare car (after spinning race car in warm-up and running backwards in forward gear) and is passed by Schumacher and Coulthard. Entering pit lane for first stop, lap 15, is told to stay out due to Villeneuve mix-up. Stops on lap 16, rejoining 13th out of 15. Recovers superbly to fifth by lap 30. Pushes hard after lap 34 second stop but finishes fifth, only 0.7s ahead of charging Gerhard Berger. For once, Damon happy to have been beaten by Schumacher, whose victory denies Villeneuve four invaluable points. By Williams' standards, a disappointing race but an exciting result for Formula One with Hill/Villeneuve championship gap reduced to 13 points.

McLAREN-MERCEDES

Very strong paddock rumours that McLaren and long-standing mega-sponsor Marlboro are to part company. After promising Friday/Saturday free sessions, using new aerodynamically-profiled front suspension, Coulthard and Hakkinen qualify disappointed fourth and sixth due to rain (Coulthard ahead for first time since Monaco). Both start well, passing Hill to third and Berger to fifth.

During first stops David and Mika run first and second, laps 15-21, but benefit of one-stop strategy lost when Safety Car emerges and field bunches up behind them. After rivals' second stops completed, lap 35, MH and DC third and fifth, but Coulthard spins out lap 38 due to handling problems. Hakkinen finishes third, convinced he could have won but for Safety Car intervention.

LIGIER-MUGEN HONDA

With major understeer, neither Panis nor Diniz able to exploit new-evolution V10 and start lowly 14th and 15th. Panis out at notorious first corner, La Source, after being hit by Barrichello. Diniz hits stationary Sauber and stops for new nosecone, lap 15, before retiring from last but one with misfire, lap 23.

JORDAN-PEUGEOT

New chassis for Brundle and new wings for both cars. Martin eighth on grid, 2.4s down, and Barrichello 10th. Revised warm-up set-up effects major improvement, with Brundle now less than a second slower than Villeneuve. Barrichello crowded by both Saubers at start and damages front suspension. Stops at end of first lap for new track rod but handling ruined and retires for safety reasons, lap 30, after being lapped twice. "At a high speed track like this you're not going to get anywhere except into a big accident." Safety Car obliges Brundle to stop twice instead of intended once. Seventh at second stop, lap 31, but retires when engine fails, lap 35. "Strategy right: performance good: result zero," says downcast Eddie Jordan.

SAUBER-FORD

Cosworth produces further-revised Ford V10 with more power. Both drivers impressed by car's improved balance. Frentzen heartening fifth fastest on Saturday morning, but qualifying spoilt by rain in final 15 minutes and he starts 11th. Herbert has engine problem on Saturday morning and loses valuable setting-up time. With substantial understeer qualifies 12th, 0.8s slower than Frentzen. But two days' hard work destroyed within seconds of start when Heinz-Harald and Johnny collide into instant retirement (same coming-together also eliminates Panis and, later, Barrichello).

TWR ARROWS-HART

With spare car now being used to test Bridgestone tyres for 1997 debut, only two cars again at Spa, both with usual built-in heavy understeer. Much-revised rear damper settings substantially reduce handling problem, but Verstappen 16th on grid, Rosset 18th. Verstappen comes into pits on lap 11 complaining of sticking throttle, but no problem found and Jos rejoins only to have a massive off exiting Stavelot at some 140 mph. Medical check reveals no serious injuries. Need to clear track brings out Safety Car. Rosset damages front wing in collision with Katayama at start and changes nosecone at lap 14 stop. Hammers on and finishes ninth of 10, one lap down.

TYRRELL-YAMAHA

Mika Salo loses half Friday morning session due to minor oil-on-exhaust fire, but subsequent times seem unaffected. Qualifies 13th, 3.5s off pace. Katayama, who loves challenging Spa circuit, is faster than Mika on Friday but has two engines fail on Saturday and qualifies 17th, 4.8s down, after resigned mechanics effect impressive Yamaha-change in only 38 minutes. Happily things much better in race, with both drivers finishing well up. Salo avoids first corner pile-up and advances to ninth by lap 5. Straight into pits when Safety Car comes out. Runs sixth, laps 16-22, and a fine fourth laps 25-28. Is caught and passed by Hakkinen, Hill and Berger to finish excellent seventh. Katayama drives untroubled race to finish eighth, 40s behind Mika. Team and Yamaha delighted at reversal of reliability fortunes.

MINARDI-FORD

Pedro Lamy struggles with set-up and also has wheel-rim fail in qualifying. Switches to spare car and starts 19th, 6.3s off pace. Races at rear of field ahead of Rosset, but has fuel-rig problem at second stop, lap 30, and comes in again for top-up, lap 38. Finishes 10th and last, one lap down. Giovanni Lavaggi has stuck-throttle problem on Friday afternoon and loses set-up time. Then has engine give up on last run and fails by 0.2s to qualify within 107 per cent of pole time. Appeals for permission to start, but this refused by stewards. Seems a harsh judgement, but rules are rules.

FIA FORMULA 1 WORLD CHAMPIONSHIP

RACE 13
BELGIUM
25 August 1996

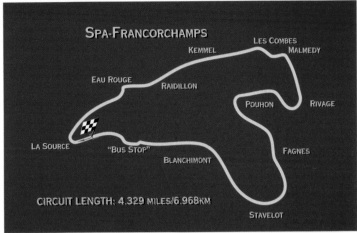

SPA-FRANCORCHAMPS

KEMMEL · LES COMBES · MALMEDY
EAU ROUGE · RAIDILLON · POUHON · RIVAGE
LA SOURCE · "BUS STOP" · BLANCHIMONT · FAGNES · RIVAGE · STAVELOT

CIRCUIT LENGTH: 4.329 MILES/6.968KM

STARTING GRID

	VILLENEUVE 1m 50.574s
HILL 1m 50.980s	
	SCHUMACHER 1m 51.778s
COULTHARD 1m 51.884s	
	BERGER 1m 51.960s
HAKKINEN 1m 52.318s	
	ALESI 1m 52.354s
BRUNDLE 1m 52.977s	
	IRVINE 1m 53.043s
BARRICHELLO 1m 53.152s	
	FRENTZEN 1m 53.199s
HERBERT 1m 53.993s	
	SALO 1m 54.095s
PANIS 1m 54.220s	
	DINIZ 1m 54.700s
VERSTAPPEN 1m 55.150s	
	KATAYAMA 1m 55.371s
ROSSET 1m 56.286s	
	LAMY 1m 56.830s

Did not qualify
LAVAGGI
(Minardi M195B)
1m 58.597s

RACE CLASSIFICATION

Pos	Driver	Nat	Car	Laps	Time
1	Michael Schumacher	D	Ferrari F310-Ferrari V10	44	1h 28m 15.125s
2	Jacques Villeneuve	CDN	Williams FW18-Renault V10	44	+5.602s
3	Mika Hakkinen	SF	McLaren MP4/11B-Mercedes V10	44	+15.710s
4	Jean Alesi	F	Benetton B196-Renault V10	44	+19.125s
5	Damon Hill	GB	Williams FW18-Renault V10	44	+29.179s
6	Gerhard Berger	A	Benetton B196-Renault V10	44	+29.896s
7	Mika Salo	SF	Tyrrell 024-Yamaha V10	44	+1m 0.754s
8	Ukyo Katayama	J	Tyrrell 024-Yamaha V10	44	+1m 40.227s
9	Ricardo Rosset	BR	Footwork FA17-Hart V8		+1 lap
10	Pedro Lamy	P	Minardi M195B-Ford V8		+1 lap

Retirements	Nat	Car	Lap	Reason
David Coulthard	GB	McLaren MP4/11B-Mercedes V10	37	Accident
Martin Brundle	GB	Jordan 196-Peugeot V10	34	Engine
Eddie Irvine	GB	Ferrari F310-Ferrari V10	29	Gearbox
Rubens Barrichello	BR	Jordan 196-Peugeot V10	29	Handling
Pedro Diniz	BR	Ligier JS43-Mugen Honda V10	22	Misfire
Jos Verstappen	NL	Footwork FA17-Hart V8	11	Accident
Olivier Panis	F	Ligier JS43-Mugen Honda V10	0	Accident
Johnny Herbert	GB	Sauber C15-Ford V10	0	Accident
Heinz-Harald Frentzen	D	Sauber C15-Ford V10	0	Accident

FASTEST LAP Gerhard Berger 1m 53.067s lap 42 (137.839mph)

DRIVERS' CHAMPIONSHIP

Damon Hill	81
Jacques Villeneuve	68
Michael Schumacher	39
Jean Alesi	38
Mika Hakkinen	23
David Coulthard	18
Gerhard Berger	17
Olivier Panis	13
Rubens Barrichello	12
Eddie Irvine	9
Heinz-Harald Frentzen	6
Mika Salo	5
Johnny Herbert	4
Martin Brundle	3
Jos Verstappen	1
Pedro Diniz	1

CONSTRUCTORS' CUP

Williams-Renault	149
Benetton-Renault	55
Ferrari	48
McLaren-Mercedes	41
Jordan-Peugeot	15
Ligier-Mugen Honda	14
Sauber-Ford	10
Tyrrell-Yamaha	5
Footwork-Hart	1

Results and Data © FIA 1996

After his breathtaking opening lap, Hill was streaking away (below) from Alesi and co...until lap six, when a pile of Goodyears did for him. Fortunately for Damon, a similar rubber stack did for his team-mate, too. Right, the upshot was yet another visit to the top of the podium for Michael Schumacher.

Everyone looks forward to Monza. With its history, its emotional atmosphere, the memories of the greats who have raced there, the fact that it is one of Ferrari's home tracks and that it's awash with good wine (and food!)...it is always a great place to be. This year though there was added drama and intrigue. Damon Hill had been brusquely told by Williams that he was to be replaced by Heinz-Harald Frentzen in 1997, while McLaren and Marlboro had announced that they were to terminate their tremendously successful 23-year-long partnership. The paddock was a hotbed of rumour and speculation, tinged with outrage on behalf of Damon.

It was a mighty tough blow for Hill, who was already under terrific pressure, knowing that he could wrap up the world championship at Monza. Realising that Frank Williams didn't think he was good enough to carry the torch, despite the fact that he had won 20 Grands Prix for the team, was

a major psychological setback, compounded by the fact that wherever he went he was besieged by the clamouring media. His demeanour was exemplary though. "I am obviously disappointed because I think I have achieved a lot and have a lot to offer, but I am totally focused on the championship and the best thing I can do is to win here."

Inevitably there was cynical speculation that, since Williams and Renault would naturally want one of their cars to carry the coveted Number One in 1997, Hill might not get as much support as Villeneuve. But anyone who knew the team immediately rejected the thought.

The first thing that Damon had to do to achieve his goal at Monza was to get pole position, and that wouldn't be easy. Formula One rookie Jacques Villeneuve, his only championship rival, knew the place well from Williams tests and from his Formula Three days. Plus, Monza was where Ferrari and Schumacher had honed

the F310 with thousands of kilometres of testing, and Benetton-Renault expected to go well in low-downforce configuration (as did McLaren-Mercedes). Not forgetting Jordan, whose Peugeot V10 had as much grunt as anything, if not more.

Schumacher was fastest on Friday, with Hakkinen top man on Saturday morning, a tenth of a second faster than Hill, but it was the afternoon qualifying hour that mattered. Things hadn't gone Villeneuve's way in the morning sessions, with a lump of concrete assaulting his Williams before he was crowded off the, track at 190 mph by Pedro Diniz. The result was that he had lost 10 vital laps of setting-up, whereas Hill had got his car beautifully balanced.

With five minutes to go, just 0.3s covered the top five when Damon raced out for his final run. It was 0.3s faster than anyone else's and an absolutely stunning lap. Pole position for the eighth time in 1996: "Particularly satisfying for a number of reasons, which I think you know," said a

very restrained Hill, who must have felt like sticking two fingers in the air. He was where it mattered most, but had no cause to relax. Villeneuve was alongside him on what was the Williams team's seventh front row monopoly of the season.

With Schumacher, Hakkinen, Coulthard and Alesi making up the top six, and only a second covering them, the opening laps looked like being terrific. As indeed they were.

Monza was bulging on Sunday. With the optimistic scent of a Ferrari win in their nostrils, the excitable hordes of scarlet-clad tifosi were in full cry. Schumacher may be German and Irvine, seventh on the grid, British, but they were driving Ferraris and could be victorious. That would do.

There was something new for the drivers: tyre walls at the major corners to prevent them hopping the kerbs. With flexible plastic bollards failing to do the job, they were an emergency measure after Villeneuve's concrete-molestation, but they had been approved by Damon Hill and Gerhard Berger. They were to ruin the race.

No bodged start for Damon this time. Off like a scalded cat, but hot-wheels Alesi was even quicker. Into the lead from the third row before the narrow Rettifilio chicane, only a couple of hundred metres after the start. Villeneuve tried to outdrag Hill but failed and, off line, by-passed the first tyre wall, Hakkinen passed him and Schumacher dropped to sixth behind Coulthard. But who said Hill lacked aggression? He was all over Alesi, thrust past the Benetton at the second Lesmo corner and rebuffed a fierce attack by Jean at the Ascari chicane. Behind them mayhem broke out as their pursuers assaulted the tyres.

Hakkinen hit one which had been dislodged by Alesi and Coulthard clouted a pile which had been moved by Villeneuve.

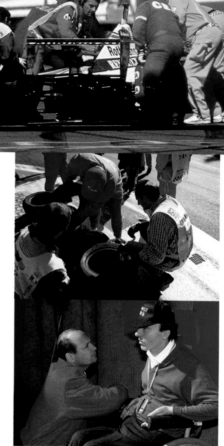

Damon Hill contemplates having a go at race marshalling (above).

The tyre walls which led to his demise were a source of contention all weekend, and required maintenance more frequently than the average British motorway (centre left).

Ron Dennis and Frank Williams (below left):

The Scot was out instantly with broken suspension. Hakkinen had to come in for a new nose and Villeneuve had bent a track rod. Magic for Hill! But not for long. Driving brilliantly, he pulled away from Alesi and on lap six, as he accelerated out of the Rettifilio, he was nearly two seconds ahead of the Benetton. Seconds later he was out of the race. "I made a mistake and hit the tyres. I made a very good start and was very pleased with the way things were going but I can't blame anyone else but myself for what happened." Typically honest, but now Hill faced the anguish of expecting Villeneuve to win and decimate his championship lead.

It wasn't to be. Unbeknown to Damon, the Canadian was in trouble. "When I clipped the tyres it bent something on the front and the car changed completely." On lap six, with Alesi now in the lead, the Ferraris of Schumacher and Irvine were second and third and the tifosi were ecstatic. Michael was bound to pass Alesi wasn't he? Well, he wasn't actually. Schumacher had started with a heavy fuel load to give him the maximum flexibility for his sole stop; although he could stay with the Benetton, he couldn't pass it. He just had to hope that Jean would be stopping before he did, and that he could then speed up with a clear track ahead to build a big enough lead to get out of the pit lane in front of Alesi. Which is exactly what happened. But not before the unfortunate Irvine rumpled his suspension on the Rettifilio tyre wall and joined the retirees.

When Alesi stopped on lap 31,

Villeneuve had already been in twice for tyres, had been lapped and was ninth out of the 11 who were still running. Hill was on his knees in the garage, praying it would stay that way as Schumacher went for it. The plan was working. On lap 30 Michael had been 0.6s behind Alesi; on lap 34 after his stop he was 4.6s ahead. All he had to do now was keep going. But would he be able to in the notoriously brittle Ferrari?

We would see. Meantime there had been plenty going on behind him. Heinz-Harald Frentzen had blotted his shining image by crashing his Sauber; Mika Salo had the umpteenth Yamaha failure of the season; and, wonder of wonders, Pedro Diniz was in sixth place. To be fair, the much-maligned Brazilian was driving an excellent race, had passed a troubled Johnny Herbert's Sauber fair and square and had kept the flying Mika Hakkinen at bay for 13 laps. No mean achievement, to put it mildly, because Mika's recovery had been superb. Stationary in the pits for 14s on lap four, whilst his new nose was fitted, he had dropped to last but had now

> "There was something new for the drivers: tyre walls at the major corners to prevent them hopping the kerbs. . . They were to ruin the race"

Villeneuve's carelessness with tyres brought a premature end to the hopes of David Coulthard, on a weekend when the McLarens were in good shape.

"Despite the fact that Damon had lost a critical race he had seemed certain to win, he was one of the happiest and most relieved people there"

Rumours in Italy suggested that Gerhard Berger might finish a race one day. Gearbox hydraulics failure brought him to an early stop (above). Former Ferrari favourite Alesi initially headed successor Schumacher (right), before the German took control; barring a Ferrari 1-2, the crowd could not have wished for a better reason to invade the track.

fought his way up to third behind Schumacher and Alesi. Admittedly he was 44s behind the Ferrari, but he was looking good for his third podium of the year after a magnificently gritty drive.

Schumacher nearly joined the Rubber Club on lap 39. "They told me to take it easy, to save the brakes and tyres, so I was driving at about 90 per cent and lost concentration. I hit the tyre barrier (yes, it was the Rettifilio again) and was very lucky not to damage the car." Indeed he was. Another two millimetres to the left and it would have been goodbye Michael. They say it isn't enough to be good in life; you need to be lucky too. Well Michael certainly had it going for him.

On lap 33, with 20 to go, Schumacher, Alesi and Hakkinen were firmly fixed in the top three places, but fourth and fifth were by no means settled between Martin Brundle and his Jordan team-mate Rubens Barrichello. Jordan really needed points to consolidate its fifth place in the constructors' championship, and both the team's drivers were scoring. They had been virtu-

ally nose to tail from the second lap, having a battle royal. Brundle: "I was having to be a bit rude at times to keep Rubens behind."

Now the orders went out to hold station. "I couldn't afford to have two drivers fighting and run the risk of them taking each other out," said Eddie Jordan.

With the tifosi's breath collectively held, Michael Schumacher not only raced reliably onwards but even put up the fastest (record) lap with only three to go (1m 26.110s, 154.67 mph). He won his first race for Ferrari on Italian soil and his third of the season by 18s from Alesi with Hakkinen third, over a minute behind after a scintillating drive. It is a tradition at Monza for the crowd to swarm over the barriers and netting, invade the track and joyously gather under the high verandah

podium and it looked as though all 160,000 of them were there to acclaim their German hero. "Never in my life have I experienced anything as incredible as this," said Michael. "With all the people going crazy below me it was fantastic to see a sea of red! I have to say it is right to let the public come (on the track) and celebrate with Ferrari on this unforgettable day." Everyone hoped the FIA would think so, too, for Michael more than deserved the adulation. He had made the whole of Italy's day.

Monza had lived up to its reputation for drama and excitement, but despite the fact that Damon Hill had lost a critical race he had seemed certain to win, he was one of the happiest and most relieved people there. With two races to go and 20 points to be won, he was actually in a stronger position for the World Championship than he had been when he arrived in Italy. Going into Portugal the gap would still be 13 points; if he finished ahead of Villeneuve at Estoril, he would be Number One in 1997.

Then he could raise his fingers to the men who had felt he wasn't up to it.

Despite his imaginative approach to Monza's chicanes, Diniz finished sixth. Frentzen takes the conventional route, for now.

FERRARI

"Our objective is one car on the podium and the other in the points," says team boss Jean Todt, but Michael Schumacher does much better than that. Using seven-speed gearbox he is fastest on Friday but drops to third on grid, with car unsettled by Saturday's windy conditions. Down to sixth after poor start, passed by Alesi, Hakkinen and Coulthard. To fourth, lap two, and third, lap three, avoiding tyres which molest Hakkinen, Villeneuve and Coulthard. Then second, lap six, after Hill also hits tyres. With heavy fuel load to maximise pit stop flexibility, sits behind Alesi in hope that Jean will stop before he does - which happens. Takes lead, lap 31, when Jean comes in and, with clear track, puts in two cracking laps which enable him to stop, lap 33, and rejoin still ahead by nearly five seconds. With car running perfectly increases lead to over nine seconds, but is lucky to get away with clipping Rettifilio tyre wall on lap 39. Told to take it easy in later stages of race and backs off, but still sets record lap with only three to go (1m 26.110s, 154.67 mph). Wins first GP for Ferrari on Italian soil by 18s to give team its first Monza victory since 1988. "Never in my life have I experienced anything as incredible as this. Up on the podium with all the people going crazy below me it was fantastic to witness a sea of red!" Not so good for Eddie Irvine. Happy enough with seventh on grid in six-speed car, although concerned about handling. Up to excellent third, lap six, avoiding tyre mayhem and stays there until lap 23 when, 13.6s behind Schumacher and due to stop, hits tyre wall and breaks front left suspension. Eddie's 10th retirement from 14 races. "We will enjoy our triumph for a few hours, and tomorrow morning at eight we will start work to improve still further," says Jean Todt.

BENETTON-RENAULT

Another good race for Alesi (rumoured to be moving to Jordan in 1997, maybe to be replaced by Hill), but another bad one for Berger. Jean goes off into Parabolica gravel trap on Friday and loses valuable set-up time. Qualifies sixth, concerned about brakes. Gerhard much happier with car after changing style to drive more smoothly, but spins on opening qualifying lap and has to drive spare to take eighth on grid. Has big off leaving pit lane during Sunday warm-up, allegedly going "too-fast, too-soon on cold tyres". Cynics suspect breakage. Alesi makes another mind-bending start, rocketing past Coulthard, Hakkinen, Schumacher, Villeneuve and Hill into lead. Fights to retain first place at Roggia and Lesmo bends but yields to very forceful Damon. Takes lead lap six, when Hill hits tyres. Makes late stop, lap 31, loses lead to Schumacher and fails to regain it when Michael stops two laps later. Finishes second, 18s down, for eighth 1996 podium. Also sets second fastest lap of race. Berger retires from fifth, lap five, with gearbox hydraulics failure. "Very frustrating, because I was overtaking Villeneuve and had a good set-up which would have made for an interesting race."

WILLIAMS-RENAULT

Formula One in uproar over Williams' decision to replace Damon Hill with Heinz-Harald Frentzen in 1997. Shocked Hill under colossal media pressure, but responds superbly by taking brilliant eighth pole position of year, 0.3s faster than team- mate Jacques Villeneuve, who breaks left front wing by hitting loose lump of concrete at Roggia chicane on Saturday morning. Then loses set-up time after being squeezed off track at 190 mph by Pedro Diniz. Team's seventh grid one/two of year. Hill makes excellent start but loses lead to super-starting Alesi. Forcefully passes Jean at Lesmo bends and then repels thrusting attack at Ascari chicane. Builds two-second lead but hits tyres exiting Rettifilio, lap six, and retires from race which could have clinched world championship. Typically makes no excuses: "I made a mistake and can't blame anyone but myself." But 13-point championship lead unaffected as Villeneuve hits tyres on first lap and deranges front suspension. Has to make three tyre stops instead of single one planned and finishes seventh, one lap down, out of points.

McLAREN-MERCEDES

McLaren and Marlboro announce parting after 23 very successful years together. West cigarettes to becomes main team sponsor in 1997. Hakkinen fastest on Saturday in car which suits Monza, but qualifies disappointed fourth. Coulthard starts fifth after losing 50m of preparation time by going off on Friday. Tyre-wall shambles destroys realistic race-winning hopes of both drivers. Coulthard hits tyres

moved by Villeneuve on lap two and retires. Hakkinen hits tyre dislodged by Alesi, lap three, and stops for new nose cone. After losing 14s makes superb recovery and is up to third at lap 32 pit stop. Retains place to finish third, but deserved better.

LIGIER-MUGEN HONDA

Powerful Mugen engine suits Monza but Panis qualifies frustrated 11th, slowed by traffic. Diniz earns wrath of Villeneuve by squeezing Jacques off at 190 mph on Saturday and also gets fist-shaking from Gerhard Berger for baulking. Qualifies 14th in spare car after parking race car with fuel leak. Panis starts last after stalling on formation lap when button-brake jams on. Hit by Katayama, lap three, and retires with broken wheel. Diniz drives well and passes Herbert to sixth, lap 18. Amazingly keeps recovering Hakkinen behind him for 13 laps until lap 25 pit stop and finishes creditable sixth, one lap down.

JORDAN-PEUGEOT

Amidst rumours that both drivers out for 1997, to be replaced by Alesi and Ralf Schumacher, Martin Brundle starts ninth, outqualifying Rubens Barrichello, 10th, who loses an hour by going off on Friday morning. Good Monza for both men, who race each other whole way. Rubens loses two places at start with clutch problem but both in points from lap six, with Brundle fifth, forcefully maintaining his position. "I had to be a bit rude at times!" Barrichello ordered to hold position to avoid collision and loss of points. Martin finishes fourth, best-yet in Jordan, with Rubens fifth, 0.2s behind.

SAUBER-FORD

Heinz-Harald Frentzen the non-stop focus of media frenzy after Williams announces he is to replace Damon Hill in 1997. H-H reports latest Ford V10 evolution has better power and torque, but spins on last lap of qualifying and, only 13th, is narrowly outqualified by Johnny Herbert. Makes bad start but catches ninth-placed Herbert, lap four, only to hit tyres, lap eight, and retire. "All three Williams drivers messed-up today!" says Frank Williams. Johnny flat-spots tyres braking to avoid Irvine at start, which slows car until lap 29 pit stop. Is then catching sixth-placed Diniz when oil pressure fails on last lap. Classified ninth, two laps down.

TWR ARROWS-HART

Jos Verstappen fully recovered after major Spa crash, except for sore neck. With major set-up changes which largely overcome season-long understeer, qualifies 15th, four places ahead of team-mate Ricardo Rosset. For once, Jos has no major problems and drives excellent race, albeit with failing brakes towards end. Takes it carefully at start, avoids tyre-wall shambles and is seventh by lap 11. With unusual two-stop strategy is down to 10th after first stop, lap 17, and to ninth after second, lap 33. Finishes for only third time in 14 races, in eighth place, one lap down. Rosset races at rear of field until retiring, lap 37, after hitting tyres and breaking steering arm.

TYRRELL-YAMAHA

After unusually trouble-free Friday, Katayama and Salo both suffer from being first on track in qualifying by picking up leaves and overheating delicate Yamaha engines. Ukyo qualifies 16th, four seconds off pace, with Salo 17th after having to switch to spare car set up for Katayama following engine damage. Mika races strongly up to 10th by lap eight, only to retire on lap 10 with another failed engine. Katayama collides with Panis, lap three, and stops for new nose. Rejoins, last and lapped, but finishes 10th, two laps down. Tyrrell mighty fed up with Yamaha engine failures and believed to be trying for Ford V10-power in 1997 (whilst TWR-Arrows is rumoured to be angling for Yamaha engines!).

MINARDI-FORD

Minardi just as frustrated with its Ford V8s as Tyrrell is with its Yamahas. At circuit where plenty of horses are essential, both Pedro Lamy and Giovanni Lavaggi do well to qualify, lining up 18th and 20th, sandwiching Rosset's V8 Hart-powered TWR-Arrows. But close for Lavaggi. Makes grid by 0.2s at Monza after failing to get on it at Spa by same fraction. Then both out of race with engine failures, Lavaggi from last but one on lap six, Lamy from last on lap 13. "There is no point in going on like this," says Gian Carlo Minardi, who is said to be trying to get Mugen engines for 1997 via new major shareholder Flavio Briatore.

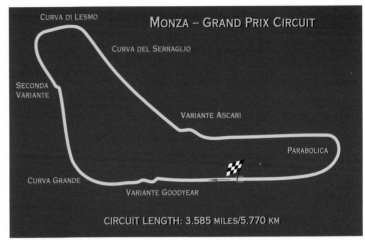

FORMULA 1 WORLD CHAMPIONSHIP

14

RACE

ITALY

8 September 1996

MONZA – GRAND PRIX CIRCUIT

CURVA DI LESMO
CURVA DEL SERRAGLIO
SECONDA VARIANTE
VARIANTE ASCARI
PARABOLICA
CURVA GRANDE
VARIANTE GOODYEAR

CIRCUIT LENGTH: 3.585 MILES/5.770 KM

STARTING GRID

HILL 1m 24.204s	**VILLENEUVE** 1m 24.521s
SCHUMACHER 1m 24.781s	**HAKKINEN** 1m 24.939s
COULTHARD 1m 24.976s	**ALESI** 1m 25.201s
IRVINE 1m 25.226s	**BERGER** 1m 25.470s
BRUNDLE 1m 26.037s	**BARRICHELLO** 1m 26.194s
PANIS 1m 26.206s	**HERBERT** 1m 26.345s
FRENTZEN 1m 26.505s	**DINIZ** 1m 26.726s
VERSTAPPEN 1m 27.270s	**KATAYAMA** 1m 28.234s
SALO 1m 28.472s	**LAMY** 1m 28.933s
ROSSET 1m 29.181s	**LAVAGGI** 1m 29.833s

RACE CLASSIFICATION

Pos	Driver	Nat	Car	Laps	Time
1	Michael Schumacher	D	Ferrari F310-Ferrari V10	53	1h 17m 43.632s
2	Jean Alesi	F	Benetton B196-Renault V10	53	+18.265s
3	Mika Hakkinen	SF	McLaren MP4/11B-Mercedes V10	53	+1m 06.635s
4	Martin Brundle	GB	Jordan 196-Peugeot V10	53	+1m 25.217s
5	Rubens Barrichello	BR	Jordan 196-Peugeot V10	53	+1m 25.475s
6	Pedro Diniz	BR	Ligier JS43-Mugen Honda V10		+1 lap
7	Jacques Villeneuve	CDN	Williams FW18-Renault V10		+1 lap
8	Jos Verstappen	NL	Footwork FA17-Hart V8		+1 lap
9	Johnny Herbert	GB	Sauber C15-Ford V10		+2 laps DNF/Eng
10	Ukyo Katayama	J	Tyrrell 024-Yamaha V10		+2 laps

Retirements	Nat	Car	Lap	Reason
Ricardo Rosset	BR	Footwork FA17-Hart V8	36	Accident
Eddie Irvine	GB	Ferrari F310-Ferrari V10	23	Accident
Pedro Lamy	P	Minardi M195B-Ford V8	12	Engine
Mika Salo	SF	Tyrrell 024-Yamaha V10	9	Engine
Heinz-Harald Frentzen	D	Sauber C15-Ford V10	7	Accident
Damon Hill	GB	Williams FW18-Renault V10	5	Accident
Giovanni Lavaggi	I	Minardi M195B-Ford V8	5	Engine
Gerhard Berger	A	Benetton B196-Renault V10	4	Electrics/gearbox
Olivier Panis	F	Ligier JS43-Mugen Honda V10	2	Collision damage
David Coulthard	GB	McLaren MP4/11B- Mercedes V10	1	Suspension

FASTEST LAP Michael Schumacher 1m 26.110s lap 50 (149.874mph)

DRIVERS' CHAMPIONSHIP

Damon Hill	81
Jacques Villeneuve	68
Michael Schumacher	49
Jean Alesi	44
Mika Hakkinen	27
David Coulthard	18
Gerhard Berger	17
Rubens Barrichello	14
Olivier Panis	13
Eddie Irvine	9
Heinz-Harald Frentzen	6
Martin Brundle	6
Mika Salo	5
Johnny Herbert	4
Pedro Diniz	2
Jos Verstappen	1

CONSTRUCTORS' CUP

Williams-Renault	149
Benetton-Renault	61
Ferrari	58
McLaren-Mercedes	45
Jordan-Peugeot	20
Ligier-Mugen Honda	15
Sauber-Ford	10
Tyrrell-Yamaha	5
Footwork-Hart	1

Results and Data © FIA 1996

Estoril was a bit of a tear-jerker for me. After 48 years with the BBC, it was to be the last European Grand Prix I would be commentating on for the Corporation. Formula One threw an unprecedented party in the paddock to mark the occasion: Ken Tyrrell, Damon Hill, Martin Brundle, Johnny Herbert and David Coulthard all made touching speeches, and Bernie Ecclestone presented us with a specially commissioned gold and silver trophy. It was a very moving occasion, and I don't mind admitting I was nearly in tears when I made my own speech.

It was an equally stressful weekend for Damon Hill, too. If he beat his team-mate Jacques Villeneuve he would be world champion. . . and in a much stronger position to negotiate his future as an ex-Williams driver. But he didn't. His defeat by the only man who could deny him his target meant that the 1996 championship was going down to the wire in Japan.

Estoril is an excellent and popular circuit. Situated on the rocky Atlantic coastline near the Portuguese holiday town of Cascais, it is notable for its long, high-G corners which put terrific demands on the tyres and, therefore, race strategy. This time Jacques Villeneuve was no stranger to the circuit. He had done hundreds of miles of testing here and knew it as well as Damon did.

It didn't look as though the Williams men were going to have any real opposition in the race, though. The Ferraris would suffer from being hard on their tyres; Benetton had yet to offer a real challenge to Williams, and McLaren and Jordan had still to get their competitive acts together. All the signs were that it was going to be a straight fight for the top honour between Frank's men. And so it was.

Michael Schumacher was fastest on Friday, but that didn't mean much. Friday times do not count for the grid and the teams spend the two sessions experiment-

ing with different set-ups and fuel loads to get things right for the race. Saturday is the day that matters. Michael was quickest again in the morning, a mere 0.009 seconds faster than Hill.

That was to be a very significant margin at Estoril, because it was that minute difference which decided pole position. It had been wet in the morning, and black clouds were threatening when qualifying began. Everyone poured out of the pit lane to set a quick time, in case of rain. Eddie Irvine put

Right. Jacques Villeneuve's pass of Schumacher around the outside of the last corner was extraordinary, but unfortunately photographers aren't allowed to stand there, so here's a shot of the Canadian being a touch less spectacular. Main pic. Believe it or not but this grand stand once had a roof.

End of an era: Murray receives a trophy to mark the conclusion of the BBC's F1 deal in Europe. Damon Hill, Martin Brundle (tipped to join him in the commentary booth, if he doesn't remain in F1), David Coulthard and Johnny Herbert shared the cakes and champagne.

"Things were looking grim for the Canadian as his championship rival pulled away in the lead"

in the first decent lap, 1m 21.362s. Villeneuve was next, 1m 21.317s. Then Hill, 1m 21.104s. But Damon hadn't finished. A crushing 1m 20.330s put things beyond doubt - by a whisker.

Villeneuve's final lap was that 0.009s slower. So Williams had its eighth front row lockout of the year, with super-starting Jean Alesi's Benetton third ahead of Schumacher, Berger and Irvine.

And then there was incredible symmetry. The McLarens of Hakkinen and Coulthard on row four, the Jordans of Barrichello and Brundle on row five, Frentzen and Herbert's Saubers on row six and the Tyrrells of Salo and Katayama on row seven. But Hill and Villeneuve were over 0.6s faster than anyone else, and the start was going to be critical.

"I don't want to disturb the championship race in front of me," said Alesi, but when the lights went out he made another of his meteoric departures, catapulting past Villeneuve and nearly taking Hill too. Only really assertive driving kept Damon ahead, whereas a slow-starting Villeneuve had both Schumacher and Alesi go by him. Things were looking grim for the Canadian as his championship rival pulled away in the lead.

Lap by lap, Damon increased his advantage, as Villeneuve pressured the Ferrari in an effort to pass. On lap 16, to Schumacher's consternation, Jacques did so with a fantastic move out of the long, 180-deg right-hander which ends the lap. Before the race, Villeneuve had said he could use that corner to gain places if his Williams was set up Indy-style. "If you try

Unlike his football team Spurs, beaten 2-1 by Leicester, Ken Tyrrell's race team had one of its most reliable weekends of the year.

Irvine's Ferrari, usually seen billowing smoke from the other end, made it into the points.

it there we'll come and peel you off the Armco!" was the team's response, but Jacques prevailed and got his dividend as, tight up behind Schumacher, he raced up to lap Giovanni Lavaggi.

With Michael astern of the Minardi and expecting Villeneuve to stay where he was, Jacques pulled out and drove round the Ferrari at nearly 140 mph. Incredible. Once past, he was gone. Now for Alesi!

The Williams drivers and Michael Schumacher were all on three-stop strategies, whereas Alesi would be coming in twice. So when Hill made his first stop on lap 17, followed by Villeneuve and Schumacher a lap later, Alesi took the lead for four laps. When he stopped, both Villeneuve and Schumacher passed him so now, on lap 23, Hill led and the two Williams-Renaults were first and second, 7.1s apart with 41 laps to go. The race for victory and - possibly - the championship was on.

For the record, Schumacher and Alesi were to retain their third and fourth places to the end, except for a nine-lap switch from laps 36 to 44, on account of their different strategies.

Meanwhile, Eddie Irvine, heading for his best result since Imola, would battle successfully with Gerhard Berger's Benetton until the last corner.

Unsurprisingly, however, the main attention was on the fight for the lead. Was the championship going to be decided in Portugal or not?

On lap 21 Hill led Villeneuve by 15s, but getting past tail-enders cost him nearly six seconds on just one lap. While Villeneuve fought his way through the same traffic, Damon's lead stabilised at about nine seconds. But, as he came in for his second stop on lap 34, Jacques took the lead until he too stopped a lap later. When he rejoined, with a stop to come, a mere three seconds separated the two of them.

Now, scenting a chance to win, Villeneuve went even quicker, setting the fastest lap of the race (1m 22.873s, 117.69 mph). Down came the gap until, on lap 48, Jacques was less than two seconds adrift when Damon stopped for the third time.

As Villeneuve took the lead, he had a clear track in front of him. If he could get

in a really quick lap and follow that up with a good stop, he could get out of the pit lane ahead of Damon. But it was going to be mighty close.

Villeneuve's 49th lap was 6.5s faster than the slowing Hill's, and his stop on lap 50 was 0.8s quicker. As Damon raced past the pits a car emerged just in front of him. "I thought it was a Tyrrell, and was thinking, 'Get out of the way!' Then I saw 'Rothmans' on the rear wing and realised it was Jacques."

Villeneuve was 1.5s ahead, but all was not lost for Damon. "At first I thought I'd set about catching him, but he was flying and there was no way I could stay with him. Then the pits told me I had got a clutch problem. I'd felt a couple of bad shifts but it didn't really affect my speed."

Honest as ever, Damon. Most drivers would have made it an excuse for their

The McLarens were closely-matched all weekend. Eventually too close, as it transpired...

"I think my oval experience helped when I passed Michael and it was actually a lot of fun"

Jacques Villeneuve

defeat, but knowing he would have a nine-point lead in the championship if he stayed where he was, with only 10 to be won in Japan, he settled for second. So Jacques Villeneuve took his fourth Grand Prix victory, 20s ahead after by far his finest Formula One drive. He'd beaten his rival fair and square after an utterly brilliant performance, and thoroughly deserved his success.

"I knew I had to beat Damon by at least four points to keep a slim chance in the championship, and that is what I did today. I think my oval experience helped me when I passed Michael and it was actually a lot of fun. After that I was just fighting to be close to Damon and to try to overtake him at the pit stop, which is what happened."

Jacques made it all sound very matter of fact, as he always does, but he had every right to be elated. Damon Hill's world title was by no means a foregone conclusion.

It looked as though Damon Hill was cruising to the world title; Villeneuve then set out to prove he was merely cruising.

Time now to consider what had happened to the other top men in a race where, most unusually, there had only been four retirements. As he had predicted, the appetite of Schumacher's Ferrari for tyres had defeated him. "I couldn't go any quicker because of a lack of grip, but the strategy and pit stops were perfect." After Michael had made two stops, his team brought him in for his last at the same time as Alesi took his second stop. The Ferrari got out of the pit lane first and stayed ahead to take third place by 1.3s.

Irvine and Berger fought together for fifth for most of the race, and the issue was only settled when Gerhard tried a banzai passing move at the last corner. He hit the Ferrari and spun it round, but damaged his own suspension. Eddie rejoined, passed the Austrian on the run up to the finish line and took the two points, his first since Imola. This lifted Ferrari to within one point of second-placed Benetton in the constructors' championship. That was something else to be settled at Suzuka.

Sauber's starting grid symmetry continued to the end, with Frentzen seventh and Herbert eighth, but Jordan's didn't.Martin Brundle was ninth, but Rubens Barrichello

failed to finish what seemed likely to be his last European race for the team. For McLaren it was a case of least said, soonest mended. Hakkinen and Coulthard battled together from the start until lap 46, when they collided. As a result Mika was out, and David slumped to 13th, two laps down. Team boss Ron Dennis was vastly unimpressed. "But," he stressed, "I am confident it will not happen again."

Oh, and one other thing: neither of the Tyrrells had any real engine or other problems for the first time for a very long time. Both Salo and Katayama finished, next to each other as they had been on the grid.

Three weeks to Japan now. The last time the drivers' championship had been decided at the final race was at Adelaide in 1994. It had all ended in tears and controversy, when Schumacher and Hill had driven into each other. Hill had won brilliantly in appallingly wet conditions at Suzuka in 1994, but had gone off and failed to finish the next year. He'd better not do so again.

Anything is possible in Formula One, and if Villeneuve took a fifth win with Hill not scoring Damon would be second in the championship for the third year in succession.

FERRARI

A workmanlike result for Ferrari, but heavily defeated by superb Williams-Renault FW18, despite brilliance of Schumacher. Michael fastest on Friday with Irvine fourth, both still trying to find right set-up. "The times are meaningless as car is not right and very difficult to drive," says Irvine. Schumacher qualifies fourth, 0.9s off Hill's pole time, pessimistic about race because of certain heavy tyre wear. ``Third is the best that is realistically possible." Irvine sixth on grid, one second off pace and much happier with car after set-up changes. Schumacher passes Villeneuve at start and stays third behind Hill/Alesi until spectacularly passed by Villeneuve whilst lapping Lavaggi at 180 degree, 140 mph Parabolica turn on lap 16. Down to eighth after lap 18 pit stop but third again, past two-stop Alesi, on lap 23. Then down to fourth behind Alesi again after second stop, lap 35. Team astutely brings him in for third stop at same time as Jean, lap 44, and Michael gets out first. Finishes third, 1.3s ahead of Alesi but nearly 54s behind Villeneuve. "I could not go any quicker because of a lack of grip." Two-stop Irvine battles with Berger for whole race. Chases fifth-placed Gerhard for 19 laps and gets past at first stop, lap 20. Loses place at second stop, lap 43, but regains it when Gerhard pits. Berger hits Irvine and spins Ferrari in banzai passing attempt at last corner of last lap, but damages Benetton suspension. Eddie recovers, passes Berger and finishes fifth, 5.7s clear, contented with first points finish since Imola. Ferrari now only one point behind second-placed Benetton in constructors' championship and looks forward to last race in Japan, "where the 310 should go well." Damon Hill certainly hopes so, for if a Ferrari wins he will be world champion.

BENETTON-RENAULT

Benetton-Renault, missing Schumacher, still lags well behind Williams-Renault with no sign of first 1996 win. Jean Alesi happy with third on grid behind Hill and Villeneuve. "I don't want to interfere with the World Championship race ahead of me, and don't expect as good a start as Monza, but I do want to win and beat Schumacher in the championship." Makes another superb start (how does he do it so regularly?) and races past Villeneuve to second, nearly passing Hill, who aggressively chops him off. Chases Hill, consistently dropping back until 13.5s behind when three-stop Damon pits on lap 17. Two-stop Alesi takes lead until own first stop, lap 22. Rejoins fourth but to third behind Hill/Villeneuve, laps 36-44, when Schumacher makes second stop. Comes in for second stop at same time as three-stop Schumacher, lap 44, and exits pit lane behind Michael. Battles to end but finishes fourth, 1.3s down and a further point adrift in championship. Berger starts fifth, one second off the pace. Two-stop strategy like Alesi. Difficult race due to throttle problem. Battles with Irvine for whole distance. Fifth laps 1-18. Loses place to Eddie at first stop and never recovers. Scrambles past the Ferrari for a few yards when both lapping Lavaggi, lap 64, but is immediately repassed. Hits Irvine during misjudged passing move on last lap and breaks suspension. Finishes sixth, 5.7s behind Eddie. Benetton now only one point ahead of Ferrari in constructors' championship, with one race to go.

WILLIAMS-RENAULT

In exciting battle for pole position, Damon Hill takes it for ninth time in 1996 - but only by 0.009s from team-mate and championship rival Jacques Villeneuve. Williams' eighth front row monopoly of season. Damon makes superb start, repulsing determined Alesi charge. Pulls away to lead Jean by 13.5s at first of three pit stops, lap 17, as Villeneuve, passed by Alesi and Schumacher, fights to recover from bad start. Hill back into lead, lap 22, but with dramatically reduced advantage of 9.1s over charging Villeneuve,who audaciously passes third-placed Schumacher on outside of 180 degree, Parabolica turn on lap 16 and advances to second at Alesi's first stop. Villeneuve continues to close and reduces gap to 3.6s, lap 36, after both have stopped twice. Jacques sets fastest lap of race (1m 22.873s, 117.69 mph) and catches Hill, lap 45. All now depends on last stops. Hill in lap 49. Villeneuve in lap 50, rejoining track just ahead of Damon. Then brilliantly pulls away to win by 20s. "Jacques did a great job getting through the traffic," says Damon. "He found some time in the pit stop and I was very surprised to see him in front of me. I could not stay with him and was told by the pits that there was something wrong with my clutch. But I can't be too disappointed, because I am only one point away from the world championship." But with a magnificent fourth win in his first GP season, Villeneuve superbly keeps his hopes alive for the last race in Japan on a track he knows well.

McLAREN-MERCEDES

Hakkinen and Coulthard start seventh and eighth, both troubled by lack of balance. Then race together with intended two-stop strategies. Seventh and eighth, lap 46, after second stops when Hakkinen, trying to pass at corkscrew, hits Coulthard. Mika in for new nose. David in for check. Team misses rear puncture, so in again for new tyre. Then yet again for pit lane speeding penalty. Mika withdrawn, lap 52, due to car damage. Coulthard finishes 13th, two laps down. Both in bad odour for "unacceptable incident between team-mates." (Ron Dennis).

LIGIER-MUGEN HONDA

Car performance disappoints at Estoril. Panis starts unhappy 15th; Diniz 18th. Olivier battles with understeer on first two sets of tyres, but goes better on third set, despite misfire, to finish 10th, one lap down. Diniz has same problem before tripping over Rosset when 17th, lap 47, and retiring. "I feel he closed the door on me."

JORDAN-PEUGEOT

Team announces Ralf Schumacher (yes, his younger brother) as 1997 driver. But who will go? Barrichello qualifies ninth, 0.1s faster than Brundle, 10th. Both feel they've done best they can for start of three-stop race. Rubens improves to seventh by lap 22 and chases Berger until second stop, lap 32. Locks rear wheels and spins out, lap 42, trying to pass Salo after second stop. Brundle finishes ninth, one lap down. Peugeot boss Pierre-Michel Fauconnier pointedly says, "The engines worked perfectly throughout the weekend. The competitiveness of the cars needs to improve for next season."

SAUBER-FORD

Cosworth produces further evolution of Ford V10 with encouraging power increase. Frentzen says top-end improvement is "remarkable", but he only qualifies 11th, two seconds slower than Hill. Herbert 12th on grid, 2.3s down, so still some way to go with whole car package. H-H won't care too much, because he is leaving, but Herbert will - he's staying for two more years. Frentzen makes "one of the worst starts of my career" and loses four places. Herbert improves by one to 11th. Frentzen recovers to drive fine race, benefiting from two-stop strategy to finish seventh, one lap down. "The engine was perfect." Herbert gets stuck behind Brundle, twice, and then a "cruising" Schumacher. Passed by Frentzen at last of three stops and finishes eighth, 3.3s behind H-H.

TWR ARROWS-HART

Verstappen loses substantial set-up time by spinning out on Friday, and having engine blow on Saturday morning. Qualifies 16th, troubled by usual understeer, as is Rosset who starts 17th. Jos happy with race set-up but says slippery conditions very hard on tyres. Is 12th, lap 47, after second stop, lap 33, when engine fails, making him one of only four retirements. Rosset follows two-stop strategy and, like Verstappen, finds car very difficult to drive on worn tyres. Angry at being held up by Lamy, as the latter leaves pit lane after delayed start, but finishes 14th, three laps down, with grossly overheated gearbox due to total loss of oil.

TYRRELL-YAMAHA

A good weekend with no engine problems, for a change. Delighted Ukyo Katayama third fastest on Friday, but this sadly only good for morale in situation where times do not count for grid. Using revised front suspension, Salo and Katayama qualify 13th and 14th, 0.2s apart but some 2.5s off Hill's pole time. Salo well pleased with set-up and drives heartening two-stop race. "The car was good all through and we were really quick through the last two corners." Finishes reliable 11th, one lap down. Katayama nearly stalls at start and loses four places. Takes early first stop (of two) to reduce oversteer by adjusting front wing. Runs consistent race, slowing at end due to "strange smell in car" and finishes 12th, one lap down. Team greatly relieved to get both cars home without major problems prior to Yamaha engine supplier's home race in Japan.

MINARDI-FORD

Very important home race for Pedro Lamy, but little joy. Stops in qualifying session with fuel pump problem and switches to spare car, only for same thing to happen. Back to repaired race car to set 19th fastest time. Lavaggi slides off on rain tyres on out-lap on Friday morning, losing whole session. Stops on second lap on Saturday morning with alternator problem so does well to qualify, albeit last. Lamy overheats clutch on formation lap and stalls at start. Is pushed to pit lane and gets away two laps down. Finishes last, five laps down and thoroughly dispirited with lack of progress in Formula One. Lavaggi sees low oil-pressure dashboard warning on lap four and cruises rest of race to save engine. Finishes 19th also five laps adrift.

FORMULA 1 WORLD CHAMPIONSHIP

RACE 15

PORTUGAL

22 September 1996

ESTORIL – GRAND PRIX CIRCUIT

CIRCUIT LENGTH: 2.709 MILES/4.360 KM

STARTING GRID

HILL 1m 20.330s	**VILLENEUVE** 1m 20.339s
ALESI 1m 21.088s	**SCHUMACHER** 1m 21.236s
BERGER 1m 21.293s	**IRVINE** 1m 21.362s
HAKKINEN 1m 21.640s	**COULTHARD** 1m 22.066s
BARRICHELLO 1m 22.205s	**BRUNDLE** 1m 22.324s
FRENTZEN 1m 22.325s	**HERBERT** 1m 22.655s
SALO 1m 22.765s	**KATAYAMA** 1m 23.013s
PANIS 1m 23.055s	**VERSTAPPEN** 1m 23.531s
ROSSET 1m 24.230s	**DINIZ** 1m 24.293s
LAMY 1m 24.510s	**LAVAGGI** 1m 25.612s

RACE CLASSIFICATION

Pos	Driver	Nat	Car	Laps	Time
1	Jacques Villeneuve	CDN	Williams FW18-Renault V10	70	1h 40m 22.915s
2	Damon Hill	GB	Williams FW18-Renault V10	70	+19.966s
3	Michael Schumacher	D	Ferrari F310-Ferrari V10	70	+53.765s
4	Jean Alesi	F	Benetton B196-Renault V10	70	+55.109s
5	Eddie Irvine	GB	Ferrari F310-Ferrari V10	70	+1m 27.389s
6	Gerhard Berger	A	Benetton B196-Renault V10	70	+1m 33.141s
7	Heinz-Harald Frentzen	D	Sauber C15-Ford V10		+1 lap
8	Johnny Herbert	GB	Sauber C15-Ford V10		+1 lap
9	Martin Brundle	GB	Jordan 196-Peugeot V10		+1 lap
10	Olivier Panis	F	Ligier JS43-Mugen Honda V10		+1 lap
11	Mika Salo	SF	Tyrrell 024-Yamaha V10		+1 lap
12	Ukyo Katayama	J	Tyrrell 024-Yamaha V10		+2 laps
13	David Coulthard	GB	McLaren MP4/11B-Mercedes V10		+2 laps
14	Ricardo Rosset	BR	Footwork FA17-Hart V8		+3 laps
15	Giovanni Lavaggi	I	Minardi M195B-Ford V8		+5 laps
16	Pedro Lamy	P	Minardi M195B-Ford V8		+5 laps

Retirements	Nat	Car	Lap	Reason
Mika Hakkinen	SF	McLaren MP4/11B-Mercedes V10	52	Accident
Jos Verstappen	NL	Footwork FA17-Hart V8	47	Engine
Pedro Diniz	BR	Ligier JS43-Mugen Honda V10	46	Spin
Rubens Barrichello	BR	Jordan 196-Peugeot V10	41	Spin

FASTEST LAP Jacques Villeneuve 1m 22.873s lap 37 (117.673mph)

DRIVERS' CHAMPIONSHIP

Damon Hill	87
Jacques Villeneuve	78
Michael Schumacher	53
Jean Alesi	47
Mika Hakkinen	27
David Coulthard	18
Gerhard Berger	18
Rubens Barrichello	14
Olivier Panis	13
Eddie Irvine	11
Heinz-Harald Frentzen	6
Martin Brundle	6
Mika Salo	5
Johnny Herbert	4
Pedro Diniz	2
Jos Verstappen	1

CONSTRUCTORS' CUP

Williams-Renault	165
Benetton-Renault	65
Ferrari	64
McLaren-Mercedes	45
Jordan-Peugeot	20
Ligier-Mugen Honda	15
Sauber-Ford	10
Tyrrell-Yamaha	5
Footwork-Hart	1

Results and Data © FIA 1996

Not everyone likes going to Japan, but I do. The culture may be very different, communication with the inhabitants virtually impossible and the food not to everyone's liking, but it certainly makes a change from custom, and the atmosphere at the superb Suzuka circuit is truly stimulating.

Japan is crazy about Formula One,. The crowds are massive and knowledgeable, the drivers are their gods and the locals go frantic if they spot one of them out of his car. Mika Hakkinen in particular, with his blonde hair and Nordic good looks, creates a giggling uproar amongst the girls and gets no peace at all.

But there was plenty for all of us to get excited about this year, for the World Drivers' Championship was to be decided in Japan. It is unusual for the 16-race series to go down to the wire, but not unknown. Suzuka, which had never previously staged the finale, had witnessed dramatic, title-settling races in the past, most notably in 1989 and 1990, when bitter rivals Ayrton Senna and Alain Prost had driven into each other, collecting one championship apiece.

This year's contestants, team-mates

JAPAN

The new world champion takes advantage of a burst champagne main, above.

Left. Slide rule: the art of never giving up, as exemplified by Jacques Villeneuve. Who says his driving style isn't reminiscent of his father's?

Damon Hill and Jacques Villeneuve, were on decidedly better terms, so no one was anticipating any unpleasantness. And to allay any suspicions of favouritism, Williams had sent four cars so that both drivers would have access to a spare . Furthermore, both technical director Patrick Head and chief designer Adrian Newey were in attendance, despite the fact that they really needed to be at the team's Grove HQ getting on with the 1997 car.

With nine points separating Hill and Villeneuve, the Canadian had to win with Damon finishing no better than seventh in order to become the first F1 rookie to snatch the championship. Although a top six finish would suffice for Hill, that was by no means a foregone conclusion. Most people were convinced that Villeneuve, on a roll after winning so well in Portugal, would do so again; Hill's enormous following in the UK was apprehensive that, for the third year in succession, something would happen to put the title he deserved beyond his reach.

133

Below. A rare shot of Jean Alesi's Benetton in one piece. The atmosphere within the team was tense before the Frenchman speared off at the exit of the first corner, inflicting a substantial amount of damage on his B196.

It was to be a fair fight. Hill had raced at Suzuka three times, scoring one of his finest wins in the appalling rains of 1994. Villeneuve had frequently performed at the circuit when he had raced in the Japanese F3 series. As a real driver's circuit, Suzuka was the perfect setting for their championship shoot-out. With its unique figure-of-eight configuration, it has plenty of gradients, just about every conceivable kind of corner and 190 mph straights. As such, it offers a daunting challenge, and the drivers love it. The facilities are superb and the viewing conditions for the massed crowds are magnificent.

Only the weather can mar things, for the local rain often defies description. After miserably wet conditions on Friday and Saturday, there were real fears that it was going to teem down on raceday. Mercifully, Sunday was the one perfect day of the meeting.

Gerhard Berger was fastest on Friday with Mika Hakkinen second, but Williams resumed their traditional dominance come Saturday. Jacques Villeneuve was in absolutely terrific form, and took his third pole position of the season. Until the last 50s Damon Hill was down in fourth, 0.6s off the pace and with Schumacher and Berger between him and his chief rival. It looked bad but, as he had done so often in the past, Damon produced a superb lap and displaced them both to preserve his record of being on the front row of the grid for every race of 1996. It was the ninth all-Williams front row of the season, and Damon was totally at ease. He had been concentrating until the last possible moment on getting his race set-up right, but he had a lot of people concerned.

Damon had every reason to be tense and terse, but I have seldom seen him as relaxed and at ease as he was on race day. Would he get a decent start this time? He had said, "I want to win the championship

Left. Eddie Irvine, accustomed to the unwanted physical attention of tall Austrians called Gerhard, awaits an unwelcome push from the eventual fourth-placed finisher. Berger's subsequent actions would earn him a suspended one-race ban.

Below. Seconds out: Schumacher hares after Hakkinen. The Ferrari driver got the better of his Finnish adversary in the end, a result which helped elevate the Italian team to second overall in the constructors' championship, albeit a couple of million points behind Williams.

by winning the race." At a circuit where passing is predictably difficult, he would need to beat Villeneuve to the first corner. On recent form, he didn't seem likely to do so, but his rapid start and Villeneuve's sluggish getaway effectively settled both the race and the championship by Turn One.

Hill's departure was meteoric. He literally left Villeneuve standing as the Canadian bogged down; by the time Jacques got going he was down to seventh, with Hill, Berger, Hakkinen, Schumacher, Irvine and Frentzen ahead of him. He rapidly took Frentzen, but he still had four very hard men between him and the other Williams as Hill raced away with Berger attached to his gearbox. But not for long. On a three-stop strategy to Hill's two, Gerhard tried an impossible passing move at the chicane on lap four in the mistaken belief that Damon would give way to avoid a collision. Hill stuck to his line, Berger broke his wing against a kerb, and the Benetton was into the pits for a new nose. When Gerhard rejoined he was down to 14th, to start a comeback that would be a joy to watch.

"Hill's departure was meteoric. He literally left Villeneuve standing"

Now Hakkinen was second, with Schumacher right behind him, Eddie Irvine an excellent fourth just ahead of Villeneuve and Martin Brundle a fine sixth. Villeneuve was the man to watch. He had to get to grips with Hill somehow, and was all over Irvine. On lap 12 Eddie yielded and Jacques was through, up to fourth. And then the first pit stops began. Most people were making two, some three and a few just one. When the first round was over, Hill was 1.5s ahead of Schumacher, with Hakkinen a further 1.7s back, Villeneuve fourth two seconds behind the McLaren, Irvine fifth and the amazing Berger up to sixth. Schumacher had passed Hakkinen during their stops, and was to stay ahead of the McLaren for the rest of the race, but it was a mighty close fight for the first three places right to the end.

On lap 32, Schumacher, Hakkinen and Villeneuve in second, third and fourth came in for their second stops, the latter thinking he had a rear puncture. With Hill staying out for another two laps, the first three positions were unchanged after the stops but Berger got ahead of Villeneuve to take fourth. Jacques then set the fastest lap of the race (1m 44.043s, 126.082 mph), but the gap to Gerhard increased to over eight seconds when the Canadian was

**Below. As Hill
steams into the
first corner,
ahead of Berger
(studying for
his PhD in
impetuosity),
Villeneuve's slim
title hopes more
or less evaporate
as he allows his
pole position
advantage to
be swamped.**

impeded by Katayama (for which Ukyo
was penalised). With 18 laps to go, Hill led
by over 16s and Berger, Hakkinen and
Schumacher cushioned him from
Villeneuve, whose championship hopes
were looking ever thinner. On lap 37, they
disappeared altogether.

In the middle of the 100 mph Turn One,
Jacques' right rear wheel came off, raced
ahead of him as he ploughed harmlessly
into the gravel trap and bounced over the
catch fencing at undiminished speed,
apparently into the crowd. But, thank heavens, it was an optical illusion. A second
row of fencing stopped it.

At that very moment, Damon Hill became
world champion. "They told me over the
radio that Jacques was out, but I couldn't
take it in, even when I saw him standing by
the side of the track. I wanted to concentrate on the race. It was a matter of putting
the championship out of my mind and concentrating on winning, which is what I
really, really wanted to do."

And he did. Schumacher did his level best
to beat him, but Damon drove brilliantly to
maintain the gap between them at around
five seconds until he eased off right at the
end. With Hakkinen trying just as hard to

**Right. Fighting to
extend his F1
career, and
thereby avoid a
perch alongside
Mr M Walker in
the TV commen-
tary booth,
Martin Brundle
finished fifth.**

pass the Ferrari, the finish of the 1996
Japanese Grand Prix saw just 3.2 seconds
covering the top three. A great ending to a
great race, with Berger a superb fourth
despite his unscheduled stop, Brundle an
excellent fifth and Heinz-Harald Frentzen,
Hill's 1997 replacement, sixth for Sauber.

But it wasn't so great for some. David
Coulthard had caused the first start to be
aborted when he stalled, a result of failing
to master his hand clutch. He then had to
start from the back. After hitting Diniz and
stopping for a new nose, he finished
eighth. Poor Irvine didn't even finish. It
had been a tough first season with Ferrari
for Eddie, but he was looking good for
fourth place when Berger nerfed him off at
the chicane. Eddie was less than enchant-

"They told me over the radio that Jacques was out, but I couldn't take it in, even when I saw him"   Damon Hill

Above. Frentzen's farewell gift to Sauber was a solitary point. Panis, Herbert, Diniz, Coulthard (having started at the back) and Verstappen follow.

ed, as were the stewards, who gave the Austrian a suspended one-race ban.

Superstarter Jean Alesi had lasted for only a few hundred yards, racing up between Schumacher and Irvine from ninth on the grid only to climb over the kerb, go off and mash his Benetton against the Armco.

So at last, after four racing years with Williams, losing the championship to Schumacher with a controversial collision at the final race of 1994 and finishing second again in 1995, Damon Hill became a very worthy world champion, the first son of a previous champion ever to have done so. His late, great father Graham would have been as proud of him as the whole British nation was. Damon is one of nature's gentlemen. He had fought his way to the top against all sorts of adversity to achieve enormous world-wide popularity, and he could now reap his reward.

It simply couldn't have happened to a nicer bloke. "This victory is for everyone at Williams, it is my leaving present to them. It is an absolutely perfect, fairy tale ending, a terrific feeling for me and a tremendous relief. I want especially to thank my wife Georgie for this championship. She has stood by me the whole way and been a tremendous strength to me throughout all the time I have been racing in Formula One."

There weren't many dry eyes in the house, least of all mine, for this great occasion had been the last Grand Prix I had commentated on for BBC Television after 48 wonderfully happy, eventful and exciting years working with a marvellous bunch of people. It would be very sad for me to leave them.

Ferrari went home happy to Maranello though. Michael Schumacher's six points for second place had snatched the constructors' championship from Benetton in the very last race. It had certainly been a season to savour, but it wouldn't be long before it all started again in Melbourne, Australia. And not a moment too soon!

FERRARI

With no changes to car since Portugal, team objective is to beat Benetton in constructors' championship. After difficult wet/dry conditions during Friday/Saturday, Schumacher third on grid 1.2s slower than Villeneuve. "The car goes better in the wet than the dry," says Michael after aborting final qualifying run due to engine problem. Irvine happy to qualify sixth following problem with gearbox hydraulics. Schumacher passed by Hakkinen at start after being delayed by slow-starting Villeneuve, but better first pit stop promotes him to second, lap 19. Stays ahead at second stop, lap 32, and is only 1.5s behind Hill following Damon's stop, lap 34. Gap increases to over six seconds but Schumacher finishes second, 1.9s down. "I tried everything I could to take Damon and nearly did it at the second stop. He deserves to win the title and I congratulate him." Michael third in championship. Irvine runs fourth, after Berger stops for new nose, laps 4-11, before being passed by Villeneuve. Back to excellent fourth, lap 37, following second stops, but hit and spun out at chicane by aggressive Berger, lap 40. "This is the second time in two races that Gerhard has driven into me. He said 'sorry' but it is not enough. This has not been a great year for me but I know I will be involved much more in the development of the new car and I expect to be more competitive next year." Schumacher very complimentary about Eddie. "Of all my team-mates, he is the one who has come closest to me in performance." (Martin Brundle wouldn't agree). Schumacher's six points result in Ferrari scoring two more than Benetton and achieving their constructors' championship goal by finishing second to Williams, albeit a massive 105 points behind. "We could not have had a better end to the season," says Sporting Director Jean Todt, "and we can now work through the winter in a calm manner with less pressure on our backs."

BENETTON-RENAULT

Unsettled atmosphere in team with belief that technical director Ross Brawn is leaving to join Ferrari. Berger fastest on Friday and qualifies fourth, happy with balance, but Alesi most unhappy and starts lowly ninth after handling problems and lack of straight-line speed. Jean has usual meteoric start but gets sandwiched between the two Ferraris exiting Turn One and smashes into Armco. Berger also makes good start, passing Schumacher and Villeneuve to lie second behind Hill. Harries Damon for three laps but tries too hard at chicane, lap four, and breaks front wing. In for new nose and rejoins 14th, 28s behind Damon. Makes great recovery to sixth by lap 17. Attacks Irvine for fourth at chicane after second stop, lap 40, and spins Eddie out. Continues to finish fourth with second fastest lap of race but team loses out to Ferrari in constructors' championship. Alesi/Berger fourth and sixth in drivers' championship. "A disappointing end to a negative season," says Flavio Briatore. Uneasy general feeling that Benetton is falling apart.

WILLIAMS-RENAULT

Determined to ensure fairness in crucial battle for drivers' championship, team takes four cars to Japan. Jacques Villeneuve brilliantly takes third pole position of first GP season with Hill second, following inspired lap in closing seconds of session. He thus preserves record of starting on front row of grid for every race of year. "I took no risks. It is fine for me and exactly where I want to be." Hill then effectively wins both race and championship by making magnificent getaway to blast past slow-starting Villeneuve, who drops to seventh, passed by Berger, Hakkinen, Schumacher, Irvine and Frentzen. Damon deals calmly with aggressive Berger, who damages front wing trying to pass at chicane on lap four, and retains lead during both pit stops , laps 18 and 34. Drives great race with no mistakes or problems, controlling things from front for whole distance. Villeneuve bottled up behind Irvine for 11 laps, but audaciously passes Eddie to fourth at chicane, lap 12. Takes second stop when fourth, lap 32, believing he has rear puncture. Sets fastest lap of race lap 34 and closes to within seven seconds of fourth-placed Berger, only for suspect rear wheel to fly off, lap 37. At that moment Damon Hill becomes world champion, before continuing to take his eighth victory of 1996 in his last race for Williams. A wonderful year for the team, for Damon and for Jacques, all of whom had performed superbly for the whole season.

McLAREN-MERCEDES

Friday sessions reveal massive front wing flutter which necessitates overnight work to strengthen supports and underwing area. Hakkinen qualifies fairly contented fifth, 1.5s off Villeneuve's pace, but Coulthard down in eighth on grid, a second slower after fraught

Saturday. He had been hit by Verstappen, spinning his race car and qualifying the spare before being fined a massive $10,000 for speeding in pit lane. Mika (very much number one in Japan) makes great start and passes Schumacher and Villeneuve to third. Second when Berger pits for new nose, lap four. Passed by Schumacher at first stop, lap 19, and stays there to end of fine race, finishing 1.33s behind Michael and 3.2s behind Hill for fourth third place of year. Coulthard causes start to be aborted by stalling engine when using hand clutch and therefore has to start from back. Hits Diniz lap one and pits for new nose. Then has "uneventful" race with two more stops, laps 16 and 34, before finishing disappointed eighth. Hakkinen/Coulthard fifth and seventh in championship with McLaren fourth in constructors' contest.

LIGIER-MUGEN HONDA

Using new evolution of Mugen Honda V10,Panis and Diniz qualify 12th and 16th. Olivier spends most of race behind Frentzen and sets sixth fastest lap before finishing seventh, 0.7s ahead of Coulthard. Diniz hit by Coulthard on first lap, suffers heavy tyre wear and fading brakes and spins out on lap 13.

JORDAN-PEUGEOT

Martin Brundle delighted to outqualify unhappy Barrichello (10th and 11th). Rubens second in warm-up but decisively beaten by Martin in race. Brundle has two-stop race (laps 14/32). In points at sixth by lap four and finishes fifth to pull away from Frentzen in championship and finish 11th. Will he now drive for team after all in 1997, following Hill's decision to join Arrows? Barrichello finishes disconsolate ninth after constant understeer, his four-season Jordan career definitely over.

SAUBER-FORD

On track he knows well, Heinz-Harald Frentzen qualifies seventh, team's best start of year. Herbert starts 13th after car problem on Friday ("something locked at the back") and major off at 155mph 130R corner five minutes into qualifying. This obliges him to use spare, set up for H-H. Frentzen passes Villeneuve to sixth at start but runs wide and drops to eighth. Races with Barrichello until passing Rubens after early second stop, lap 29. To sixth, lap 40, after Villeneuve and Irvine retirements and stays there for second successive Japanese GP sixth place, scoring Sauber's 53rd GP point on Peter Sauber's 53rd birthday. "A great way to end with the team!" Herbert suffers from oversteer but finishes full-distance 10th. Both drivers use latest evolution Ford-Cosworth V10 for race.

TWR ARROWS-HART

Team announces officially that it will use Yamaha engines and Bridgestone tyres with Damon Hill and Pedro Diniz as drivers in 1997, Diniz allegedly paying $12 million for the privilege. So last races with team for Jos Verstappen and Ricardo Rosset, who qualify 17th and 19th. Both plan one-stop strategy but Rosset given 10s penalty for blocking and stops twice. Reliable race for both ,with Verstappen finishing 11th, one lap down, and Rosset 13th, two laps adrift.

TYRRELL-YAMAHA

Suzuka a major disappointment for Japan's Ukyo Katayama and for Yamaha on home track. No engine problems on Friday and Katayama, 14th, outqualifies team-mate Salo. "Reliability has been good. We look forward to a trouble-free race," says Harvey Postlethwaite, who speaks too soon. Fifth and eighth in wet warm-up Ukyo and Salo look good, but both retire from race. Salo, on one-stop strategy, feels engine tighten and then sees smoke when 15th on lap 20. Retires to pits. Katayama battles with Verstappen until first stop when 13th, lap 15. Hits Jos at chicane, lap 25, stops for new nose and is given 10s penalty for blocking Villeneuve, lap 35. Engine problem in pits prevents him from rejoining. "So now we say 'Sayonara' to Yamaha," (and a few other choice things, no doubt) says Harvey. "It is time for us to move on," (to Ford V8 power for 1997). "This is not the end of the association with Tyrrell we were hoping for," says Yamaha project leader Takaki Kimura. They'll need to do better for Arrows next year with Tom Walkinshaw and Damon Hill to contend with.

MINARDI-FORD

Using latest evolution Ford-Cosworth ED4 V8, Lamy starts 18th and finishes 12th, two laps down, but Giovanni Lavaggi fails to qualify by nearly a second..

RACE 16

FORMULA 1 WORLD CHAMPIONSHIP

JAPAN

13 October 1996

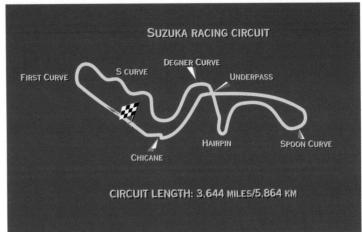

SUZUKA RACING CIRCUIT

FIRST CURVE
S CURVE
DEGNER CURVE
UNDERPASS
HAIRPIN
SPOON CURVE
CHICANE

CIRCUIT LENGTH: 3,644 MILES/5,864 KM

STARTING GRID

VILLENEUVE 1m 38.909s	**HILL** 1m 39.370s
SCHUMACHER 1m 40.071s	**BERGER** 1m 40.364s
HAKKINEN 1m 40.458s	**IRVINE** 1m 41.005s
FRENTZEN 1m 41.277s	**COULTHARD** 1m 41.384s
ALESI 1m 41.562s	**BRUNDLE** 1m 41.600s
BARRICHELLO 1m 41.919s	**PANIS** 1m 42.206s
HERBERT 1m 42.658s	**KATAYAMA** 1m 42.711s
SALO 1m 42.840s	**DINIZ** 1m 43.196s
VERSTAPPEN 1m 43.383s	**LAMY** 1m 44.874s
ROSSET 1m 45.412s	

Did not qualify

LAVAGGI
(Minardi M195B)
1m 46.795s

RACE CLASSIFICATION

Pos	Driver	Nat	Car	Laps	Time
1	Damon Hill	GB	Williams FW18-Renault V10	52	1h 32m 33.791s
2	Michael Schumacher	D	Ferrari F310-Ferrari V10	52	+01.883s
3	Mika Hakkinen	SF	McLaren MP4/11B-Mercedes V10	52	+03.212s
4	Gerhard Berger	A	Benetton B196-Renault V10	52	+26.526s
5	Martin Brundle	GB	Jordan 196-Peugeot V10	52	+1m 07.120s
6	Heinz-Harald Frentzen	D	Sauber C15-Ford V10	52	+1m 21.186s
7	Olivier Panis	F	Ligier JS43-Mugen Honda V10	52	+1m 24.510s
8	David Coulthard	GB	McLaren MP4/11B-Mercedes V10	52	+1m 25.233s
9	Rubens Barrichello	BR	Jordan 196-Peugeot V10	52	+1m 41.065s
10	Johnny Herbert	GB	Sauber C15-Ford V10	52	+1m 41.799s
11	Jos Verstappen	NL	Footwork FA17-Hart V8		+1 lap
12	Pedro Lamy	P	Minardi M195B-Ford V8		+2 laps
13	Ricardo Rosset	BR	Footwork FA17-Hart V8		+3 laps

Retirements	**Nat**	**Car**	**Lap**	**Reason**
Eddie Irvine	GB	Ferrari F310-Ferrari V10	39	Accident
Ukyo Katayama	J	Tyrrell 024-Yamaha V10	37	Engine
Jacques Villeneuve	CDN	Williams FW18-Renault V10	36	Lost wheel
Mika Salo	SF	Tyrrell 024-Yamaha V10	20	Engine
Pedro Diniz	BR	Ligier JS43-Mugen Honda V10	13	Spin
Jean Alesi	F	Benetton B196-Renault V10	0	Accident

FASTEST LAP Jacques Villeneuve 1m 44.043s lap 34 (126.062mph)

DRIVERS' CHAMPIONSHIP

Damon Hill	97
Jacques Villeneuve	78
Michael Schumacher	59
Jean Alesi	47
Mika Hakkinen	31
Gerhard Berger	21
David Coulthard	18
Rubens Barrichello	14
Olivier Panis	13
Eddie Irvine	11
Martin Brundle	8
Heinz-Harald Frentzen	7
Mika Salo	5
Johnny Herbert	4
Pedro Diniz	2
Jos Verstappen	1

CONSTRUCTORS' CUP

Williams-Renault	175
Ferrari	70
Benetton-Renault	68
McLaren-Mercedes	49
Jordan-Peugeot	22
Ligier-Mugen Honda	15
Sauber-Ford	11
Tyrrell-Yamaha	5
Footwork-Hart	1

Results and Data © FIA 1996

Below. The changing face of Formula One: Michael Schumacher had to get used to the 'P2' board.

Expectations had been high for 1996, with more top driver changes than there had been for years. Schumacher to Ferrari, to drive an exciting new car with an exciting new engine; Alesi and Berger to Benetton; an enthralling new prospect in Jacques Villeneuve. These were only some of the things that had my senses tingling at the thought of what was to come. By and large, however, it didn't happen. The in-depth strength and continuity of Williams, allied to the reliability of the all-conquering Renault V10 and two very competent drivers, proved too much for them all. But if the Williams steam-roller which flattened everything in its path made the winners predictable, there were brilliant flashes which made it a memorable and satisfying year.

Chief of which was Damon Hill's superb title success. They say nice guys come last; they don't in Damon's case. Prior to 1996 he had won 13 times for Williams, but had never gained the recognition he deserved. "It's the car, not him, the knockers main-

tained. Where others received praise, he received criticism. Under terrific pressure the whole season, he typically kept his head down, worked, thought and trained ceaselessly and let his driving do the talking. This year it all came good. Eight wins, nine pole positions, on the front row of the grid for every one of the 16 races and championship leader all the way. He richly deserved the success that made him the first son of a world champion to emulate his father, and it couldn't have happened to a nicer bloke. Being fired by Williams seems a strange kind of gratitude from the team he had served so well, but in a funny

sort of way it may turn out to his advantage. I'm convinced that, with Tom Walkinshaw's drive and leadership and Hill's driving talent, the revitalised Arrows team will get to the top far sooner than most people expect.

It was his new team-mate that gave Damon the hardest time. When Jacques Villeneuve made the switch from top Indycar driver to Formula One, no one really knew what to expect. Nigel Mansell had made a gigantic success of the reverse move in 1993, but that was Nigel, wasn't it? Villeneuve took to F1 like a duck to water, sensationally proving his talent by starting his first Grand Prix from pole position and very nearly winning the race. His success in winning four races in his debut year and taking the championship down to the wire was a magnificent achievement which clearly marked him out as a champion in waiting. Like next year, I'd say. What's more, Jacques is a breath of fresh air in Formula One. Ever cheerful, bursting with talent, laid back and incredibly matter-of-fact, he regards the whole thing as fun. But I've seldom seen such determination and will-to-win. A great acquisition for the sport.

Michael Schumacher said all along that he was expecting 1996 to be a learning year with Ferrari, with no hope of winning

Left, Damon Hill might have taken longer than everyone expected to wrap up his first World Championship title, but eight victories from 16 starts made him a worthy champion.

Jordan (below): high on potential, short on results.

men, but Schumacher endeared himself to the team with his cheerfulness and uncomplaining nature (in public anyway!), giving new heart to his Maranello colleagues and the whole of Italy. His performance in the appallingly wet conditions in Barcelona was one of the most outstanding I have ever seen, and his victory before the euphoric tifosi at Monza was certainly one of the most emotional of all. For years we have

Schumacher's three victories enabled the Prancing Horse to achieve its pre-season target.

the championship, but I doubt that even he realised just how tough it was going to be. Time after time he was let down by the brittle and unreliable F310, but he calmly kept working away at making it better. The dispiriting run of double retirements at the successive Canadian, French and British Grands Prix would have destroyed lesser

been hearing Ferrari say that next season it would be better, only for the team to fail to deliver. In 1997, with Schumacher, I think it will. And whilst I'm on the subject of Ferrari, hats off to Eddie Irvine. Being in a team with Schumacher is no picnic, as Johnny Herbert and others have discovered. Michael's talent is daunting to a team-mate, and he makes sure he gets virtually all the testing. Irvine had too little opportunity to master the tricky F310, but he accepted his lot with dignity and common-sense and impressed everyone with his commitment. In 1997 he should get his reward.

If Williams ran true to its commanding form and Ferrari mostly flattered to deceive, with Schumacher doing the impressing rather than the car, the rest were frankly disappointing. Despite its massive resources, Mercedes-Benz power,

"Depressing, too, was the fact that what started out as an already thin 22-car series turned into a 20-car series after Forti withdrew"

Forti's struggle to raise funds ensured that its cars literally spent more time in the pits than they did on the track. At least Andrea Montermini was able to keep up with Brookside (opposite). Gerhard Berger (above) and Jean Alesi (above left) swapped the glamour of driving for Ferrari for the, erm, glamour of driving for Benetton.

two very good drivers and unrivalled experience, McLaren failed to win a race for the third year in succession. Benetton, so composed when Schumacher was there, struggled to integrate new drivers and to develop a difficult car. Jordan found that the last slopes to the top are desperately difficult to climb, even with an engine as good as the Peugeot V10. The rest were nowhere, with the exception of Ligier's extraordinary victory at that amazing Monaco race, where only three drivers went the distance. Depressing, too, was the fact that what started out as an already thin 22-car series turned into a 20-car series after Forti withdrew. The spectacle was still there, thanks to the quality at the front, but any more defections and there would have been real cause for concern. So it is more than reassuring to know that, next season, the Arrows team will be strong and lusty rather than weak and ailing, and that Jackie Stewart's potentially successful new team will be increasing the numbers.

Memories of 1996? Schumacher going off at Monaco. Ligier's Olivier Panis driving round Monte Carlo with an enormous tricolour. Villeneuve's first win at the

143

McLaren made progress, but Mika Hakkinen (above) has still to win a Grand Prix. Inset, the post-race parc ferme` was a familiar scene of mutual celebration for Hill and Villeneuve. Right, the sun set on the Tyrrell /Yamaha relationship at the end of the season.

Nurburgring. Race leader Hill's engine blowing at Monaco. Berger's doing the same at Hockenheim. Schumacher's incredible mastery at Barcelona and his first pole position for Ferrari in the heady atmosphere of Imola. Martin Brundle's frightening crash at Melbourne. Pedro Diniz's fire in Argentina. David Coulthard's superb starts at the Nurburgring and Imola. Alesi's in Italy and Portugal. Hill's fumbled pit stop in Belgium. Villeneuve and Schumacher crossing the line 0.8s apart at the Nurburgring. The tifosiís course invasion at Imola.

But most of all, for me, there were some very special, personal highlights. Receiving a magnum of champagne from Michael Schumacher at Silverstone, a gift which all the drivers had signed, and then sitting in the magnificent vintage Rolls-Royce which took Damon and Jacques on their parade lap in front of 90,000 flag-waving, cheering and joyful spectators. The lump-in-my-throat delight of watching Damon embracing his wife Georgie immediately after getting out of his Williams at Suzuka, as world champion. The realisation, as I put my microphone down in Japan, that I had made my last Grand Prix broadcast for the BBC. I won't forget 1996 in a hurry.